GLENN NEAL

The Second American Revolution

One Way Or The Other

2nd Edition

Flyover Country Press, L.L.C.
Beckley, West Virginia

ISBN: 0-9843761-0-0
ISBN-13: 978-0-9843761-0-0

DEDICATION

To Bredga, whose love and support
kept this writing project alive during the dark days.
Thank you for putting up with me.

Acknowledgments

Special thanks to Steve Vassey and the members of Columbia I Chapter
of the South Carolina Writers Workshop, who taught this lawyer
how to write for real people, not just other lawyers.
In particular, thanks to Bill Kaliher, Mickey Burriss, Hope Clark, and Rachel
Haynie
And to Patrick Neal, M.D., Tallahassee, Florida, my first editor.

TABLE OF CONTENTS

List of Illustrations

Forward

This country was founded upon principles of freedom and a system of checks and balances. Our forefathers framed a Constitution based on these doctrines. As my good friend, Glenn Neal will remind you: the Constitution of the United States was a 'grant of power, in trust, by the people to the government to be exercised in accordance with the mandate of the people.'

Unfortunately, this is not the status quo in today's America. Today's Supreme Court regularly oversteps its bounds, amending the Constitution as it sees fit anytime 5 justices agree on a new "interpretation." Federal courts have seized the power to levy taxes (a power constitutionally granted only to Congress and State Legislators); our government 'of the people, for the people and by the people' is slowly slipping away and it is YOUR, MY, and OUR DUTY to restore it.

Glenn Neal will show you, using their own words, how the Supreme Court disregards its Constitutional authority in order to usurp power for itself, how justices substitute their own feelings and intuition in the place of the regular language of the law, and how THEY DON'T CARE if it is right or wrong. I can remember a time when our leaders were elected by the people and they made the law of the land. Today, even if our Congress can manage to pass a law, the Supreme Court no longer feels bound by it.

It is a shame—and a far cry from the vision set forth by those who pledged their lives, their fortunes, and their sacred honor in a Declaration of Independence more than 230 years ago to establish this system. It is an insult to them that we, the people, have allowed this to come to fruition and stand idly by while the foundation of our beliefs as a nation are mindlessly cast aside and trampled on. It is time for us, EACH of us, to stand up and correct these grievances, to restore OUR government to its proper state of function, to rally in our beliefs and stand firm in our convictions that this Great Nation is OURS and Our Responsibility. It is time to pledge OUR lives, OUR fortunes and OUR sacred honor and stand against any foe or force who may stand in our way until our system is reinstated and these atrocities are ended.

In 1773, a group of men rallied together and tossed tea into a harbor in protest, stirring the hearts and minds of their countrymen, which led to the Revolution that set this country apart. Is it any wonder then, as federal courts tax today without representation, that 'Tea Party' Movements are stirring the hearts and minds of our countrymen? I think not, and Glenn Neal agrees.

In *The Second American Revolution*, Glenn Neal details how to familiarize your-self with our current system of government and how to change it. He offers a step-by-step guide to influencing transformation in our country. Glenn Neal has mapped the path, now the question is—do you have the moral fiber to stand for what is right and walk it?

The Honorable Shirley Love
West Virginia State Senate (Ret)

Prologue

This book is an update and revision of *How Dangerous Are They? Supreme Court Justices in Their Own Words,* © *2005,* which was offered for publication in the spring of 2004. After being accepted and going through a year-long editing process, it was listed in the publisher's spring 2005 catalogue (*see*: listing on Amazon.com). The author withdrew the manuscript prior to printing because of a last-minute dispute—with what the author perceived to be an *uber*-liberal editor—over certain content involving a legal issue which was accurate but not politically correct.

When I set out to write this book, I realized I was not an investigative reporter, nor did I want to become one. I wanted to see what information was out there "in plain view," accessible to anyone with a computer and a connection to the Internet. For that reason I have used as many Internet sources as practical.

My views are necessarily influenced by my training and practice as a trial lawyer. At the time I retired I was employed as an assistant prosecuting attorney. My first priority was prosecuting criminals; however, my boss assigned me the additional duties of advising the county government, our employer. My job required I be thoroughly familiar with state and United States Supreme Court decisions on the full range of law as they affect state and local government, contracts, land use, and the freedoms guaranteed by the Bill of Rights, among others.

I conducted training for law enforcement officers in search and seizure, civil rights, family violence, and domestic issues, as the U.S. Supreme Court cases and state law evolved and changed.

I, like all lawyers have been "brainwashed" by law school and the practice of law; however, I have tried to be as objective as possible in looking at some trends of the Supreme Court lawyers rarely discuss in public. There is substantial peer pressure among lawyers not to criticize the Supreme Court or judges in general—one American Bar Association official went so far as to recommend that lawyers, who are also elected officials, be disciplined (to include disbarment) if they criticize judges.

Another reason not to criticize judges is that every lawyer knows in future cases he or she will be appearing again and again before this same judge. It does no service to clients if the lawyer becomes the target of a judge with a grudge. Judges have a lot of discretion—how to interpret and apply the law, what evidence will be admitted—and they have the power to dismiss cases without even letting them go to the jury for consideration.

I encourage the reader to read the book, but don't just take my word. Go online and read the original sources, if you have the time and inclination, then you decide: *How Dangerous Are They?*

PART I
Identifying the Problem

Chapter 1: Can We Have a "Living Constitution" and the Rule of Law?

Experience should teach us to be most on our guard to protect liberty when the government's purposes are beneficent. Men born to freedom are naturally alert to repel invasion of their liberty by evil-minded rulers. The greatest dangers to liberty lurk in insidious encroachment by men of zeal, well meaning but without understanding.
—Justice Louis Brandeis, *Olmstead v. U. S.* (1928)[1]

The Second American Revolution is imminent. Whether it is peaceful or violent depends on whether you, as an individual, are willing to do something to restore the government the Founding Fathers created, and which served us well until the middle of the twentieth century. These first pages, describing the problem, are sometimes filled with doom and gloom.

The content of **Part I** may even sound familiar if you have read books by Judge Robert Bork, Mark Levin, or Judge Andrew Napolitano. *The Second American Revolution* differs in two significant ways: first, I quote extensively from published Court decisions, public speeches, and other sources to give the reader a view of U.S. Supreme Court justices in their own words. **Part II** is a clear solution, which can be accomplished if you are willing to accept your own responsibility and "git'er done."[2]

To telegraph the ending of the play at the opening curtain, we cannot get rid of the scoundrels in government without term limits, and we can't have term limits without amending the Constitution. The United States Supreme Court, in *U.S. Term Limits, Inc. v. Thornton*,[3] struck down an amendment to the Arkansas State Constitution limiting the number of terms a federal senator or representative may serve.

The Court said the qualifications for federal officials are spelled out in the U.S. Constitution and the states have no authority to change that. Based on that reasoning, neither would Congress—in the unlikely event we could persuade it to try.

I have been exposed to a "senator for life" in the person of nonagenarian the Honorable Robert C. Byrd (D-WV), elected to Congress in 1952—while the author was still in high school—and the longest-serving senator with over fifty years in that chamber.

I also knew a "president for life," Franklin D. Roosevelt. Both served honorably but for way too long. Term limiting all elected officials is one of several reforms proposed in **Part II,** detailing how you can get involved and effect the changes. In my lifetime, I have watched the Supreme Court go from what Alexander Hamilton called "the least dangerous branch" to the most overbearing and oppressive. The

Court routinely overturns laws passed by Congress; now the president has gotten into the business of overriding Congress.

President Barack Obama asked for a commission to study how to reduce the federal budget deficit. [It's pretty simple, actually—quit spending money you don't have]. The Senate turned him down; his response was to "move forward" on the commission by issuing an executive order.[4] This raises some interesting constitutional questions. There is no authority in the Constitution for the president to override Congress; and who will fund the commission? Only Congress has the constitutional authority to levy taxes.

❖   ❖   ❖

Few would deny America is more polarized along political and ideological lines than at any time since the Civil War. What has been a center-right country since its founding is being steered hard left by a president who, during his campaign, promised "transformational change." He is delivering on his promise.

Individual freedom seems to stand helpless against assault from its left flank.

How much government do we want? "A government big enough to give you everything you want, is strong enough to take everything you have."[5] The government has taken over two of the "big three" automakers; it is in the banking business, and it's using its muscle to coerce big business to bend to the president's will. The president is firing CEOs of private businesses—never done before and clearly not within the president's power granted by the Constitution. The health care system is under siege.

As this is being written, the federal government enthusiastically supports the theory of global warming, even in the face of the unraveling science, and tries to pass cap and trade legislation (some call it "cap and tax"). The government is running *trillion* dollar deficits—if you want to see what a trillion dollars looks like, go here: http://www.pagetutor.com—and the price of gold bullion reached $1,200 an ounce for the first time in history.

In the countryside, a group called "Oathkeepers" is encouraging enlisted military personnel to make individual decisions about which orders they will obey and which they will not. On the surface this seems like a good idea—the Nuremberg Trials established the principle that "I was just following orders" will no longer be a defense to war crimes.

After the war, most civilized nations adopted, through the United Nations, the new "Nuremberg Rules" as a part of international law. The first nation to test the rules was Canada during the trial of a conscientious objector who had fled America to avoid military service. A Canadian court ruled:

> An individual must be involved at the policy-making level to be culpable for a
> crime against peace...the ordinary foot soldier is not expected to make his or
> her own personal assessment as to the legality of a conflict. Similarly, such an

individual cannot be held criminally responsible for fighting in support of an illegal war, assuming that his or her personal war-time conduct is otherwise proper.

On November 20, a group of Christian leaders—Catholic, Protestant, evangelical—called on all Christians to practice civil disobedience if the government tries to impose laws that do not conform to their deeply held traditional Christian values.[6]

Meanwhile, the Supreme Court of the United States uses its "Living Constitution" to make any laws it wants any time it wants. A "Living Constitution" is anathema to the rule of law. It was "invented" for the sole purpose of giving the Court power to amend—unilaterally and *unlawfully*—the Constitution any time five justices agree on what it *should* say.

Article V: How to Amend the Constitution of the United States

The only legitimate method of amending the Constitution is the procedure in Article V of the Constitution. De facto amendments through decisions of the Supreme Court are not lawful and do not conform to the rule of law. But we must obey them.

> *De Facto* is used to characterize an officer, a government, a past action, or a state of affairs which must be accepted for all practical purposes, but is illegal or illegitimate....Thus an officer, king, or government *de facto* is one who is in actual possession of the office or supreme power, but by usurpation, or without lawful title.—*Black's Law Dictionary,* 5th ed.

The Supreme Court said, "The Constitution was written to be understood by the voters; its words and phrases were used in their normal and ordinary as distinguished from technical meaning; where the intention is clear there is no room for construction and no excuse for interpolation or addition."[7]

The Tax Day Tea Parties are about a people, born in freedom, who now see those freedoms being stripped away by an oppressive government. Taking their theme from the Boston Tea Party, which began the American Revolution, the underlying anger and frustration now, as then, is with a government remote from its people—a people who are being taxed and regulated without having a say in the process.

This book is about a dysfunctional United States government. A poll in June 2008, toward the end of the Bush administration, confirmed what most Americans already knew—only 17 percent of *all* Americans believe the United States government represents the will of the American people.[8] Most of the people's distrust is aimed at Congress; however, no branch of government enjoys a majority approval of the way it is conducting business.

Several writers have identified the problem. This book is the first to offer a specific solution and a road map on how to solve that problem. The solution is simple in concept—relatively more difficult, but not impossible, to achieve.

We will focus initially on the Supreme Court. That does not imply that the Court is the sole dysfunctional branch. The Congress and the president each warrant a separate book in order to deal with the problems and the disconnect from the American people.

After the section on the Supreme Court, this book will touch briefly on why reform of the legislature will be necessary before the people trust Congress enough to allow it to get the Supreme Court under control. We must also examine how Congress has unlawfully delegated much of its lawmaking power to the president, who now can make laws, enforce those laws, and sit in judgment of those who disobey his laws. Legislative, executive, and judicial power, all in the hands of one man.

Unfortunately, few people see the hubris of the high court or the dangers of a monstrously huge federal government. Or so much power in the hands of the president. Most Americans don't seem to care.

But What Can the Supreme Court Do to Me?

A lot—and it already has!

- Did you know federal courts can levy taxes on your property without waiting for the legislature to do it? It doesn't happen often because most legislators know they have no choice so they go ahead and do what the courts ask—in spite of what the voters want. There may be a time, as in an election year, when the legislatures can't afford to act as an instrument of the Supreme Court. So anticipating that the legislature may balk someday, the Supreme Court went the next step: it gave the lower federal courts direct taxing authority—in violation of Article I of the Constitution. (See chapter 7). Article I gives taxing authority exclusively to Congress.

- The Supreme Court gave local and state governments the power to seize your home or business and give it to another private individual who will use the property however it wishes as long as it pays more taxes than you do.[9]

- The Supreme Court has given foreign terrorists the right to sue us in our own courts, even if the terrorists are not within the territorial jurisdiction of any federal district court in the United States.[10] It has extended to the terrorists greater civil rights than we give our own GIs in the field. One example: a person serving in the armed forces and subject to trial by military courts martial cannot petition for a writ of habeas corpus demanding to be tried in a civilian court

- The Supreme Court has assumed—without any authority—the right to amend the United States Constitution any time five justices can agree with each other about what they want the Constitution to say.

The reader looking at the bulleted points above will probably think, "Naw— that can't be true. Surely, that has to be hyperbole. The Supreme Court can't be that bad." Bear in mind, however, that the opinions expressed herein are not just those of the author.

Whenever there is a five-to-four decision to strike down or extend some law, there are four justices on the Court—justices that are equally intelligent, equally learned, and equally qualified in every respect—who are looking at the same facts, the same evidence, reading the same Constitution, and the same case law, who disagree with the majority opinion.

When that five-to-four split repeats over time, most often with the same justices voting together on each side of the issue, one may reasonably infer that *the different interpretations must come from some personal philosophy or political ideology,* not from any reasonable interpretation of the law. Or the Constitution.

The Constitution or Ideology—Which Controls?

During the 2006-2007 term, the first in which Sandra Day O'Connor was not a player, Justice Anthony Kennedy was the deciding vote in all twenty-four of the five-to-four decisions.

He may not be the best man for the job. "Justice Kennedy likes to wander all over the constitutional law like an errant voyager," according to John Yoo, former deputy assistant attorney general, Office of Legal Counsel. "No one knows where he is going to end up."[11]

Insofar as practical, the author has done most of the basic research for this book online. This was a conscious choice so that readers who want to read the original materials for themselves may do so in the comfort of their own home or office. One needs only a computer and an Internet connection.

How Dangerous Are They?

An understanding of the threat to liberty posed by the Court also will require at least a cursory examination of the other two branches of the government and their own dysfunction—how each in its own way encroaches on the liberty of the people and the concept of self-government.

Adding to the problem, Congress knowingly acts in ways not authorized by the Constitution. The federal government has *only* the powers delegated to it by the Constitution. Congress exceeds that mandate during almost every session.

The elected members know they are acting contrary to their role spelled out in the Constitution. For example, every year since 1995, John Shadegg, an Arizona Republican, has introduced legislation in Congress to require every bill to cite the specific part of the Constitution from which it, Congress, draws its authority to legislate. (The 2009-10 version is HR 450/S 1319

Each year since 1995, the bill has failed to pass. The members of Congress know full well that many of the laws they pass *are not authorized by the Constitution.* They just do whatever they want and the Constitution be damned!

The president of the United States, who has no authority in the Constitution to legislate or to judge the laws he makes and enforces, in fact does all three. He makes law, just like the legislators, he enforces the laws as the Constitution intended him to do, and he judges the laws that he makes in his administrative courts separate from the regular court system created under Article III.

President Franklin D. Roosevelt seized the power to make laws as an "emergency" measure during the Great Depression. The Court, perhaps to preserve its own power, overturned many of Roosevelt's laws, but Congress wimped out and did nothing.

Executive branch agencies did not begin with Roosevelt or the Administrative Procedure Act (APA), of course. Some administrative agencies date to the Civil War; however, the massive expansion of administrative agencies—and the size of the federal government—date only to Roosevelt's New Deal.

But even Roosevelt eventually became concerned by what he saw as the administrative agencies developed as a fourth branch of government.

Congress actually enhanced the unlawful presidential law making power by passing the APA, which formalized Roosevelt's power grab. There has been heated debate among scholars about whether Congress has authority to delegate its law-making powers. The author sides with those who believe Congress does not have that power. (See Article I, U.S. Constitution.) However, in reality, the sheer volume of laws passed by the president—measured by the paper they are printed on—is greater by far than the all the current laws passed by Congress.

Most county courthouses have a law library. Go by and look at the shelf space the U.S. Code (passed by Congress) occupies compared to the Code of Federal Regulations (the "rules" by the president that have the force and effect of law).

❖   ❖   ❖

It will become clear as you read this book that the Court rulings are most often all about ideology and only incidentally about the Constitution. The author believes once readers see how screwed up the government has become, they will want to do something about it.

In his first inaugural address, President Abraham Lincoln said, "This Country, with its institutions, belongs to the people who inhabit it. Whenever they grow weary of the existing government, they can exercise their *constitutional* right of amending it, or their *revolutionary* right to dismember, or overthrow it."

The final chapters of this book will provide a road map on how to create the peaceful revolution Lincoln spoke of—by amending the Constitution. There is so much palpable anger at government out here in "fly-over" country that it would not take much for some demagogue to stir up a violent revolution unless we take steps now to peacefully take back our country from an overly zealous federal government and reinstitute representative government.

Chapter 2: Who Told the Supreme Court It Can Amend the Constitution?

What today's decision will stand for, whether the Justices can bring themselves to say it or not, is the power of the Supreme Court to write a prophylactic, extra-constitutional Constitution binding on Congress and the States.—Justice Scalia's dissent in *Dickerson v. United States (2002)*. [12]

Should the Supreme Court be able to amend the Constitution at its own will and pleasure? Article V establishes a political procedure requiring a two-thirds vote of Congress or two-thirds of the state legislatures calling for a convention to offer amendments, then ratification by three-fourths of the states.

It does not grant any power to the Supreme Court to change the Constitution.

Article V is the only lawful way to change the Constitution; in 1956, the Supreme Court said if there is something in the Constitution we don't like, "the thing to do is to take it out of the Constitution, not to whittle it down by the subtle encroachments of judicial opinion."[13] But now, even without any *lawful* authority, the Supreme Court routinely amends the Constitution. It requires only that any five of the nine justices vote for the change.

The Court won't admit it amends the Constitution, of course. Like any good political spin doctor, it calls what it does by a different name—"interpretation."

Overruling the Constitution

Remember Y2K? As the year 2000 approached, there was fear computers would crash, airliners would not be able to find their way in the sky, and power grids would go down, leaving us all to freeze in the dark. Without telephones. Well, there was no electronic cataclysm. What may prove to be an even greater catastrophe, however, did occur, and hardly anyone noticed. The United States Supreme Court decided *Dickerson v. United States*.[14]

The Supreme Court in *Dickerson* announced it had the power to rewrite the Constitution.

One of the unintended consequences of that decision was the loss of one of the most fundamental rights guaranteed to a citizen of the United States of America by the First Amendment—the right to petition the government.[15]

In previous cases, the Supreme Court rated the right to petition the government for redress of grievances as one of "the most precious of the liberties safeguarded by the Bill of Rights."[16] That fundamental right had extended to all branches and all departments of government.[17]

Dickerson so emasculated that right that for all practical purposes your right to petition the federal government has been abolished in any area of law where the Supreme Court has ruled. You can still write your letter, of course, but Congress and the president—and all of the people of the United States acting together—are powerless to act on any subject area where the Supreme Court has made law.

There were even more serious consequences still to come.

In *Dickerson*, the Supreme Court gave itself the *overt* power to rewrite (amend) the Constitution. Again, that is not just the author's opinion. (See Justice Scalia's dissent, which headed this chapter.) The Court had already demonstrated in earlier cases its overriding authority to strike down any action of a state legislature with which it disagrees—not just for failure to comply with the Constitution, but with which the justices *personally* disagree on philosophical grounds.

As will become apparent in the chapters which follow, our written Constitution has been subordinated to the whims of the Court; the "Living Constitution," which is incompatible with the rule of law, is being interpreted by the Court in ways that are de facto amendments to the Constitution.

In its legal definition, de facto "is used to characterize an officer, a government, a past action, or a state of affairs which must be accepted for all practical purposes, but is illegal or illegitimate."[18]

"*Rule of Law* is a legal principle, of general application, sanctioned by the recognition of authorities, and usually expressed in the form of a maxim...provides that decisions should be made by the application of known principles or laws without the intervention of discretion in their application."—*Black's Law Dictionary,* 5th Ed.

If a judge follows a personal motive, employs her unique life experience as "a wise Latina," or views a case with "empathy" for one side or the other, by definition that judge is not following the rule of law. The law must not change each time a new president is elected and appoints his cronies to the Supreme Court.

If a military officer stages a coup d'état and seizes the government, he may announce that he has absolute power to govern. And he has, as long as his army is loyal to him. But it is *de facto* power seized at the point of a gun. It is not legitimate power. Nonetheless, you must obey the military dictator because his de facto power carries with it the power to kill anyone who crosses him. The fact that his power is *unlawful* in that example would not make you any less dead.

Just so, we must follow the dictates of the Supreme Court, which has assumed the power to amend the Constitution.

Because citizens were not interested in the Court's work and did nothing, the usurped power became de facto power. That power, assumed by the Court, is so clearly alien to the document itself that it is manifest the Constitution has no meaning or life in and of itself. It has become merely a symbol.

Justices on the Court invoke the Constitution as authority for their distorted decisions much like old-time evangelists in the hills and hollers of West Virginia (where the author grew up) selectively invoked the name of God and the Bible to bolster their point of view, no matter how misguided that personal point of view may appear to an educated clergy.

Think of *Roe v. Wade*[19] as an example of the Court amending the Constitution. Before the *Roe* decision, a woman had no constitutional right to have an abortion. After the decision in *Roe,* there was a constitutional right to have an abortion.

Play whatever semantic games with that you want, but *Roe v. Wade* is a de facto constitutional amendment, creating new federal rights where none existed before. The author expresses no opinion on the merits of *Roe v. Wade*, merely that if it was desirable to have legalized abortion, Congress, and not the Court, should have legalized it.

As it is, *Roe* has divided this country more than almost any other issue since the Civil War. A discussion of *Roe* and other Supreme Court amendments to the Constitution will be the subject of some of the following chapters.

Overturning Legitimate Acts of Congress

The authority to overturn an act of Congress has been around for a long time, dating back to the 1803 case *Marbury v. Madison*. That authority, because it was an unlawful usurpation of Congress' constitutional powers, was used sparingly for the next 150 years, thus gaining the patina of long-established precedent without creating any further controversy. That changed radically beginning in the second half of the twentieth century.

By the time the Court decided *Dickerson* in the year 2000, the Court felt comfortable enough in its self-given power that it announced that it can overturn any act of Congress it doesn't like. If you read the decision carefully, that means not just cases that do not comply with the Constitution, but any law with which five justices disagree personally.[20]

The Court needs only to frame the question in terms of a conflict with the United States Constitution and then decide that the question does, in fact, conflict with the Constitution. It doesn't make any difference what the issue is or whether the issue has merit. As it demonstrated in *Dickerson,* the Court can make a sophist argument then decide whatever any five justices agree with each other to decide.

The justices don't even have to agree with each other on why they want a particular outcome; it only requires five of them to vote for that outcome for whatever reason. This will become apparent in the *Bakke* decision[21] in chapter 3. Justice Powell wrote the plurality opinion for a Court so badly fractured that none of the six separate opinions spoke for a majority of the Court.

Any good lawyer worth her salt would know how to frame a question to get the conflict with the Constitution she wants. Homer Cummings, President Franklin Roosevelt's attorney general, said, "In the uncertain condition of our constitutional law it is not difficult for the skillful to devise plausible arguments and to raise technical objections to almost any form of legislation that may be proposed."[22]

Once the lawyer frames the conflict, the Supreme Court then resolves it in the way it wants, and, once decided, there is no appeal from a decision of the United States Supreme Court. No one can override the court. Justice Scalia's dissent in *Dickerson* states bluntly: "What today's decision will stand for, whether the Justices can bring themselves to say it or not, is the power of the Supreme Court to write a prophylactic, extra-constitutional Constitution, binding on Congress and the States."[23]

Can the Court Repeal the Bill of Rights?

Let's examine one fundamental right negated by the *Dickerson* decision. The United States Constitution guarantees every citizen the right to petition the government for redress of grievances. The American colonists codified that right in the First Amendment because they had some bad experiences with their previous government ignoring their reasonable pleas for fairness.

England's King George III routinely ignored their petitions for relief from what the colonists considered unreasonable taxation without any voice in the government that imposed the taxes.

The king also ignored their appeals to rein in his royal governors, who were grossly abusing their power. He ignored their requests when they asked to be afforded the same basic human rights that other Englishmen in the home island took for granted.

At least King George had an excuse. He may have suffered from a hereditary disease, porphyria, the intermittent symptoms of which, by the time of the American Revolution, may have seriously impaired his good judgment. He had some sort of learning disability and did not become a proficient reader until he was eleven years old. After the revolution, his erratic mental state deteriorated further, and it became impossible to keep it hidden. He was certifiably insane by 1811.[24]

The eventual response of the American colonists to the repeatedly unfair treatment by the king was to rebel and to form a new and independent country that would be more responsive to its citizens' voices. To ensure that the Americans who came after them would not find it necessary to rebel and throw off this new American government, the founders wanted to have some effective way to petition the government for relief.

Having learned that a people can throw off an abusive and unresponsive government, Americans would need to have some reasonable expectation that they could communicate with their government. They needed to know their petitions would be heard, and acted upon, by someone in government with the power to make and enforce decisions one way or the other.

The petitioner may not *like* the decision.

For example, if the government believes some overriding interest of the whole country is more important than relieving the particular burden complained of by the individual, it might deny the relief sought. But the citizen had an absolute right to be heard.

For more than two hundred years after the founding of our nation, the process worked. One could write a letter to one's congressional representative or to the president and expect that if the request was reasonable, someone in government would have the power to help solve the problem or grant the request.

That is no longer true.

Here's how the process is supposed to work: Let's say a person was the victim of a career criminal who voluntarily confesses to a police officer, in the presence of the victim, admitting that he committed the crime. It looks like a slam-dunk case. This criminal will be convicted and punished for his crime, right? Well, not necessarily. The police officer had not read the criminal his *Miranda*[25] rights before he admitted that he committed the crime, so the confession cannot be used against him. He walks away free.

The victim feels outraged, so she calls her congressional representative. Congress had been getting thousands of similar calls over the past few years from other crime victims and police officers. As a result, Congress passes a law. Let's call it "18 U.S.C. § 3501."

Now the trial court will listen to all the evidence, out of the presence of the jury, and determine whether the defendant confessed voluntarily. If the court is satisfied that it was voluntary, the confession could be admitted as evidence in court whether or not the criminal got the technical *Miranda* warnings.

The jury then gets to hear the evidence surrounding the giving of the confession, as well as the confession itself, and the jury also has to decide whether it was voluntary. The jury is another layer of protection for the criminal defendant to ensure there was no coercion. If the members of the jury determine, independently of the judge's ruling, that the confession was voluntary, it may give the confession whatever weight it feels is warranted. If *either* the court or the jury believes the confession was coerced or forced in any way, it cannot be used as evidence.

The aggrieved victim petitioned her government for redress of that grievance, and the government agreed that a too-technical application of the *Miranda* rules was wrong. As a result, Congress changed the law. *Miranda* is intended to protect the defendant from police coercion, not from the criminal's own stupidity or arrogance. That's how it is supposed to work. And in fact, that is how it did work—until the year 2000.

Justice Scalia began his dissent in *Dickerson* this way:

Those to whom judicial decisions are an unconnected series of judgments that produce either favored or disfavored results will doubtless greet today's decision as a paragon of moderation, since it declines to overrule *Miranda v. Arizona*.... Those who understand the judicial process will appreciate that today's decision is not a reaffirmation of *Miranda,* but a radical revision of the most significant element of *Miranda* (as of all cases): the rationale that gives it a permanent place in our jurisprudence.[26]

The decision in *Dickerson* turned *Miranda* into a constitutional right where none existed before. By elevating *Miranda* to the status of a constitutional right (it had been merely a rule of court and *not* a constitutional right prior to 2000), the Supreme Court is then able to say that the law passed by Congress, 18 U.S.C. § 3501, which in effect overruled the excessively technical application of *Miranda,* is unconstitutional.

What Does *Miranda* Require?

The *Miranda* decision was meant to stop certain police practices that were excessively coercive—which *might* lead to false confessions. It was limited in scope. Several subsequent cases emphasized the limited effect of the ruling: for example, the court ruled there is no requirement to give warnings before asking a suspect, "Where did you plant the bomb?"

Because of the gradual evolution of the case law leading up to the *Dickerson* decision, *Miranda* had taken on the "penumbra" (the author's word, not the Court's—and with apologies to the late Justice Harry Blackmun) of a constitutional right. The Court dictated that from now on, Miranda *would* be treated as a constitutional right.

That rendered the citizen's petition for redress, and Congress's law in response, null and void.

Chief Justice Rehnquist claimed, in the face of Scalia's dissent, that the Court is not really elevating *Miranda* warnings to constitutional status per se.[27] He was being disingenuous. All the fancy verbal footwork to try to avoid calling *Miranda* a constitutional right was to no avail. If you look at a duck and call it a horse, that doesn't make it a horse.

It's still going to waddle around wearing feathers, quacking like a duck, and eating snails and slugs and whatever other repulsive things it may find on the ground that it thinks taste good.

Make no mistake, after *Dickerson,* the *Miranda* warnings are a de facto constitutional right, and that fact will become abundantly clear in future decisions of the Court.

With few exceptions, changes brought about by the Court are subtle but always in one direction—giving the Court more power and, in the process, making our government less responsive to its citizens and less democratic.

The Court by its very nature is undemocratic. It is not elected by the people and is not accountable to the people. The people have no say over what the Supreme Court does. The people do not get to vote for Supreme Court justices. The justices serve for life. The Court's decisions, even if arbitrary and capricious, can never be questioned or overturned except by the Court itself.

"Dictatorship" is the name we usually give to an autocratic ruler. In Roman law, a dictator "[was] a magistrate invested with unlimited power, and created in times of national distress and peril...and had unlimited power and authority over both the property and lives of the citizens."[28]

At least in Rome, the dictator could serve for a limited term of six months only.

Miranda as we know it today did not spring full-blown from the Court. It evolved.

Another example of the evolution of the Supreme Court's expanding power and encroachment are the religious freedom cases discussed in the next chapter. They will demonstrate a group of decisions which individually, on their face, do not seem to be that threatening to individual rights. But taken together, the incremental changes have abolished any public expression of religious faith at most public places and events.

It is important to understand that the Bill of Rights did not confer any rights on the citizens of the United States. That is worth saying again: the Bill of Rights did not give anybody *any* rights. The first ten amendments *prohibited* the federal government from *taking away* the natural human rights that the people already had.

Those religious freedom cases will also help to put into context Justice Scalia's comment in *Dickerson*: "Those to whom judicial decisions are an unconnected series of judgments that produce either favored or disfavored results will doubtless greet today's decision as a paragon of moderation."[29]

For lawyers who follow the Court, individual decisions of the Court are not "an unconnected series of judgments."

Don't be distracted by Rehnquist's sophist arguments in *Dickerson* over whether *Miranda* is now a constitutional right. The two really important issues to come out of *Dickerson*: (1) the Supreme Court's restricting your constitutional right to petition your government for redress of grievances, and (2) the Court's giving itself the overt power to rewrite the Constitution.

Actually, the Court has been rewriting the Constitution since *Marbury v. Madison*,[30] decided in 1803. *Marbury* was the Court's first ever amendment to the Constitution, asserting the power of "judicial review," the power of the Court to review and overturn an act of Congress.

The drafters of the Constitution had considered and specifically rejected giving the Court that much power. The founders feared that if the Constitution gave the Court the power to override Congress, the states would never ratify it.

Thomas Jefferson and others of his party vociferously denounced *Marbury*, but they were not in a legal position to do anything about it: they won. It's the losers who appeal Court decisions.

But Chief Justice John Marshall heard the outrage—and the threats to impeach him—and the Court moved cautiously for the remainder of Marshall's tenure as chief justice. That set the paradigm for the next 150 years until Earl Warren became the chief justice in 1953. Now the gloves were off.

The Supreme Court Trumps the "Co-Equal" Congress

Rehnquist announced unequivocally in the *Dickerson* case that the Supreme Court has the power to override an act of Congress if the Court believes the act is in conflict with the Constitution. In the hands of a clever lawyer, any question about *any* act of Congress can be framed in such a manner that it will conflict with the Constitution.

Every lawyer is trained in law school how to nitpick in order to distinguish one set of facts from another. For example, if there is an accident and A, B, and C happen as a result, but D, E, and F also happen, the lawyer for the plaintiff is going to emphasize A, B, and C in her argument while the defense lawyer will focus on D, E, and F to support her case.

Both are telling the absolute truth—just not the whole truth. It is only the witnesses who must "swear to tell the truth, the *whole* truth, and nothing but the truth." All of those events, A, B, C, D, E, and F, resulted from the accident. But lawyers choose to emphasize the facts that support their client's case.

They do not hide any legal precedent from the court, but they do not voluntarily bring forth the facts that do not favor the outcome they seek. That's the other lawyer's job. Under the Code of Conduct, lawyers do have an obligation of candor to the Court insofar as they must reveal any binding *legal precedent* to the contrary that they know about.

So the conflict with the Constitution gets framed, and then who gets to decide? Well. The Supreme Court, of course.

In a post-*Dickerson* world, where does one turn for relief? Suppose a citizen is aggrieved by the unintended consequences[31] of a far-reaching Supreme Court decision, decided on an entirely different point of law, but which coincidentally infringes on some important right everyone had always taken for granted but now has been lost. Where does one send one's "petition for redress"? One's congressional representative?

That probably won't do much good. *Dickerson* says that Congress has no power to override a decision of the Supreme Court. The president? He has no more power than Congress to overrule a bad Court decision. Ah—go back to the Supreme Court itself! That is easy to say but not so easy to do. Apart from the fact that the Supreme Court has virtually absolute discretion to choose which cases it wants to accept for review, there are a very limited number of "appeals as of right," none of which are relevant to this discussion.

The Court Controls Its Own Agenda

The Court chooses to hear fewer than seventy to eighty of the approximately seven thousand petitions it receives each year. Add to that an additional barrier, the cost of the appeal, and a petition for redress in this class of cases is prohibitive for the average citizen.

As the seven thousand petitions come into the Court, they are screened by law clerks who then brief the justices on the case. The several justices then may or may not actually read all of the petitions for review. The justices themselves decide if they want to read all the briefs or just the sampling their clerks recommend.

In other words, your petition must first pass the critical scrutiny of at least four law clerks—the best and the brightest of each year's graduating law students, usually from the best schools, are the ones who usually become Supreme Court clerks, but inexperienced young lawyers nonetheless—who will then pass the case up to their respective justices, four of whom must be sufficiently impressed to vote to hear the appeal before the case can be docketed. Some justices rely more on their clerks than others.

The odds against any particular case being among the seventy or eighty which get docketed are at best nearly one hundred to one, and in fact are much worse than that—the Court alone decides which cases to hear. As stated above, there is no right of appeal to the United States Supreme Court; the rule itself specifies that accepting a petition for review is a matter of "judicial discretion" and will be granted "only for compelling reasons." The Court has indicated a strong preference for hearing cases where:

(a) a United States court of appeals has entered a decision in conflict with the decision of another United States court of appeals...; (b) a state court of last resort has decided an important federal question in a way that conflicts with the decision of another state court of last resort or of a United States court of appeals; (c) a state court or a United States court of appeals has decided an important question of federal law that has not been, but should be, settled by this Court.[32]

Although not in the rules, there might be one other class of cases: those that may advance the Court's own agenda. And the Court does have its own agenda.

An appeal to the Supreme Court, therefore, is not like writing a letter to one's congressman. It's going to cost much more than a postage stamp, and there is only the slimmest of chances that a particular petition will be among the few the Court chooses to hear, even after the petitioner has spent substantial sums of money on court costs and lawyers' fees getting the case in a position to be appealed.

There is another barrier to appeals: it is absurd to think that the Court will take up the challenge to revisit a new decision it just handed down just because some innocent citizen, not a party to the case, was unintentionally injured by its ruling.

If you are aggrieved by the unintended consequences of a Supreme Court decision, the Supreme Court is the only one who can "fix" it. Which means, for all practical purposes, no one will fix it. The ruling in *Dickerson* is explicit: Congress has no power to second-guess a Supreme Court decision, although the Court routinely second-guesses Congress.

Is the First Amendment Right to Seek Redress Still Valid?

So how much good is the First Amendment right to petition the government for a redress of grievances? Not much good at all if the Supreme Court is the culprit who violates your rights. Oh, it is still possible to write to one's congressional representative or send an e-mail, but he has the power to act only where the Supreme Court has not yet made law.

Compare that to the lip service Chief Justice Rehnquist pays to the Constitution in *Dickerson* when he says the Court's "power to judicially create and enforce nonconstitutional 'rules of evidence for the federal courts exists only in the absence of a relevant Act of Congress.' " He then demonstrated that the opposite is true as he proceeded to strike down a relevant act of Congress—18 U.S.C. § 3501—ruling, in effect, that the *Miranda* warnings themselves are a constitutional right.

Rehnquist acknowledges Congress's power to regulate the Court's procedural rules except where the Court has ruled on something of a constitutional nature. The only thing that can trump an act of Congress is the Constitution. Therefore, ipso facto, *Miranda* warnings must be a constitutional right; otherwise the Court could not have overruled the act of Congress at 18 U.S.C. § 3501.

Article III of the Constitution gives Congress the explicit power to set regulations for the Court. Section 2 of Article III says, in part, "the supreme Court shall have appellate Jurisdiction, both as to Law and Fact, with such Exceptions, and under such Regulations as the Congress shall make" (capitalization as in the original).

Chief Justice Rehnquist's hypocrisy in preserving the Court's power at the same time he claims the Court is not creating a new constitutional right becomes all the more apparent when you look at Rehnquist's own previous writings on *Miranda*:

> The Court recognized that these procedural safeguards were not themselves rights protected by the Constitution...The rule is calculated to prevent, not to repair. Its purpose is to deter—to compel respect for the constitutional guaranty in the only effective way—by removing the incentive to disregard it....
> The deterrent purpose of the exclusionary rule necessarily assumes that the police have engaged in willful, or at the very least negligent, conduct which has deprived the defendant of some right. By refusing to admit evidence gained as a result of such conduct, the courts hope to instill...a greater degree of care toward the rights of an accused. Where the official action was pursued in complete good faith, however, the deterrence rationale loses much of its force.[33]

Miranda was merely a procedural safeguard imposed by the Court, and not by the Constitution. It need not be slavishly followed in all cases if law enforcement officers act in good faith. The chief justice's view that *Miranda* was a mere procedural rule was reaffirmed as he joined with Justice O'Connor's opinion in the *Elstad* case, decided in 1985, some nineteen years after *Miranda*:

> The Miranda presumption does not require that fruits of otherwise voluntary statements be discarded as inherently tainted. It is an unwarranted extension of Miranda to hold that a simple failure to administer the warnings, unaccompanied by any actual coercion or other circumstances calculated to undermine the suspect's ability to exercise his free will, so taints the investigatory process that a subsequent voluntary and informed waiver is ineffective for some indeterminate period.[34]

The "flip-flop" in Rehnquist's position as expressed in *Dickerson* came about because he had a dilemma. If the Supreme Court allowed the Fourth Circuit decision upholding 18 U.S.C. § 3501 to stand, it would be admitting that Congress, and not the Court, was the real lawmaker who decides public policy and law in this country. The Court would be ceding back to Congress the power which the Court had carefully, incrementally usurped from Congress over the years.

Was the Court being Machiavellian? It would be sheer speculation to guess. But either way the result is the same: Rehnquist, and six other justices, voted to keep the power. Only Justice Scalia, joined by Justice Thomas, openly voiced the real impact of the decision.

Can this be how, facing sure death if they failed, the people who rebelled against King George "in order to form a more perfect union, establish justice...and secure the blessings of liberty" wanted the new Constitution to work?

The idea that you would risk your life to secure liberty from one imperial power (King George) only to voluntarily turn it over to another imperial power (the nine appointed, life-tenured Supreme Court justices) is too ridiculous to contemplate.

When there is a conflict between two ostensibly equal branches of government, normally one looks to the Constitution to resolve the conflict. But what happens when one of the "coequal" branches is the only one that can say what the Constitution means?

The right to petition the government for redress is not one that comes as readily to mind perhaps as the other First Amendment guarantees of freedom of speech or of the press and freedom of religion.

If one thinks of the Bill of Rights at all, the other protections with which we are most familiar are the Fifth Amendment right against self-incrimination or the Fourth Amendment right against unreasonable search and seizures—and maybe the Second Amendment right to keep and bear arms. Except for lawyers, political activists, and political science teachers, most people probably don't think much about petitioning the government for redress.

It Is an Important Right, Nonetheless

Every person has the right to talk to lawmakers and to express a position on issues and ask for their support. It does not have to be a formal "petition" with a lot of signatures. It's every person's right to talk to his government and be treated with respect. But if the subject matter conflicts with something the Supreme Court has ruled on, your representative is going to say, "Sorry, I can't help you."

Look again at that conflict between two ostensibly equal branches of government: only one of the "coequal" branches gets to say what the Constitution means!

Metaphorically, it's as if the Constitution was written in Latin and the Supreme Court comprises the only people left alive who still know how to read Latin.

The other branches of government must rely on the Supreme Court to tell them what the Constitution says and if the Supreme Court has a hidden agenda and deliberately misrepresents what is in the Constitution, Congress and the president just have to accept it because they don't read Latin.

Some congressional representatives or the president may go home and try to dig out their old high school Latin books (if any of them are old enough to have had high school Latin books) and translate for themselves what the Constitution says. But the Supreme Court will always say, "Nope, you guys are amateurs. We are fluent in Latin and the official translators of the Constitution. End of discussion."

Let's Try the *Legitimate* Way to Amend the Constitution

The usual process leading to a constitutional amendment is for the United States Congress to vote by a two-thirds majority to enact a resolution calling for an amendment, then send that proposed amendment out to the several states to be ratified. But that may be a hard sell. The lawyers in Congress will not permit any restrictions on the Supreme Court, and most members certainly won't vote to term-limit themselves.

On the other hand, never has there been such a disconnect between our elected representatives in Washington and the people who elected them. Precisely the reason the founders provided a bypass mechanism for a Congress who has forgotten it is the servant of the people. The time is ripe to use method two!

The people of the United States have not used the second procedure in Article V even though the Supreme Court has declared that it is lawful—two-thirds of the states can demand a convention to propose amendments. Many people fear a convention for offering amendments to the Constitution because they fear a runaway convention where everything is on the table. Their fears are unfounded.

There are substantial differences between the Constitution and the Articles of Confederation, which were scrapped in order to adopt the Constitution we have now. The definitive difference is the language of the Constitution of the United States: Article V states unequivocally, "Congress...or, on the Application of the

Legislatures of two thirds of the several States, shall call a Convention *for proposing Amendments*, which in either Case, shall be valid to all Intents and Purposes, as *Part of this Constitution*."[35] All amendments must be ratified by the ¾ of the states

❖   ❖   ❖

There has never been this much cynicism about the federal government and such a feeling of hopelessness that the people have no meaningful input into what the elected representatives do.

Many in Congress—most lawyer-congressmen, in fact—may try to sabotage any effort to reform the government, particularly if it curtails, even in the slightest, the power of the Supreme Court—and lawyers. If one should also mention tort reform, the lawyers will go nuts. If the proposal for reform begins in Congress, it will be spiked before it gets out of committee.

Most lawyers are very deferential toward the Court.[36] The Constitution gave Congress the exclusive lawmaking power before the Supreme Court decided it, too, wanted to set policy and make laws. Lawyers like the courts making law because it gives them more power.

Any effort to amend the Constitution will need to overcome the resistance of the lawyers serving in Congress and the institutional inertia of that body. Apart from their demonstrated bias in favor of the court system, there is tremendous peer pressure among lawyers to maintain the status quo.

"One ABA [American Bar Association] official proposed professional discipline, including disbarment, for politicians who are also lawyers and who criticize judges."[37] In the 110th Congress, 236 members hold a law degree—178 in the House and fifty-eight in the Senate.

As the Court over time seizes and consolidates more and more power for itself, the country is becoming less and less democratic as a result. In addition, because we are ruled by judicial fiat rather than laws passed by our elected representatives, there is not a consensus of what the law should be. Therefore, there is polarization and conflict among citizens. To paraphrase comedian Rodney Dangerfield, "[the law] don't get no respect."

The Court by its nature is an antidemocratic institution. Its members are political appointees, not elected by the people. Once appointed, they have the right to serve for life. They are not accountable to the people, or to anyone. The Supreme Court consists of nine old people who totally control their own agenda. Only three of the justices currently serving are under the age of sixty-five.

Most are near or past seventy; one justice, Stevens, was ninety years old when he retired in April 2010. He was the third oldest ever to serve on the Court. Justices impaired by age or illness occur all too frequently.

Mental decrepitude and incapacity have troubled the United States Supreme Court from the 1790s to the 1990s. The history of the Court is replete with repeated instances of justices casting decisive votes or otherwise participating actively in the Court's work when their colleagues and/or families had serious doubts about their mental capacities.[38]

Law Professor David J. Garrow wrote a law review article that studied the problem in depth: about once every ten years, on average, a justice of the United States Supreme Court suffers from such serious mental or physical illnesses that he cannot meaningfully participate in the work of the Court. Some were certifiably insane, others demented to the point their colleagues on the Court would not decide a case if the impaired justice's vote would be decisive.[39] Some stayed on the Court for as much as two years in this impaired condition.

The members of the Court debate in secret and hand down laws that are binding on the people and on Congress. After one such secret debate, a former law clerk for the late Justice Harry Blackmun wrote about one of his "most vivid memories":

> The sight of the Court's three most liberal Justices returning to their offices after one of the Court's Friday morning conferences spoke volumes. Justices Blackmun and Brennan, both frail and slight, walked down the plush maroon carpet, arm in arm, leaning upon one another for support. Brennan, who had been ill, appeared unsteady on his feet. Behind them, arms outstretched, either out of protectiveness toward his diminutive colleagues, or to derive support, loomed the wheezing figure of Justice Thurgood Marshall.[40]

The Elected Congress Should Be Making Our Laws

If we are to live in a free society, where we actually vote for the people who make our laws—as we incorrectly believe we do now—it is imperative that we bar the Supreme Court from making law in defiance of the elected Congress.

To be sure, the Congress does enact much of the law we live under. But on many issues that are *really* important, it is the Court that makes law *and policy.*

Reigning in the Supreme Court can begin with the state legislatures. Article V of the United States Constitution contains two methods to add amendments: (1) Congress by a two-thirds vote can approve a proposed amendment and send it out to the states to ratify. Given the nature of the needed reform and the anticipated resistance of the lawyer-members, it is highly unlikely that Congress will initiate this kind of amendment; and (2) two-thirds of the state legislatures can demand that Congress call a convention for offering amendments.

This second method has at least two advantages. First, instead of a two-thirds vote of Congress—probably impossible to muster—it requires only a simple majority vote of two-thirds of the state legislatures. Given the demographic and political makeup of the country and the dissatisfaction with the federal government, this should not be an impossible goal to meet.

In June 2007, only "19% of voters [thought] Congress is doing a good or excellent job."[41] A Reuters-Zogby poll in September 2007 saw the number of people who considered Congress was doing a good or excellent job fall to 11 percent. Another Rasmussen poll, published July 8, 2008, saw Congress' approval in single digits—only 9 percent thought Congress was doing a good or excellent job.

The second advantage is that if you have two-thirds of the states participating in the convention they asked for, they probably will vote for ratification of their work and would need only a few more states to join them in order to make up the three-fourths majority to ratify.

Unlike federal representatives and senators, who go to Washington and forget who sent them there, almost all state legislators live in the communities that elected them. Since they must run for reelection, they are quite happy to meet constituents and listen to their views.

Don't expect that your conversation with your representative, standing alone, will change his mind. But I guarantee that if you and several friends and neighbors begin to talk to the representative, either alone or together, he or she will hear you. CAUTION: do not start an organized letter-writing campaign, and don't form a "committee" to go see your representative in a group. Legislators are more likely to listen to the concerns of individual citizens in the community, according to Bill Wooten, a West Virginia lawyer and member of the West Virginia House of Delegates. Mr. Wooten believes "the best way is to call" your delegate or state senator. Most legislators are always eager to know what citizens have on their minds.

Mr. Wooten is an attorney and has an office where he can be reached; legislators who are not otherwise well known may be more difficult to track down, but they are just as easy to talk to once you find them. On the state level, legislators are still very close to the people they represent. Anyone, I mean *anyone,* can pick up a telephone and talk to his or her legislator; and if you cannot reach him or her immediately, everyone I have ever known or known about returned telephone calls to constituents.

Mr. Wooten reminded me of something I already knew from my own experience. Most people, not just legislators, are more likely to listen to people they know or with whom they have some "connection"—for example, the people one goes to church with, people that one sees in the barber or beauty shop every few weeks, or people one meets at the Moose Lodge or the Knights of Columbus. But they do not ignore *any* constituents.

Of all the people you ever want to meet, politicians are the easiest. If you don't happen to belong to the Elks or any other organizations to which he may belong, every politician has to run for office. Volunteer to help. You can work in the kitchen helping prepare those "rubber-chicken dinners," or you can work on the serving line (you may need a food handler's permit from the local health department), or you can stuff envelopes for direct mailings, or just hang around campaign headquarters and schmooze or answer telephones.

Chapter 3: Animus Toward Religion

Believing with you that religion is a matter which lies solely between a man and his God; that he owes account to none other for his faith or his worship; that the legislative powers of the government reach actions only, and not opinions, I contemplate with sovereign reverence that act of the whole American people which declared that their legislature should "make no law respecting an establishment of religion or prohibiting the free exercise thereof."—Thomas Jefferson, letter to the Danbury, Connecticut Baptists[42]

The author once read, "These statements ["Congress shall make no law respecting an establishment of religion, or prohibiting the free exercise thereof"] are so brief, and consequently so vague, that there is much debate as to what they actually mean when applied to specific issues."[43]

That comment immediately brought to mind the lyrics from the country song "What Part of No Don't You Understand?"[44] "Congress shall make no law" means exactly that: Congress shall make no law!

The First Amendment was ratified in 1791, a dozen years before the Supreme Court's 1803 decision in *Marbury v. Madison*. At the time of ratification, it was axiomatic that the First Amendment did not give either the Supreme Court or the president any power to make laws. Therefore, the phrase should be understood to mean "the *federal government*" shall make no law restricting the free exercise of religion.

It effectively denies to the whole federal government the power to regulate religion or religious thought. Religious freedom came from God, according to Thomas Jefferson, not from the government; therefore, the government had no power to diminish or curtail in any way its free expression.

Joseph Story, whose *Commentaries on the Constitution of the United States* is still considered the standard treatise on the subject, wrote:

> In some of the states, episcopalians constituted the predominant sect; in others, presbyterians; in others, congregationalists; in others, quakers; and in others again, there was a close numerical rivalry among contending sects. It was impossible, that there should not arise perpetual strife, and perpetual jealousy on the subject of ecclesiastical ascendancy, if the national government were left free to create a religious establishment....Thus, the whole power over the subject of religion is left to the state governments...and the Catholic and the Protestant, the Calvinist and the Arminian, [sic] the Jew and the Infidel, may sit down at the common table of the national counsels, without any inquisition into their faith, or mode of worship"[45] (spelling as in the original).

That is the key to understanding the First Amendment establishment clause. Imagine the backlash if the United States government had tried to impose the Anglican religion, established in Virginia, on all the colonies—the Quakers in Pennsylvania, the Congregationalists in New England, and the Baptists and Catholics wherever they may be found. The Anglicans were obliged by law to attend church; taxpayer dollars supported the mission of the Church.

What is so difficult to understand? Unless, of course, one doesn't want to understand. Unless someone wants to be able to argue his or her own antireligious point of view without the meddlesome inconvenience of the plain words of the Constitution.

This chapter will examine the Court's cases touching on religion with the twofold purpose of showing (1) the way the Court builds on precedent to change the law incrementally in ways that seem innocuous and benign at the time; and (2) how the Court shows antagonism, consciously or unconsciously, against free religious expression. Only in hindsight do you see the Court's larger purpose and direction. The result is obvious: the Supreme Court of the United States, in direct violation of the First Amendment, has prohibited the free exercise of one's religion in public events.

First, Some History

At the time Congress debated whether to adopt the First Amendment, state law established the Church of England (Anglican Church) as the official religion in the colony of Virginia, as it had been in the mother country, England. White Americans were required to support that church through their taxes, and they were required to attend church.[46] Another example of an established church was the Puritan Congregational Church of Massachusetts, which was not disestablished until 1833 by an amendment to the state constitution.[47] (Ten of the original thirteen colonies had established churches.)

Establishment of Anglicans in Virginia occasionally broke up evangelical church services. There was some tolerance from time to time for non-Anglicans, but it was not uncommon to see a Baptist minister preaching from his jail cell. At all times, even during the periods of relative tolerance for differing Christian views, there was a continuing effort to stamp out the "pagan" religious beliefs of African slaves and Native Americans and turn them all into Christians.

The First Amendment Was intended to prevent the federal government or its subdivisions or agents from that kind of direct interference either in support of or in opposition to religion.

Freedom of Religion

The guarantee of freedom of religion in the First Amendment did not promise freedom from religion. As President John Adams said, "Our Constitution was made only for a moral and religious people. It is wholly inadequate to the government of any other."[48]

The population centers in this country, stretching from New England through New York and Pennsylvania, were settled in large part by people who came here because they could not freely practice their religion in their native country.

Of all the free people who came here early, the vast majority professed some sort of Christian faith, which gave some common background and helped smooth the rough edges where different ethnic groups came together.

By the year 1702, all thirteen American colonies had some form of state-supported religion. This support varied from tax benefits to religious requirements to restricting voting or serving in the legislature.[49] All of the government tax support went to Protestant denominations, and only Christian Protestants were eligible to serve in elected office.

Although Delaware quit government support for religion as early as 1792, some colonies/states continued state support for religion and/or restrictions on anyone but Protestants holding public office until after the American Civil War. The last states to cease all government support for religion were Maryland (1867), South Carolina (1868), North Carolina (1875), and New Hampshire (1877).

Religious observations are deeply imbedded in our laws: religious holidays, opening sessions of Congress and other public functions with prayer, the Declaration of Independence, which refers to the "protection of divine Providence," the swearing of oaths on the Bible, and in other ways too numerous to mention. The military service academies still require attendance at chapel, and the government recruits and pays chaplains for the military. Even sessions of the Supreme Court begin with the words "God save the United States and this Honorable Court."

In one religious freedom case, Chief Justice Burger wrote:

> Some who trouble to read the opinions in these [religious freedom] cases will find it ironic—perhaps even bizarre—that on the very day we heard arguments in the cases, the Court's session opened with an invocation for Divine protection. Across the park a few hundred yards away, the House of Representatives and the Senate regularly open each session with a prayer. These legislative prayers are not just one minute in duration, but are extended, thoughtful invocations and prayers for Divine guidance. They are given, as they have been since 1789, by clergy appointed as official chaplains and paid from the Treasury of the United States. Congress has also provided chapels in the Capitol, at public expense, where Members and others may pause for prayer, meditation—or a moment of silence.[50]

The westward expansion of our frontiers was based on "manifest destiny," a belief that Americans had a God-given right to conquer and control the North American land all the way to the Pacific Ocean.

The Holy Bible—and a Christian Nation

The King James Bible "entered, as no other book has, into the making of the personal character and public institutions of the English-speaking peoples"[51] and, in particular, the immigrants to America. The two books, and often the only books, found in the homes of pioneers moving west were the Holy Bible and the Sears, Roebuck catalog. At the beginning of the nineteenth century, 130 separate Bible societies gave away Bibles to new European immigrants who had none when they arrived.

Enter Congress, who inadvertently gave the Supreme Court reason to begin to interpret—and make—laws regulating religion.

When Congress enacts a law exempting religious organizations from certain taxes, for example, or creates a tax exemption for charitable contributions to religious organizations, without adequately defining exactly what a religious organization is, Congress has just invited the Supreme Court to get involved. Somebody has to decide, "What is a religious organization?"

From the settlement in Jamestown in 1607 to the Declaration of Independence in 1776, the American colonists—overwhelmingly Christian—had been living under the common law as British subjects. They had been conditioned, therefore, to believe that "judge-made law" was legitimate, normal, and necessary. The people of this country never questioned whether the courts had the right to interpret what the elected representatives intended when Congress passed a new law.

That belief permitted John Marshall to get away with his power grab in *Marbury v. Madison* notwithstanding the singular lack of such authority in the Constitution. The plain wording of the newly drafted Constitution for the governance of the United States of America gave Congress the exclusive lawmaking authority.

Only Thomas Jefferson and a handful of his contemporaries saw the danger in Marshall's newfound power of "judicial review."

America has always been a Christian nation; the early settlers strongly believed that religious faith and moral teachings made for a better and more law-abiding citizen. Although most states had discontinued direct tax support for churches by the early nineteenth century, some states continued to restrict public office holders to Protestant Christian males.

Maryland's law requiring that one had to believe in God to hold public office was not challenged in the U. S. Supreme Court until 1961.[52] It was no surprise when the Court struck down the law, given the Court's assault on religion freedom begun in 1947 with the *Everson* case.

Incredibly, South Carolina still tried to enforce a law requiring a belief in God in order to hold public office in 1993. In 1997, the South Carolina Supreme Court unanimously invalidated the law. Six other states had similar laws on the books but never tried to enforce them.

The idea that America is a Christian nation began to change after World War II.

The Assault on Belief

The Court began its assault on religious freedom in 1947 with the case *Everson v. Board of Education*.[53] The holding in that case is less important than the fact that the Supreme Court assumed the power to rule on it at all.

Until *Everson,* the court's ruling on religious issues followed a path of noninterference in religious matters. In 1878, the Court addressed the issue of whether a man could use his religious belief to circumvent and disobey the law of the land. The Court established the primacy of the law when it ruled in *Reynolds v. United States*[54] that a polygamous Mormon, living in Utah Territory, could be prosecuted under the federal laws against bigamy.

But that decision is consistent with the Christian view that one should "render therefore unto Caesar the things which are Caesar's, and unto God the things that are God's."[55] Christians are expected to obey the civil and criminal laws of the country where they may be living.

In an 1899 case, *Bradfield v. Roberts*,[56] the Court refused to stop government funding for a Catholic charity hospital in the District of Columbia which served indigent patients. In 1908, *Quick Bear v. Leupp*[57] allowed the government to transfer funds belonging to the Sioux Indians, but held in trust by the government, to Catholic schools designated by the Sioux to educate their children.

In each case, there was a federal question: a violation of a federal statute in the one case, and a question about direct federal funding of programs operated by religious organizations in the other two. In each of the latter cases, the federal government was directly paying out money to institutions, a hospital and a school, which happened to be run by a religious organization, the Catholic Church, for the benefit of the people. The United States Supreme Court did not find any conflict in that.

Other cases considered by the Court favored noninterference by the government in religious matters. Various cases held that ministers, theological students, and others whose religion forbade them to make war may be excused from the draft;[58] states may not discriminate against religion by requiring all children to attend public schools;[59] immigrants in the process of being naturalized cannot, on moral grounds, avoid the oath to uphold the Constitution.[60]

Freedom of the press and of religion figured into the Supreme Court striking down a city ordinance which had prohibited the distribution of religious tracts;[61] a city has no authority to impose a tax on religious activity;[62] and the state may not compel students to recite the Pledge of Allegiance to the flag if it violates their religious principles.[63]

On the other hand, the cases which follow *Everson* represent an epiphany on the part of the Court. It began to push the idea that any laws which have the effect of "accommodating" religion generally (not establishing an official state religion, mind you, just allowing spontaneous expressions of religious thought by citizens), and, more recently, any action whereby the government even acknowledges religion, must be stamped out.

Everson should never have gotten to the United States Supreme Court.

A New Jersey state law allowed local school districts, in lieu of providing school buses, to reimburse parents for the cost of public transportation to get their children to and from schools. Catholic children going to parochial schools were eligible for the transportation aid the same as children attending public schools.

Everson sued the board of education to stop the practice as it applied to parochial schools. The local court ruled in his favor, and the board appealed the decision to the New Jersey Supreme Court, which reversed it, allowing the practice to continue. That should have been the end of it. It was a state issue, and the highest state court had decided it.

At that time there were few direct federal funds going to help elementary and secondary education. The Smith-Hughes Act of 1917 and its successors provided a small amount of federal funds for vocational education; the Servicemen's Readjustment Act of 1944 (GI Bill of Rights) following World War II provided opportunities for returning veterans to attend college.

But direct funding to state and local school districts for academic education wouldn't happen for another fourteen years—spurred by the "education gap" when the Russians launched the first artificial earth satellite, Sputnik. After Sputnik, the federal government suddenly became interested in supporting education at every level to try to stamp out the "education gap."

Everson's dispute with a local school board happened at a time when most local school boards nationwide were supported by local tax funds, usually from property taxes, with some supplemental funds from the states. The dispute was settled, and should have remained settled, by the New Jersey courts. To borrow a cliché, "The federal government didn't have a dog in that fight."

The Court Acts Without Authority

There was no constitutional authority for the U.S. Supreme Court action since there was no federal issue to be resolved. New Jersey law mandated school attendance but permitted parents to satisfy the mandate by sending their children to religious schools so long as the religious schools met the same state criterion as to teacher qualification and curriculum as public schools. That state law was neutral toward religion, and the United States Supreme Court did not question or even analyze that neutrality.

But the Court did accept the case for review and, by a narrow five-four margin, upheld the decision of the New Jersey Supreme Court. It could have, and should have, just declined to accept the case for review because it was a state issue. That would have produced the same result. However, it would not have advanced the Court's antireligious agenda, which was just beginning to emerge.

If you look at the merits of the state law case, Catholic parents were paying the same taxes as non-Catholics; some of those taxes went to support public schools, which Catholic children did not use. The relatively small amount of money involved in the transportation subsidy was minuscule when compared with the cost of hiring more teachers and building additional classrooms that would become necessary if Catholic families utilized the public schools (as they were entitled to do) instead of exercising their religious choice.

The suit by Everson obviously could have had only one motive: anti-Catholic bias.

Planting the Seed of Religious Suppression

Having agreed to hear the case, and just as Chief Justice Marshall had in *Marbury,* the *Everson* court added other gratuitous findings, not necessary to the outcome of the case, that there was "a wall of separation between church and state" mandated by the First Amendment of the Constitution.

That was disingenuous. But true or not, the "wall of separation" finding became the bludgeon that later courts would use over the next six decades to rule against free religious expression in almost every case.

The language about the wall of separation is not in the Constitution. It comes from the letter from Thomas Jefferson to a group of Baptists in Danbury, Connecticut.[64]

In context, the letter had the opposite meaning of what that language now means to the Supreme Court. In Jefferson's letter, the "wall of separation between church and state" meant no one in the federal government would ever interfere with your religious freedom. Religious freedom came from God, and government had no power to take it away. But the Supreme Court has taken it away. At least insofar as public expressions of religious faith at any public function which is remotely connected with or funded by any amount of tax money.

In the Supreme Court, the phrase "wall of separation" evolved to mean the Court will ferret out and suppress any expression of religious ideas by any person remotely connected by any means with any level of federal, state, or local government employment or on government property or using government funds.

There are even attempts to deny the factual history of settlement in the West and Southwest, carried out by Catholic missionaries, by removing crosses and religious icons from state and local government seals and from monuments on public land.

This goes against two fundamental rights guaranteed in the Constitution: the free exercise of religion and the right to free speech. The Court has elevated the latter right to such an exalted position in the case of protesters of various ilk that it seems strange the Court would suppress religious (free) speech—unless one accepts the premise that there is a deeply held bias against religion felt by a majority of the members of the Court.

Supreme Court justices are intelligent and very well educated. It is difficult to believe that they "misunderstood" where the "wall of separation" language came from. Of course, each justice who voted against the free expression of religion would deny that he was antireligious. But "you will know them by their fruits."[65]

The four dissenters in *Everson*—Jackson, Frankfurter, Rutledge, and Burton—would have overturned the New Jersey Supreme Court and prohibited any tax money going to help transport Catholic children to their religious schools. If you read the dissenting opinions, you will already see the animus toward religion, which expands exponentially in later decisions.

The year following the decision in *Everson,* the Court ruled that an Illinois school district could not allow children to attend optional religious education classes on campus during regular class hours.[66] The classes on religion were held once a week for thirty minutes, and children could not attend unless their parents signed written permission forms. Children who did not attend those classes continued to study nonreligious subjects as a part of the regular school curriculum.

The instructors for the optional religious classes were from a rotating group of different religious denominations and beliefs who came to the school at no cost to the school board.

If there were no bias against religious instruction, the optional classes were in many respects no different from optional classic literature classes or optional foreign language courses or optional sports programs held during school hours. No students were required to play football; no child was required to take Latin—although students who hoped to pursue a career in law or medicine at that time may have been encouraged to take Latin—and no students were required to take the religious classes.

A Biased Court

However, the Supreme Court is not neutral. It has an agenda to advance secularism at the expense of Judeo-Christian values and traditions. The Court chose to focus on the "establishment clause" while completely ignoring the "free exercise clause" in the same sentence of the First Amendment.

A New York City program tried to comply with the Court's ruling, prohibiting religious classes on public school property, by allowing its students to go off campus to religious education classes held in churches. The U.S. Supreme Court allowed that practice. The Court acknowledged, "We are a religious people whose institutions presuppose a Supreme Being. We guarantee the freedom to worship as one chooses."[67]

The majority also found "no constitutional requirement which makes it necessary for government to be hostile to religion and to throw its weight against efforts to widen the effective scope of religious influence."[68] That tolerant attitude would change substantially in future decisions of the Court.

Those findings in the New York case are consistent with our history of religious freedom and nongovernmental interference in religious matters. The findings of the Court are also consistent with the Court's own precedents prior to *Everson*. The New York decision drew strong condemnation from the dissenters. Mr. Justice Black wrote the "establishment of religion" prohibited in the Illinois case should also apply here. Justice Frankfurter agreed. Justice Jackson, sounding histrionic—or worse—went so far as to say that New York's release time program used "the State's power of coercion"[69] to *force* children to engage in religious activity. Such hyperbole would get worse.

If you ignore the dissent for a moment, this case seemed to temporarily draw back from the Court's headlong rush to outlaw religion in public life. However, a minority of justices continued their hostility to children learning about religion and moral values in the public school. Soon, that minority would become the majority. What followed was a series of cases aimed at eliminating all religious expression in public life.

- *Engle v. Vitale*[70] prohibited prayer in public schools.
- *Abington School District v. Schemp*[71] prohibited reading the Bible in public schools.
- *Walz v. Tax Commissioner*[72] prohibited local governments from exempting religious organizations from paying property taxes on real estate they own (the Court said that amounted to a taxpayer subsidy for religion).
- *Lemon v. Kurzman*[73] prohibited any kind of government assistance for teachers in parochial schools, even if those teachers taught only secular subjects such as science or math.
- *Santa Fe Independent School District v. Doe*[74] prohibited students from publicly offering a prayerful invocation before football games because that amounted, according to the Court, to the state endorsing religion.

The net effect was demonstrated in 2002 when a federal judge in Iowa carried the trend to extremes: he outlawed the Lord's Prayer. "Judge Charles R. Wolle of the Federal District Court in Des Moines ruled that the principal effect of having the high school choir sing the prayer was 'to advance the Christian religion.'"[75]

The executive department has finally gotten into the fight to restore some balance: the U.S. Department of Education, invoking the free speech clause, has issued guidelines that say that a school may not in any way assist or organize prayer at school events; however, the school must remain neutral toward religion or lose their federal school funding. (See "Guidance on Constitutionally Protected Prayer in Public Elementary and Secondary Schools."[76])

That "neutrality" means if a speaker is chosen "evenhandedly," the free speech clause dictates that school authorities may not prohibit the speaker from making religious or, for that matter, antireligious comments. Such free speech is not "attributable" to the school. The Supreme Court decisions prohibiting the school from sponsoring prayer or religious comments at school events do not apply.

Will the Supreme Court rule against the executive department as it did when it struck down the Religious Freedom Restoration Act (42 U.S.C. § 2000bb) passed by Congress? Actually, several federal appeals courts already have.

The divide between the appeals courts, which uphold the executive branch "guidance," and those who do not can be seen in geography—whether the ruling court is in what is generally thought of as a "liberal" part of the country or whether the region is more "conservative," i.e., the South and the West (but not the Far West).

The Third Circuit (Pennsylvania, New Jersey, and Delaware) has ruled that a school board policy which permits a graduating class to vote whether to have a graduation prayer (with a disclaimer that the decision was entirely that of the graduating class and not of the school) violated the establishment clause.[77]

The Ninth Circuit (California, Oregon, Washington, Idaho, Montana, Nevada, and Arizona) held that a school must prevent students from giving an invocation at graduation to avoid any appearance that the government is sponsoring religion.[78]

In contrast to those views, courts in the South and in the West (excluding the Far West) uphold the executive branch attempts to ease the restrictions on religion.

The Fifth Circuit (Texas, Louisiana, and Mississippi) allows student-initiated, nonsectarian prayer by students at graduation.

The Eleventh Circuit (Alabama, Georgia, and Florida) upheld the right of graduating seniors, if they choose, to elect a student from among themselves to give a two-minute speech at the beginning and/or end of the graduation ceremony. The chosen student has the absolute discretion to say whatever he or she wants to say, including a prayer. Since the school has no input into monitoring or dictating what the student says, the "speech" is not attributable to the school and therefore does not violate the establishment clause.[79]

The case restoring some religious freedom in the Eleventh Circuit was *Adler v. Duval County Sch. Bd.* and is particularly interesting because the Supreme Court remanded the original case to the Eleventh Circuit Court for reconsideration in light of *Santa Fe. v. Doe*[80] decided in 2000.

The Eleventh Circuit reaffirmed its prior decision in *Adler*, distinguishing it from *Sante Fe v. Doe*. Again, the decision (*Adler II*) was appealed to the Supreme Court, which declined to rehear the case, allowing the decision to become the new standard for when prayer may be permissible at school functions—at least in the Eleventh Circuit.

The Differences Are in Ideology, Not in the Law

Even as the Supreme Court in religious cases grudgingly allows students to exercise their free speech rights under the First Amendment, Congress and the president are on the same page in support of the people's agenda, which is pro-religion. Is it just coincidence that the president and our representatives in Congress have to stand for election and the Supreme Court does not? And wasn't that what the founders intended? Shouldn't those *elected* be the policymakers?

Do we want the unaccountable Supreme Court justices, who do not have to answer to the people, making the policy and laws that the people must follow?

Why is the Supreme Court so hostile to religion that the government must resort to the "free speech clause" when the "free exercise" of religion has its own place in the Constitution? And how did the Supreme Court gain such power that the executive department must find creative ways to circumvent the will of the Court?

Apparent Authority Becomes Real Authority

Let's examine a hypothetical: suppose there is a person that we will call "Homeowner" who has a neighbor with a tree growing in his backyard. The tree is beginning to die and drop dead limbs on Homeowner's property. A man says he will cut the tree for Homeowner. And he does. He didn't ask the neighbor's permission; he just went over and cut it. The neighbor didn't complain. Maybe he wanted it cut but just didn't have the money.

A neighbor on the other side also has a tree on his lot, which shades Homeowner's garden. The man says he'll cut that tree, too. And he does. For some reason that neighbor doesn't complain either.

The word spreads that this man is cutting trees on other people's property and getting by with it, so eventually some person who doesn't know any better will say, "Well, he's getting by with it, so it must be legal." Now the tree-cutting man has the weight of people's *belief* that he has the lawful authority to cut other people's trees. He keeps cutting maybe a tree a week, and after about a year, the man shows up at Homeowner's place with a chain saw.

"Your majestic two-hundred-year-old white oak tree, which your pioneer great-great-great-grandfather planted, is blocking your neighbor's view of the lake, so I am going to cut it," he tells Homeowner. "Like hell you are!" Homeowner replies.

Anticipating that Homeowner may not want to give up his tree, the man with the chain saw has the foresight to bring along a naïve young police officer who believes the man's "apparent" legal authority is real authority, and he restrains Homeowner while the would-be Paul Bunyan proceeds to cut the wonderful two-hundred-year-old oak tree. On Homeowner's property. Without Homeowner's permission.

That, metaphorically, is what the Supreme Court has done with judicial review. The Court appears to have the authority to make law, even though the Constitution gives it no such authority, and it can use its apparent authority because we acquiesce—we allow it to use the apparent authority without protest.

In 1947, the Court gave itself the right to interfere in religious freedom in the *Everson* case. The Court expanded its activism into the criminal law under Chief Justice Earl Warren; it now touches on virtually every aspect of our lives.

Unfortunately, while the Court is achieving its goals, it is not necessarily achieving its intent: in many cases, the Supreme Court rulings have not fostered tolerance of minority views; it just polarizes opinions. Abortion and religious freedom are but two examples that one could cite.

So how does one restrain a Court that knows no restraint? By amending the Constitution to give back the power to Congress that the Constitution intended for Congress to have, Congress should be able to override a Supreme Court decision by a supermajority; (like overriding a presidential veto). Or maybe the Court should be stripped of authority to override Congress under any circumstances. In other words, it should follow the document we call the Constitution.

Look at Article I of the Constitution. Congress is the sole and exclusive lawmaker, although if one looks at power being exercised by the federal government, that's not what actually happens on the ground.

Even though Congress is the immediate victim of the Supreme Court's power grab, the people suffer the most harm. Still, don't expect Congress to pass legislation, or propose an amendment, to reform the Supreme Court. Or itself.

Following the ratification in 1791 of the first ten amendments, known as the Bill of Rights, only seventeen additional amendments have been ratified out of some five thousand to ten thousand proposed.[81] Several recent attempts to amend the Constitution have been proposed in the Congress only to die in committee.

As stated in the first chapter, there are advantages to having the states petition Congress to call a convention. While it takes two-thirds of the state legislatures to successfully petition Congress, it takes only a simple majority vote within each legislature of each state—much easier than trying to persuade two-thirds of both houses of Congress to propose amendments for ratification.

Another advantage would be that attendees at the conference could consider more than one amendment. For example, term limits for all federal elected officials, not just the president, preventing the Supreme Court from exercising its de facto power to tax or to amend the Constitution, and demanding control of our borders—the sine qua non of a sovereign nation.

The need for reform will be discussed in more detail in the following chapters; however, the one amendment which is absolutely vital to the survival of representative government is to abolish the Supreme Court's self-given power to amend the Constitution. (See discussion in chapter 6.) Throughout this manuscript, the author will refer to de facto Supreme Court amendments to the Constitution in order to emphasize the Court's lack of authority to make changes to the Constitution through "interpretation." The so-called Living Constitution is anathema to the rule of law, which we claim to value.

Restoring the Status Quo Ante

Many of the proposed Article V amendments offered during the past decade are about restoring religious rights or promoting traditional values: prayer in schools, display of religious symbols, prohibiting desecration of the flag, and defining marriage as the union of one man and one woman. They propose to restore the status quo ante for unauthorized Supreme Court amendments to the Constitution.

There have been proposals floated to prevent the courts from mandating that a legislature levy or raise taxes, limiting the term federal judges serve from life tenure to a term of years, and other substantive reforms.

If all of the people now promoting single-issue amendments were to join in the effort to give Congress back the power that has been hijacked by the Supreme Court, we would all have a much better chance of getting an amendment passed and then petitioning Congress for our individual projects once Congress has the power to overturn the Court.

And you know what? That's exactly how the people who promoted independence from England and drafted the United States Constitution and the Bill of Rights thought it should work.

It will never be possible to amend the Constitution quickly enough or often enough to keep up with the agenda of an activist Supreme Court. The process is too burdensome and too slow and is successful in only a rare handful of cases.

The Supreme Court should not unilaterally decree amendments to the Constitution. The Supreme Court's overturning of two acts of Congress, the Religious Freedom and Restoration Act, and 18 U.S.C.A. § 3501 (to restore the voluntariness test to criminal confessions) demonstrate the hubris of a Supreme Court which has usurped legitimate congressional powers and now feels free to substitute its judgment for that of our elected legislators.

Justice Stevens spelled it out in *Atkins v. Virginia*: "Our own judgment is 'brought to bear,'...by asking whether there is reason to disagree with the judgment reached by the citizenry and its legislators."

That goes far beyond deciding whether a particular law is permissible under the Constitution. It means any law can be declared "unconstitutional" if at least five of the justices personally disagree with it. The disagreement with the law may be personal prejudice, it can be capricious, it may be misguided "good intentions." It doesn't matter.

It is all about getting five votes. Any kid just out of law school and certainly Supreme Court justices know how to parse words, to twist meaning, and to pervert the English language to make a logical argument to support their subjective thoughts and desires. That is what lawyers learn to do.

But when the Supreme Court does it, those tortured words that allow the Court to reach a predetermined goal become the supreme law of the land.

Justice Antonin Scalia wrote a dissent which stated the problem simply:

> It is just a game, after all. In the end, it is the *feelings* and *intuition* of a majority of the Justices that count—the perceptions of decency, or of penology, or of mercy, entertained...by a majority of the small and unrepresentative segment of our society that sits on this Court. (Emphasis in original.)

We must deny the Supreme Court the power to amend the Constitution or lose still more of our liberty.

Chapter 4: What Does "5-to-4" Mean? (It Depends on Whose Gore Is Being "Oxed")

Our own judgment 'is brought to bear'...by asking whether there is a reason to disagree with the judgment reached by the citizenry and its legislatures.—Justice Stevens, writing for the majority in *Atkins v. Virginia*[82]

Seldom has an opinion of this Court rested so obviously upon nothing but the personal views of its members.[83] *[I]n the end, it is the feelings and intuition of a majority of the Justices that count.* (Citing his earlier dissent in *Thompson*[84])—Justice Scalia's dissent in *Atkins v. Virginia* (Emphasis in the original.)

"In republican government, the legislative authority necessarily predominates."[85] James Madison's words ring hollow when one looks at what the Supreme Court of the United States is doing today.

Imagine living in an imperial country where one woman, who was appointed to her office for life, if she wants to stay, with virtually nothing to restrain her power. She can make laws, which are binding and enforceable against everyone in the country—citizen and alien alike, the president, the Congress, and each of the political subdivisions—and, further, there is no way for the people in the country to change her laws. The president can't do it. The legislature can't do it. The ordinary citizen wouldn't even know how to begin to get her newly passed laws changed. They are final.

And her laws are based, in part, on her reading and consideration of foreign laws and world opinion, not based solely on her own country's Constitution and traditions.

"Tyranny!" you say. "Dictatorship!"

The author knows such a woman. Here in America. The author met her when he was a student at Washington and Lee University School of Law, and she came there as a guest speaker. He wrote a story about her for the law school's student newspaper, where he was the managing editor. He followed her career on the Supreme Court with interest.

She was very likable. She seemed levelheaded and intelligent, gracious and charming.

That woman, who wielded such imperial power until her retirement in 2006, was Associate Justice of the United States Supreme Court Sandra Day O'Connor. She, like the late Lewis Powell in his time, was the decisive vote in the majority of the close cases decided by the Court. In 2003, for example, she alone decided which side won in 92.8 percent of the very important five-to-four decisions where the Court is making new law. And her power was not just in the five-to-four rulings she decided.

The Swing Vote Retires—Long Live the Swing Vote

Because everyone knew she was the "swing vote" who could go either way, other justices modified or tailored their own opinions in order to win her over to their side in the tense tug-of-war that goes on behind the scenes when the justices deliberate. Lawyers arguing cases before the Court were aware that she alone might decide their case, and so they tailored their arguments accordingly.

We don't know much about the secret wheeling and dealing that goes into the Court's deliberations, but we got a brief glimpse when the late Justice Blackmun's papers were made public. We learned how, at the last minute and after much lobbying by the other justices, Justice Kennedy betrayed the chief justice and voted with the other side after promising to support Rehnquist in his effort to overturn *Roe v. Wade*. O'Connor was instrumental in getting Kennedy to change his mind.[86]

Chief Justice Rehnquist thought he had the votes to overturn or at least greatly diminish the scope of *Roe*. When Kennedy changed his mind at the last minute, *Roe* was spared and continues to be the law of the land. O'Connor, along with Kennedy, voted with the five-to-four majority in the decision to uphold a woman's right to have an abortion.

The Court is split ideologically between three or possibly four justices who hold what are described for convenience as "liberal" or "progressive" views—Justice Breyer sometimes joined with Kennedy or Rehnquist, making him the most "moderate" of the liberals—versus four justices, Chief Justice Roberts and Associate Justices Scalia, Thomas, and Alito, generally regarded as "conservatives."

One justice, Kennedy, whose inconsistent votes and written opinions appear almost capricious at times, emerged as the new "swing vote," replacing O'Connor following her retirement in 2006. According to the *Harvard Law Review*,[87] Sandra Day O'Connor was the fifth vote in thirteen of the fourteen cases decided by a five-to-four majority in 2003. Kennedy has topped O'Connor's record.

A majority of the cases reaching the Supreme Court call for a straightforward decision based on whatever remains of so-called settled law, often resulting in unanimous decisions or at least decisions reached on an eight-to-one or perhaps seven-to-two vote. It is the controversial (to paraphrase Admiral Farragut) "Damn the Constitution, full speed ahead" decisions, wherein the justices write new law, that the five-to-four votes come into play.

In other words the more important and controversial the decision, the more likely Sandra Day O'Connor was in her time, and now Justice Kennedy is in his, to be the lone vote to decide it. In the 2006-2007 term, the first in which O'Connor did not play a role, Justice Kennedy was the deciding vote in all twenty-four of the five-to four decisions. The Court decided seventy-two cases, so Kennedy alone determined the outcome in one-third of all the cases that term.

Bush v. Gore, "giving" the presidency to George W. Bush in 2000, is a good example of the kind of contentious, divisive cases that split the Court—and the American people.

O'Connor's and Kennedy's power to decide close questions of law are all the more alarming because neither feels constrained by the United States Constitution. By her own admission, O'Connor relied on international law and *world opinion* in formulating her judicial opinions. O'Connor stated publicly that "conclusions reached by other countries and by the international community, although not formally binding upon our decisions, should at times constitute persuasive authority in American courts."[88]

Kennedy also relies on foreign law to interpret the U.S. Constitution. In *Roper v. Simmons*,[89] he said:

> The overwhelming weight of international opinion against the juvenile death penalty is not controlling here, but provides respected and significant confirmation for the Court's determination that the penalty is disproportionate punishment for offenders under 18...The United States is the only country in the world that continues to give official sanction to the juvenile penalty. It does not lessen fidelity to the Constitution or pride in its origins to acknowledge that the express affirmation of certain fundamental rights by other nations and peoples underscores the centrality of those same rights within our own heritage of freedom. [Internal citations omitted.]

Kennedy does not seem to notice that American culture is different from the rest of the world. We have more freedom, more guns, and more "political correctness," which gives violent criminals "understanding" rather than retribution. That takes away the "fear factor" for many criminals, as demonstrated by the *Roper* case. The crime at issue in *Roper* was particularly depraved and brutal. Justice Kennedy's recitation of the facts includes the information that:

> [A]t the age of 17, when he was still a junior in high school, Christopher Simmons, the respondent here, committed murder. About nine months later, after he had turned 18, he was tried and sentenced to death. There is little doubt that Simmons was the instigator of the crime. Before its commission Simmons said he wanted to murder someone. In chilling, callous terms he talked about his plan, discussing it for the most part with two friends, Charles Benjamin and John Tessmer, then aged 15 and 16 respectively. Simmons proposed to commit burglary and murder by breaking and entering, tying up a victim, and throwing the victim off a bridge. Simmons assured his friends they could "get away with it" because they were minors.
> The three met at about 2 a.m. on the night of the murder, but Tessmer left before the other two set out. (The State later charged Tessmer with conspiracy, but dropped the charge in exchange for his testimony against Simmons.)

Simmons and Benjamin entered the home of the victim, Shirley Crook, after reaching through an open window and unlocking the back door. Simmons turned on a hallway light. Awakened, Mrs. Crook called out, "Who's there?" In response Simmons entered Mrs. Crook's bedroom, where he recognized her from a previous car accident involving them both. Simmons later admitted this confirmed his resolve to murder her.

Using duct tape to cover her eyes and mouth and bind her hands, the two perpetrators put Mrs. Crook in her minivan and drove to a state park. They reinforced the bindings, covered her head with a towel, and walked her to a railroad trestle spanning the Meramec River. There they tied her hands and feet together with electrical wire, wrapped her whole face in duct tape and threw her from the bridge, drowning her in the waters below.

Simmons, meanwhile, was bragging about the killing, telling friends he had killed a woman "because the bitch seen my face."

Simmons was convicted by a jury and the trial judge gave him life. He appealed. The Supreme Court overturned because Simmons was a juvenile when he committed the crime.

What a Difference a Day Makes

Supreme Court decisions are absolute and inflexible; therefore, a person cannot be executed if he is seventeen years and 364 days old when he commits a capital crime. A day later, on his eighteenth birthday, if he kills someone—in the words of comedian Ron White—"we'll kill you back."

A year earlier, in October 2003, O'Connor began her keynote address to a meeting of the American Society of International Law this way:

> What I wanted to tell you tonight is that I do not deserve to be your speaker. I do not know much about international law. I am just learning; I am trying to learn and I have no words of expertise to give you on that subject. I am here because I think it is important and because I think I need to know more.[90]

That lack of knowledge did not prevent her, during the Atlanta speech, from criticizing her fellow justices on the Court for not relying more on foreign law. "There has been reluctance," she said, "on our current Supreme Court to look to international or foreign law in interpreting our own Constitution and related statutes."[91]

The Traditional View

O'Connor's favorable view of using foreign law and world opinion to decide issues for America is diametrically opposite to the views the Supreme Court held about its own role in American society during the early years of the republic:

> In considering this important case, I have thought it best to pass over all the strictures which have been made on the various European confederations; be-

cause, as, on the one hand, their likeness to our own is not sufficiently close to justify any analogical application; so, on the other, they are utterly destitute of any binding authority here. The Constitution of the United States is the only fountain from which I shall draw; the only authority to which I shall appeal.[92]

The modern Court routinely embraces European opinion and laws.

Atkins v. Virginia[93] is a death penalty case in which the European Union filed an *amicus curiae* (friend of the court) brief severely critical of the death penalty. Briefs are filed "ostensibly on behalf of a party but actually to suggest a rationale consistent with its own views."[94]

The European Union is, in effect, acting as a lobbyist before the United States Supreme Court—and the Court is listening and acting on the advice of that "lobbyist," who was trying to persuade the Court to adopt the European version of the law as its own. It did.

Chief Justice Rehnquist said the decision in *Atkins* "more resembles a *post hoc* rationalization for the majority's subjectively preferred result."[95] He was severely critical of the "Court's decision to place weight on foreign laws, the views of professional and religious organizations, and opinion polls" of questionable scientific reliability ["An extensive body of social science literature describes how methodological and other errors can affect the reliability and validity of estimates about the opinions and attitudes of a population derived from various sampling techniques" (from Rehnquist's dissent)].

Justice Scalia joined that dissent and went on to write his own in which he called "irrelevant" the "practices of the 'world community,' whose notions of justice are (thankfully) not always those of our people."[96]

Scalia continues, "We must never forget that it is a Constitution for the United States of America that we are expounding...Where there is not first a settled consensus among our own people, the views of other nations...cannot be imposed upon Americans through the Constitution."[97]

He was right in principle, wrong on the facts. A majority of five on the Court did indeed believe they could impose views contained in the European Union's *amicus* brief on the American people. So they did. Just like Chief Justice Burger said, "We are the Supreme Court and we can do what we want."[98]

This is particularly alarming because the *Atkins* decision contains the bold assertion that the Supreme Court does not believe it is bound by the laws and rules enacted by Congress and perhaps not even those written in the Constitution!

Justice Stevens, writing for the majority, said, "In addition to objective evidence, the Constitution contemplates that this Court will bring its own judgment to bear by asking whether there is reason to agree or disagree with the judgment reached by the citizenry and its legislators."[99]

Does that include the "citizenry" who wrote the Constitution? Almost certainly, if you read the recent opinions of the Court. Adding insult to injury, it seems that a majority of justices are approaching a mind-set where they are perfectly at ease with consulting foreign law as they blithely ignore our own. Nor do they seem to abide by the United States Constitution.

Atkins seems to answer the question as to whether the Court feels bound by the Constitution—*Dickerson v. United States* unequivocally announced that the Court cannot be constrained by any acts of Congress. But *Atkins* and subsequent decisions give a strong indication that the Court is not bound by the *Constitution*—or anything but its own judgment and "feelings" about what the law should be.

Following the decision in *Dickerson,* it is absolutely clear that Supreme Court decisions, even those decisions that are based on international law and world opinion rather than on our own Constitution, are not open to question or change by Congress. The Supreme Court trumps every other branch of government.

It Wasn't Supposed to Be That Way

Article III of the Constitution, creating the federal courts, gives Congress the authority to regulate the Court's appellate jurisdiction and to impose "such Exceptions and...Regulations as the Congress shall make." Every Supreme Court case cited in this work was brought under the Court's appellate jurisdiction. Throughout the Constitution, if there is a "first among equals," it is the Congress. Congress is the exclusive lawmaking body; it does not share that duty with the Court.

In the Federalist Papers, we find "the great security against a gradual concentration of the several powers in the same department, consists in giving to those who administer each department the necessary constitutional means and personal motives to resist encroachments of the others."[100]

That's why the Constitution gave Congress the exclusive authority to pass laws and raise revenue. The president cannot be compelled to enforce laws that he believes are unconstitutional. The Constitution gives the Court life tenure so it can do its job without interference from the other two branches.

Federalist no. 51 continues:

> If men were angels, no government would be necessary. If angels were to govern men, neither external nor internal controls on government would be necessary.... But it is not possible to give each department an equal power of self-defense. In republican government, the legislative authority necessarily predominates.[101]

Since 1947, the Court has been insidiously increasing its power. After *Dickerson v. United States* was decided in 2000, the Court's acquisition of unconstitutional power is no longer insidious. It is blatant.

To understand the power of the swing vote on the Court, it helps to know that the Court does not in fact have nine independent and intellectually honest members. There are justices with strong ideology on both sides of the arguments. They almost always take sides consistent with their own private philosophy and personal bias.

There is nothing necessarily wrong with that—we all do it because we view the world through a "filter" of our own experiences, values, prejudices, and beliefs—but the net effect is often a standoff between conservative and liberal forces.

How the Votes Split

Dr. Lawrence Sirovich has analyzed the Supreme Court's voting record mathematically and found since Associate Justice Breyer joined the court in 1994 (the last new justice to be appointed at the time of Sirovich's analysis) the vote tally is what you would expect if the court consisted "of 4.68 ideal justices."[102] An ideal justice is one whose vote is not correlated in any way with any other justice's. If two members of the Court nearly always voted alike (Scalia and Thomas, for example, or Souter and Ginsberg often vote the same way), the Court would behave mathematically as if there were only eight justices.

If there were nine totally independent judges voting solely on the merits of individual cases, over time their votes should be randomly spread out over the 512 patterns mathematically possible. But that clearly is not what happens.

Those statistically "4.68 ideal justices" usually end up as the majority in a five-to-four voting block that determines the outcome of many important cases. If one actually reads the decisions, in many cases it is the same four who vote together on each side with Sandra O'Connor in her day, and now Justice Kennedy, deciding the outcome.

This is not a new phenomenon. The first Court under Chief Justice Earl Warren voted as if it were "5.16 ideal justices."[103] The second Warren Court, according to Dr. Sirovich, was even more liberal. Dr. Sirovich, who is a mathematician at Mount Sinai School of Medicine in New York, imputes no political motives to the court but simply extracts mathematical patterns from the information about the votes.

The author, on the other hand, is a lawyer who has read a lot of Supreme Court cases; he has no such reticence about looking at the decisions and finding clear patterns of political bias. On both sides. The so-called first Warren Court covered the period 1959 to 1961. With the appointment of Arthur Goldberg in 1962, Warren had a solid, dependable fifth vote to ram through his liberal political agenda. By Goldberg's own admission, his tenure on the court was "a time when the Warren Court absolutely got into high gear."[104]

In the "second" Warren Court (1967-1969), Thurgood Marshall dissented only once. Warren had five votes and a political agenda. With them, he changed the face of American law.

Prior to O'Connor joining the Court, the late Justice Lewis Powell was the swing vote on a more or less evenly divided court. Everyone who studied the Court, and that includes each of the lawyers who argued cases there, knew the makeup of the court and could predict with a fair degree of certainty how individual justices would vote on a particular issue. Therefore, they tailored their presentation to try to persuade Powell to vote their way in the case before the Court.

Judge Bork's comments in his book *Coercing Virtue* reinforced the author's own belief, formed over his career in the law, that it is more important to know the judge's personal philosophy than it is to know the law.[105]

Reverse Discrimination

Justice Lewis Powell wrote the opinion in *University of California Regents v. Bakke*,[106] a 1978 case stamping the Supreme Court's seal of approval on affirmative action. *Bakke* was a case growing out of the medical school at the University of California at Davis having set aside sixteen seats in the class of one hundred entering students each year for minorities who could not meet the regular admissions standards.

Other minority students who could compete successfully on their own merits, without the set-aside, could apply using the regular admissions process. If they did not gain admission, they could then ask the admissions office to reconsider their application for one of the sixteen seats set aside for minority students. The medical school admitted approximately eleven minority students per year through the regular process in addition to the sixteen set-aside or quota seats. In the four years preceding Bakke's filing suit, about twenty-seven medical students on average out of a class of one hundred were minorities.

Bakke, a white student, was denied admission even though most of the sixteen students admitted through the quota set-asides had substantially lower qualifications; he claimed he had been the victim of unlawful reverse discrimination.

Bakke's Medical College Admissions Test (MCAT) scores were 3.44, seven hundredths of a point lower than the average score (3.51) for students admitted under the regular admissions program the first year he applied; his scores were actually better than the average score of students admitted through the regular admissions process (3.36) in the second year he applied. In each of the two years he applied for admission, his scores were substantially higher than the average for the sixteen students admitted through the "special" program, 2.62 and 2.42, respectively; the latter score nearly a full point lower than Bakke's.

Bakke's claim of racial discrimination was based on the equal protection clause of the Fourteenth Amendment, a provision of the California State Constitution, and § 601 of Title VI of the Civil Rights Act of 1964. The trial court found that the UC Davis admissions policy was an unlawful racial quota since sixteen of the one hundred seats were set aside for minorities and no whites could apply—the minority students competed only against each other.

However, the state court would not order UC Davis to admit Bakke since he could not prove that he would definitely have been admitted had the racial quotas not been in place.

The California Supreme Court agreed that the admission policy was an unlawful racial quota system but disagreed with the trial court on the standard of proof that Bakke needed to show in order to warrant his admission to the school. The California high court went the next step and ordered UC Davis to approve Bakke's admission to the medical school.

The UC Regents appealed to the United States Supreme Court. After reviewing the evidence, members of the Court could not agree on anything. When Justice Powell finished the plurality opinion, neither it nor any of the six separate opinions spoke for a majority of the squabbling Court.

Powell's opinion consisted of fourteen parts: part 1; part 2 A and B; part 3 A, B, and C; part 4 A, B, C, and D; part 5 A, B, and C; and part 6. A slim five-to-four majority could agree on the eventual outcome, but there was wide disparity for the reason or reasons the particular justices gave for voting to affirm that part of the decision of the California Supreme Court granting Bakke admission.

White joined Powell in parts 1, 3-A, and 5-C. Brennan, Marshall, and Blackmun joined only in parts 1 and 5-C; Brennan, White, Marshall, and Blackmun filed a separate opinion in which they concurred in the judgment but dissented to much of Powell's reasoning justifying the opinion. White, Marshall, and Blackmun then went on to write separate individual opinions.

Justice Stevens wrote an opinion concurring in part and dissenting in part. He was joined by Chief Justice Burger and Justices Stewart and Rehnquist. These four wanted to affirm the decision of the California Supreme Court admitting Bakke solely based on Title VI of the Civil Rights Act, which prohibited discrimination because of race. They thought it unnecessary to reach the Fourteenth Amendment issue.

Four justices—Brennan, White, Marshall, and Blackmun—wanted to reverse the California Supreme Court and hold that racial quotas were permissible in some cases in order to overcome past discrimination.

Bakke demonstrates that even when the Court reaches a decision, the justices on the Court don't always agree about why they reached that decision. An interesting phenomenon to think about when one considers that these people have the ability to profoundly affect the way you live your life as you attempt to conform your conduct to the law.

It Takes Five Votes, *Not* Lawful Authority
Ultimately, it is five *votes*, not the justices' reading of the Constitution and laws passed by Congress, which determine what the law will be in the future.

The *Bakke* case reinforces the author's belief that Supreme Court decisions often are not about the law at all. They are about the personal preferences of the justices who serve on the Court. Surely if there was something called "law," that had some meaning, some of those nine people on the Court could have agreed on *something* and come up with a majority opinion.

Ellen Goodman, reacting to the 2000 presidential election, wrote in the *Boston Globe* about "the deep fractures in the magisterial Supreme Court. The same five-to-four majority that had stopped the recount made time the enemy of fairness. The clock and the court decided for George W. Bush."[107]

Maybe she never heard how fractious the Court was in *Bakke*. Or all those five-to-four decisions of the liberal Warren Court. Or the five-to-four cases that O'Connor has decided over the years, or that Kennedy is deciding now. Maybe it all depends on whose Gore is being oxed.

If you don't like the outcome, you scream loudly about the illegitimacy of a five-to-four decision. But if you like the outcome, not a whisper about the vote tally. By emphasizing the slim five-to-four decision, Goodman attempts to discredit the result of the Supreme Court's ruling in the 2000 presidential election. At least that decision was a clear five-to-four vote.

Bakke, for all its failure to have a majority vote for the opinion, is just as much the law as *Brown v. Board of Education*,[108] which was unanimous. So is *Bush v. Gore*.[109] So is the badly fractured *Planned Parenthood of Southeastern PA v. Casey*,[110] preserving *Roe v. Wade*. So are all of the other five-to-four decisions of the Court.

The fact is, the law is what five justices say it is. Any five justices. Never mind the Constitution, never mind Congress. Five justices voting together can determine what the law is, and their decision is not subject to question.

The Warren Court decided many of its important cases by a five-to-four majority vote. After Arthur Goldberg joined the court in 1962, he became the fifth vote on what would be the most radically activist Court in the history of the republic. Goldberg was a New Deal liberal who was a labor lawyer before he began his government service.[111]

It is important to understand that Supreme Court justices are just people. They behave according to their own intuitions and feelings formed existentially from their own experiences over a lifetime. They come to the court with desires, ambitions, prejudices, faith, preconceived notions, perhaps a little hubris, and their own ideas about how and why things happen. They also must be political—at least to some degree; the president appoints justices, so they necessarily must have political connections in order to come to the attention of the president.

In addition, they come with a mind warped by law school.

All of that is hidden by a veneer of education, experience, and sophistication. But it's there. Law schools train students to be analytical, but the primordial feelings are still there; and those feelings inevitably influence how they approach and solve problems, how they "filter" and prioritize information.

Now Justice Stevens has admitted the decision in *Atkins* really did depend on the *feelings* and *intuition* of the justices who voted in the majority, not on a reading of the law.

Justices have their own agenda, political views, prejudices, and opinions just like the rest of us. They also have the power to act on their views and to impose those views on the rest of us in the laws they "pass" and the constitutional amendments they routinely impose.

All the more reason to be extremely wary of any individual who has the sole, decisive, irrevocable vote on momentous issues of liberty, life, and death.

So in the end, what does "five-to-four" mean? It means Justice Kennedy, with his own personal worldview and biases, gets to make laws that you and your children and grandchildren will live under for the rest of your life. He does not have to compromise with a few hundred people gathered from all over the country as Congress must do. He only has to choose which side of the four-to-four split he wants to affiliate with and then decide the case in front of him.

That may be fine for people who like Justice Kennedy's philosophy on life. But what happens when he is no longer on the Court? Doesn't it make sense to put the elected Congress back in the business of making the laws we live under? Congress does, of course, make some of the laws. Laws raising or lowering taxes—most of the time—or deciding which criminal laws of the states it wants to federalize and duplicate.

However, Congress is very much aware that it often is the U.S. Supreme Court that sets the agenda for the country on important policy matters. That is why the Senate Democrats used the filibuster to block President Bush's court nominees.

There is a better way. Let's give back to Congress the sole and exclusive lawmaking power bestowed on it by Article I, § 1 of the Constitution. "All legislative Powers herein granted shall be vested in a Congress of the United States, which shall consist of a Senate and House of Representatives."

Notice that the Constitution gives none of the lawmaking powers to the Supreme Court or to the president. Any lawmaking powers exercised by the Supreme Court are de facto (unlawful and illegitimate), seized in *Marbury v. Madison* (1803) and expanded in numerous decisions since.

President Franklin D. Roosevelt tried to pack the Court and use it to expand presidential power; shortly after that, the Supreme Court began to expand its own unlawful use of power. Today unlawful usurpation of legislatiive power by the judiciary the president has the Supreme Court's fingerprints are all over it.

President Barrack Obama, for the first time in history, has overruled Congress by issuing an executive order

Chapter 5: Judges Decide, Criminals Slide

What secret knowledge, one must wonder, is breathed into lawyers when they become Justices of this Court, that enables them to discern that a practice which the text of the Constitution does not clearly proscribe, and which our people have regarded as constitutional for 200 years, is in fact unconstitutional?—Justice Scalia, *Bd. Of Comm'rs v. Umbehr*, (1996).[112]

Think about a career criminal whose rap sheet runs to three single-spaced, typewritten pages. He has heard the *Miranda*[113] warnings at least forty or fifty times while he was being arrested. During the more than ten years he spent in prison on various sentences, he watched at least one cop show a week in which at least one criminal suspect has been read his *Miranda* rights.

He heard *Miranda* warnings on TV at least 520 times while in jail and forty or fifty times in person when he was arrested. He knows *Miranda* so well he can lip-sync the words with the officer when he is "giving him his rights."

When he got out of prison the last time, he was a little short of cash, so he mugged a little old lady, in the nighttime, on a dimly lit street. The little old lady yelled, "Help!" The perpetrator took off running as fast as he could, with her purse; and as he turned the corner at a dead run, he saw a police car, which just happened to be in the neighborhood on patrol, coming his way. He turned and ran the other way. Naturally, that attracted the police officer's attention.

The police officer chased him down, and the perpetrator said, "I didn't do nothin' why you stoppin' me?" The officer brings the suspect back to where the little old lady is still screaming "help," and she immediately blurts out: "That's him. That's the [expletive deleted] who stole my purse." The police officer in a spontaneous moment of outrage says, "Where's the purse?" The perpetrator, with an attitude born of experience and knowing the less evidence you have the more difficult it is to get a conviction, says defiantly, "I threw it in the back of a pickup truck that was drivin' by."

With the suspect in his car, the officer then drove around the block, hoping to catch sight of the vehicle; by luck, the pickup truck had stopped at a gas station to get fuel. "That's it!" the perpetrator blurts out in surprise. (Many perpetrators aren't very bright.) The purse, unknown to the truck driver, is still in the back of the pickup, which has out-of-state license plates.

The perpetrator was arrested, an investigation ensued, and eventually a grand jury indicted him for strong-arm robbery. He is a three-time loser several times over, and this time the prosecutor is going to "put the 'bitch' on him." (Criminal slang for the habitual criminal statute calling for a life sentence.)

He was appointed counsel, Clever Lawyer, who moved pretrial to suppress the statement, "I threw it in the back of a pickup truck drivin' by," because the cop asked, "Where's the purse?" before he read the suspect his *Miranda* rights.

Now, the suspect knows his *Miranda* rights, maybe better than the police officer. The officer knows he knows, because he personally has arrested this criminal multiple times before and has seen the bored, disinterested look in the criminal's eyes as he has said impatiently, "Yeah, yeah, I know," while this officer was reading him his rights. But because of the spontaneity of the police officer's question, he did not read him his rights on this particular occasion.

At the suppression hearing pretrial, the judge finds (1) the suspect was in custody; (2) the police officer had restricted his freedom of movement when he took the suspect back to where the little old lady was yelling for help, and his asking, "What did you do with her purse?" amounted to a "custodial interrogation"; and (3) everyone who had been present agreed the police officer had not read the suspect *Miranda* warnings before blurting out the question.

The judge ruled that prosecutor could not use the statement as evidence at trial.

Clever Lawyer then moved to suppress any evidence of the purse because the purse was the "fruit of the poisonous tree."[114] In other words, the police would not have found purse (fruit) except for the unlawfully obtained statement (the "poisonous tree").

The pickup truck was from out of state and would have returned home as soon as it refueled. It is highly unlikely the police officer would have known where to look for the purse if not for the criminal's statement. Whether the driver would have turned in the purse when he found it is speculation. It was not inevitable that the purse would have been discovered absent the defendant's statement.

There are two exceptions for the "fruit of the poisonous tree" doctrine: (1) if the evidence (fruit) inevitably would have been found anyway notwithstanding the unlawful confession;[115] and (2) if the "fruit" was a firearm, bomb, or other dangerous instrumentality which would present a danger to the public or to the officer's safety if not recovered.[116] This case did not fit within either exception, so the judge told the prosecutor he could not use the purse as evidence at trial.

At trial it was a "he said/she said" kind of case with no physical evidence. The little old lady proved to be an inadequate witness—she had recently had her glasses changed to a new type of "no-line" bifocal, which she wasn't quite used to—the street was dimly lighted, and she had only a fleeting glimpse of the defendant as he snatched her purse and run.

She is absolutely certain of her identification of the defendant, however. He was taller than she was, so she was looking up at him through the top part of her glasses, the part without the bifocal feature; what light there was from a nearby streetlight came from behind her and shone fully in the defendant's face, and she could see him clearly, from no more than two feet away.

Clever Lawyer has her demonstrate *reading* in the courtroom, and she takes a minute to focus her eyes, bobbing her head up and down until she finds just the right spot on the new bifocals. Clever Lawyer naturally calls attention to how long it takes her to focus her eyes, even in a well-lighted courtroom.

He is able to plant a seed of doubt in the mind of the jurors as to whether she could have gotten a clear look at the perpetrator in the fleeting second, in dim light, when he snatched her purse. The jury finds him "not guilty." The robber walks away a free man.

At this point readers may be thinking that the author must surely be exaggerating about the extent to which *Miranda* and other technical loopholes are used by defense lawyers to get obviously guilty criminals off. Be assured he is not. What follows is an actual example, a Fourth Circuit Court of Appeals case, *United States v. Dickerson,*[117] and the U.S. Supreme Court case, *Dickerson v. United States,* that overturned it.

A Catch-22

In the year 2000, the United States Supreme Court faced a classic "Catch-22" in the *Dickerson* case. It came to a decision that greatly expanded the scope of *Miranda.* The author will discuss the facts of *Dickerson* later in this narrative, but it is sufficient for now to state the dilemma: as Justice Scalia stated in his dissent, "Justices whose votes are needed to compose today's majority are on record as believing that a violation of *Miranda* is *not* a violation of the Constitution."[118] (Emphasis in original.)

Chief Justice Rehnquist, writing for the majority, acknowledged that the Supreme Court's own power to set out "rules of procedure and evidence for the federal courts exists only in the absence of a relevant Act of Congress." Rehnquist continued, "Congress retains the ultimate authority to modify or set aside any judicially created rules of evidence and procedure that are not required by the Constitution.... But Congress may not legislatively supersede our decisions interpreting and applying the Constitution."[119]

The Supreme Court reversed the Fourth Circuit Court of Appeals. Although the trial court made a finding of fact, that the confession was voluntary, it could not be used because of a *possible* technical violation of *Miranda.* The Supreme Court did not disturb the finding of fact. The Court, therefore, tacitly agreed that the confession was voluntary.

It still overturned the decision because the suspect, *Dickerson,* may not—*may* not—have received the *Miranda* warnings prior to his statement. From that, it should be clear that the case was not about the warnings but about whether the Congress has the power, given to it by the Constitution, to make procedural rules for the

Court. Even a cursory reading of the Constitution will confirm that Congress has that power. The Supreme Court said Congress does not.

Suddenly, *Miranda* has become a constitutional right, in and of itself, even though Rehnquist in the very same opinion states that the Court does not agree with *Miranda's* holding and probably would have decided it differently if looking at that case as one of first impression. Why did the Court overturn the Fourth Circuit's decision? Well the reason Rehnquist gave is *stare decisis.*

The real reason?

To rule otherwise would be to admit the obvious, apparent to anyone who actually reads the Constitution and not a Supreme Court interpretation of it: that the United States Congress is the only governmental body the Constitution trusts with the power to make laws. The Court would be limiting its own power if it ruled against Dickerson.

They teach you in law school that a trial is a "search for truth." So how did we get to the point where a jury in a criminal trial, searching for the truth, is not permitted to hear the truth?

Two words: *judicial review.*

Judicial review is the process whereby the Supreme Court gets to substitute its idea of what the law should be for the actual laws that Congress (or a state legislature) enacts. Judicial review is a creation of the Court, beginning with *Marbury v. Madison* and expanded in later decisions until the court had assumed important parts of the legislative power for itself.

"Whoever hath an absolute authority to interpret any written or spoken laws, it is he who is truly the lawgiver, to all intents and purposes, and not the person who first spoke or wrote them," Bishop Hoadly's sermon preached before the king (1717).[120] We have known for almost four hundred years that judicial review makes the Court the de facto lawmaker.

For that reason, the men who wrote the Constitution considered and then rejected the idea of giving the Court the power of judicial review. The United States Constitution makes no mention of judicial review. Nor does the constitution of the republican federation of Switzerland. A legislative act in Switzerland is not subject to judicial review. France and Germany have only limited review in special courts, and in fact some analysts have suggested that France has no judicial review as that term is understood in the United States.

The parliamentary system of our mother country, England, while not a constitutional republic like America, also has no judicial review. English courts cannot challenge an Act of Parliament. In fact, the Law Lords, a subset of the House of Lords who sit in the upper chamber of Parliament as legislators, is as close as the English come to our Supreme Court. They are the court of last resort, just as our Supreme Court is, but obviously they are more deferential to the legislature since they are a part of it.

The English took Bishop Hoadly at his word back in 1717. No judicial review for the Brits! Or the Swiss.

In contrast to those systems, only the people of America gave in to Chief Justice John Marshall's grab for power in 1803. Scholars still debate whether judicial review is a good idea; however, it is considered sacrosanct and not open to question among law professors, judges, and most practicing attorneys today.

The practice has now spread to other countries and has profoundly affected the whole body of laws, not always in beneficial ways. As one example, the Supreme Court, in assuring that criminals' rights are protected, seems not to consider the rights of victims of crime or the rights of the people as a whole to be free from predation by criminals.

Ninety-five percent of all criminal cases are brought in state courts.[121] As late as 1948, when Title 18 of the United States Code was revised, the federal government made minimal intrusion into state prosecution of crime, although "judicial review" was alive and well. Since then Congress has increasingly federalized what used to be a purely state matter, and the Supreme Court has interjected itself even more aggressively into the state law process without any constitutional authority so to do.

Usurping Congressional Power

The usurpation of congressional power did not happen at any single moment in time or with any particular case. Law builds on precedent. The changes are gradual, insidious, and rarely discernable to the average citizen who may try to keep up with events by reading newspapers or watching TV news. But as Justice Scalia pointed out in his dissent in *Dickerson*, a case decided by the Supreme Court is not a discrete event. It is closely related to the history of the Court and to the future direction of the law.

From the ratification of the first ten amendments to the Constitution in 1791 until 1925, those amendments—known as the Bill of Rights—were thought to control only federal government action. Then, in 1925, the Court in *Gitlow v. New York*[122] looked at the First Amendment anew.

Note that date—the Fourteenth Amendment had been ratified in 1868; for the next fifty-seven years, no one believed that it gave the federal government any control over the states other than banning slavery and preventing discrimination against former slaves.

This was still apparent in the Supreme Court case *Twining*, decided in 1908. By 1925, however, the Court began expanding the Fourteenth Amendment to "incorporate" the First Amendment into state law by way of a three-stage process over a period of the next twenty-two years.[123] By the end of eighty years after the Fourteenth was ratified, the Supreme Court had used it to effectively repeal the Ninth and Tenth amendments to the Constitution.

Powell v. Alabama [124] applied the Sixth Amendment right to counsel to trials in state court, saying it was "incorporated" through the Fourteenth. *Twining v. New Jersey,* [125] that meddlesome 1908 case, was still considered good law so far as it maintained that the Fifth Amendment right against self-incrimination applied only in federal proceedings and did not apply to the states.

The issue in *Twining* was a state procedure whereby a prosecutor could comment to the jury about the defendant's failure to rebut or explain an incriminating document the state introduced as evidence at trial.

Twining is difficult to reconcile with the other Fourteenth Amendment cases unless you understand the concept of *stare decisis. Stare decisis* is one of the most important concepts in the American practice of law. At least it used to be. It is defined as:

> [The] Policy of courts to stand by precedent and not to disturb settled point. Doctrine that, when court has once laid down a principle of law as applicable to a certain state of facts, it will adhere to that principle, and apply it to all future cases, where facts are substantially the same; regardless of whether the parties and property are the same. [126]

What had the justices been smoking when they decided that the First and Sixth amendments applied to trials in the state courts but the Fifth Amendment did not, one might ask.

Even with *stare decisis* in play, the decisions are still troublesome. The Supreme Court in *Twining* (1908), ruling on the issue for the first time, decided the Fifth Amendment did not apply to trials in state court. That seemed like a very reasonable decision at the time. Later Supreme Courts would uphold that ruling even though they may have disagreed with it, just as the Rehnquist Court upheld *Miranda* in 2000.

Later, when considering whether other amendments should be applied to state trials, the justices believed they were writing on a blank slate. No previous Supreme Court had ever ruled on that particular issue. Thus, in the First Amendment cases, there were no cases on point dealing with this exact subject matter—whether free speech protections should be applied to the states—so the Court felt free to say that the First Amendment was "incorporated" by the Fourteenth and therefore applied to the states.

What had happened in the law since *Twining* to make the justices change their mind? Well, uh—nothing actually. What did change? The only thing that changed was that some new justices, with a more "progressive" political philosophy, were appointed to the Court.

Arguably, the First Amendment cases should have been controlled by *Twining*. But judges can split some pretty thin hairs when they want a particular outcome.

The mechanism by which they do that in the First Amendment cases was to focus on the "right" instead of on the "amendment." If one looks at the right of free speech, you have a case of first impression. No Court has ruled on free speech before, so one can rule as it wishes.

If you look at whether the First Amendment should be incorporated by way of the Fourteenth, and therefore binding on the states, you have a controlling precedent that was set in *Twining* which says the First Amendment cannot be incorporated.

When *Powell v. Alabama* came up on appeal, the Court was faced with an outrageous injustice. A group of Negro defendants in a southern courtroom, without any meaningful assistance of counsel, were tried for the crime of rape of two white girls. The crime of rape carried the possibility of the death penalty at that time. With no prior Court decisions on that particular subject matter restraining them, the Supreme Court felt free to apply the Sixth Amendment's right to counsel to trials in state courts.

Although *Twining* had its critics on the Court and its impact was limited by other decisions, its holding that the Fifth Amendment did not apply to the states was not specifically overruled until 1964 by the Warren Court.

Laying the Groundwork to Interfere

As the Supreme Court "reviewed" those state cases, it began the infuriating habit of planting metaphorical "land mines," which would blow up in some future case coming before the Court, and some new "right" would be found for a criminal defendant prohibiting his prosecution for the crime he committed. This newly found "right" restricted what evidence the prosecution could introduce in future trials.

This is all well and good for the criminal; it is devilishly difficult for a prosecuting attorney to explain to a victim of crime who sees a criminal go free even though there is overwhelming evidence of his guilt which cannot be used at trial because of some procedural technicality.

The court wrote in *Twining,* "[I] t is clear that the 14ᵗʰ amendment in no way undertakes to control the power of a state to determine by what process legal rights may be asserted or legal obligations be enforced" by state courts. It went on to say, "Much might be said in favor of the view that the privilege [against self-incrimination] was guaranteed against state impairment as a privilege and immunity of national citizenship, but, as has been shown, the decisions of this court have foreclosed that view."

The Court did not rule on the merits of the case, but instead let the judgment of the New Jersey Court of Errors & Appeals (state supreme court) stand because any guarantee against "self-incrimination in the courts of the states is not secured by any part of the U.S. Constitution." "Any part of the U.S. Constitution" would seem to cover all the amendments in the Bill of Rights, but hey! We are dealing with the Supreme Court here. As Chief Justice Warren Burger said, "We are the Supreme Court. We can do what we want."[127]

Nor was there any federal prohibition against a state statute that allowed appeal of a criminal court conviction when the trial judge had misinterpreted the law. *Palko v. Connecticut*[128] was about double jeopardy. Frank Palko had been tried and convicted of second-degree murder, a lesser included offense, on an indictment charging first-degree murder.

Because there had been substantial misapplications (errors) of law by the trial judge, a Connecticut statute allowed the state to appeal. The state supreme court ruled in favor of the prosecution—and Palko was tried a second time on the same indictment, found guilty of first-degree murder, and sentenced to die.

He appealed the second conviction on double jeopardy grounds, but the supreme court of Connecticut affirmed the conviction. He then appealed to the United States Supreme Court, claiming the federal right against double jeopardy was violated by his second trial on the same indictment in state court.

The U.S. Supreme Court affirmed the decision of the Connecticut court but planted one of those aforementioned "land mines." Even while upholding the state's highest court, the U.S. Supreme Court ruled that certain pledges of the amendments, specifically the First and Sixth, which bind the federal court, "have been found to be implicit in the concept of ordered liberty, and thus, through the Fourteenth Amendment, become valid as against the states."

That language, "implicit in the concept of ordered liberty," was unnecessary to the finding in *Palko*. The case was not about the First or Sixth amendment, it was a *Fifth* Amendment case. Nevertheless, the Court "planted" a finding that the Fourteenth Amendment carried in it certain rights "implicit in the concept of ordered liberty." That language appears nowhere in the amendment. Later, that language would be cited as a reason for the massive federal interference with state criminal law that was to follow.

The Court that decided *Palko* was the same Court that overturned much of President Franklin Roosevelt's New Deal legislation.

A decade later, the Warren Court, looking for an excuse to abandon *stare decisis*, would seize upon that *Palko* language to find all kinds of new rights in the Constitution that had not been manifest to generations of learned judges on earlier Courts.

In *Adamson v. California*,[129] the Supreme Court ruled, "It is *settled law* [remember those words] that the clause of the Fifth Amendment, protecting a person against being compelled to be a witness against himself, is not made effective by the Fourteenth Amendment, as a protection against state action" (emphasis added). The part of the Fifth Amendment to the United States Constitution absolutely forbidding a second trial under any circumstances applied only to procedures by the federal government, not to state trials.

Allowing the prosecutor to appeal makes a lot of sense if you consider fairness and the context of the ruling. If you have a lazy or stupid or corrupt judge (there are a few) whose rulings make it impossible for the prosecution to put on its best case and to get a fair trial for the state, why shouldn't the prosecutor have the same right of appeal as the defendant? At least in this limited type of cases.

Adamson was decided in 1947. A mere sixty-three years ago. That was the condition the law found itself in one hundred fifty-six years after the adoption of the Bill of Rights and six years before Earl Warren became chief justice of the United States Supreme Court. *Adamson* would be overruled by the Warren Court less than twenty years after the earlier Court handed down the ruling. Warren did not believe in *stare decisis* if it prevented him from creating a new law that he liked better than the old one passed by Congress and upheld by generations of judges.

A New Millennium and a New Constitutional Right

Most people who grew up watching cop shows on TV assume the requirement for a law enforcement officer to read a suspect his *Miranda* rights comes straight from the Constitution. It doesn't.

The constitutional right to have the *Miranda* warnings was elevated to that status by the Rehnquist Court in the year 2000! Prior to 2000, the Court considered *Miranda* a "prophylactic" rule to prevent police misconduct. In another case the Court said explicitly that *Miranda* warnings are "procedural safeguards…not themselves rights protected by the Constitution."

The defendant in *Harris v. New York*[130] made incriminating statements to police before he received *Miranda* warnings. Then, while testifying at trial, he told a different story. The Court allowed statements taken in violation of *Miranda*—that would have been inadmissible by the state as direct evidence—to be used to impeach false statements made by the defendant as he testified in his own defense. *Miranda* was not a license to lie.

If the lack of *Miranda* warnings kept the state from using the defendant's statement in its own case, it could certainly use the previously suppressed statement in rebuttal if the defendant gets on the witness stand and fabricates a story that is very different from what he initially told the police.

The holding in *New York v. Quarles*[131] created a public safety exception to *Miranda*. If the police are trying to locate a dangerous instrumentality (i.e., a gun or a bomb), police can ask, "Where's the gun?" without giving *Miranda* warnings.

But in *Dickerson*, Chief Justice Rehnquist, writing for the majority, said, "*Miranda,* being a constitutional decision of this Court, may not be in effect overruled by an Act of Congress [18 U.S.C. § 3501]."

Justice Scalia, in a scathing dissent joined by Justice Thomas, wrote that the constitutional rule announced in *Dickerson* means "that this Court has the power, not merely to apply the Constitution but to expand it, imposing what it regards as useful "prophylactic" restrictions upon Congress and the States. That is an immense and frightening antidemocratic power, and it does not exist."

Except it does exist now. The Supreme Court just made it exist. They made it up and told the rest of us, "This is the law." And there is absolutely nothing we can do about it under the present laws and Constitution (as interpreted by the Supreme Court).

It is important to know what the law is. It is vital to know that, given the same or very similar facts, a court will rule the same way tomorrow as it did today and as it had ruled yesterday. That's how the common law developed. In a society where we are "governed by laws and not by men," it is absolutely essential that a person be able to know what the laws say.

If you don't personally know, at least you should be able to consult someone who does know. But without *settled law* (remember that term?), not even the lawyers know what the law may be on a given day in a particular court.

The Warren Court simply ignored *stare decisis* when there was a particular outcome it wanted to reach in a particular case. There was no settled law. Building on Warren's work, the modern Supreme Court created what it calls the Living Constitution. Now, there are no limits on what the Supreme Court can do.

Imagine a conversation something like this.

Detective: "I just busted this guy for assault, and when I went to search him for a weapon, for my own safety, I found a bag of green leafy vegetative matter that looked and smelled like marijuana." (Yes, policemen do talk like that—you are not permitted to call the marijuana "marijuana" because you don't have the lab report back yet and you can't prove it's marijuana). "His lawyer said he would have the drug evidence thrown out of court because I didn't have a warrant. Can he do that?"

Prosecuting Attorney: "Well, I'm not sure. The court probably wouldn't throw out the evidence right now, but you know, this case might not come to trial for a year or so, and I'm not sure how a judge might rule then. That's too far ahead to make predictions."

"Ridiculous," the average person would assert, "the law doesn't change that way."

Then consider this: the retirement or death and the subsequent appointment of a single justice to the Court can tip the balance from a five-four decision to follow precedent to a five-four vote to dishonor the received wisdom of previous decisions and create new law. One has only to look to the appointment of Arthur Goldberg to the Warren Court in 1962 to see how the appointment of a single justice can fundamentally change the law as we know it.

Goldberg gave Earl Warren a dependable fifth vote and solidified what came to be known as the Warren Court. In his own words, Goldberg's tenure on the Court was "a time when the Warren Court absolutely got into high gear." Goldberg was the fifth vote and wrote the opinion in *Escobedo v. Illinois*,[132] the precursor to *Miranda*. A five-to-four vote decided both cases.

Overruling Established Law

A better example is *West Virginia Board of Educ. v. Barnette*.[133] The *Gobitis* case, decided a mere three years earlier, had upheld the saying of the Pledge of Allegiance in the public school. With the appointment of two new justices to the Court, the *Barnette* case overturned *Gobitis* and prohibited the saying of the pledge in public schools.

The Court today is so evenly divided that a single new appointment of a justice to the Court could have a profound effect on the law.

When you look at the facts, it becomes obvious that the *Miranda* ruling in the *Dickerson* case was not about the defendant's civil rights being violated; it was about the Court hanging on to its power to promulgate rules, which it can then treat *as if* the rules are contained within the document we call the Constitution.

Those Warren Court decisions present a dilemma for a more conservative Court, which might consider itself bound by *stare decisis.* The Warren Court, in making all its new laws, knew no such restraint. As stated before, Warren simply ignored *stare decisis* when it suited his purposes so to do. However, the Rehnquist Court said in *Dickerson*, "Whether or not we would agree with *Miranda*'s reasoning and its resulting rule, were we addressing the issue in the first instance, the principles of *stare decisis* weigh heavily against overruling it now."

The *Dickerson* case started out with a man robbing a bank in Alexandria, Virginia. An eyewitness to the robbery gave the FBI a description of the getaway car and a license number; that led them to Charles T. Dickerson's apartment in Tacoma Park, Maryland. There they found a large amount of money, which Dickerson claimed he had won gambling; he refused the FBI's request to search his apartment. All of the federal agents left the apartment, but some continued to observe the place from outside until their fellow agents could obtain a search warrant.

After obtaining the warrant and notifying the agents outside Dickerson's apartment, the lead investigator, FBI Special Agent Lawlor, returned to the interview room where Dickerson was waiting and told the suspect that agents were searching his apartment. Dickerson then said he wanted to make a statement. He confessed to driving the getaway car for a series of robberies in Maryland and Virginia, and he identified Jimmy Rochester as the actual bank robber.

The search of Dickerson's apartment pursuant to the search warrant found "a silver .45 caliber handgun, dye-stained money, a bait bill from another robbery, ammunition, masks, and latex gloves." He was subsequently indicted by a grand jury and scheduled for trial for conspiracy, three counts of bank robbery, and three weapons charges.

His attorney claimed Dickerson had not been properly "Mirandized" and made a pretrial motion to suppress the confession and any independent evidence that was obtained as a result of information contained in the confession.

Whose Law? Or Is It Just Ideology?

The U.S. district court ruled that the confession was voluntary; however, because of a dispute over when *Miranda* warnings had been properly given, the evidence would not be admissible at trial. Dickerson claimed that he was not given his *Miranda* warnings prior to confessing, and there were some conflicting documents from Special Agent Lawlor that seemed to support that.

A judge approved the search warrant at 8:50 p.m., according to Lawlor's handwritten notation on the warrant. The *official FBI waiver* of rights form indicated that Dickerson waived his rights at 9:41 p.m., some fifty-one minutes later.

From the author's personal experience while prosecuting drug crimes for a joint state-federal task force, it is not uncommon for the FBI to transcribe the information in a defendant's handwritten statement onto a standard waiver of rights form and have the defendant sign that form also.

On the other hand, another police officer who was present, Detective Thomas Durkin of the Alexandria Police Department, presented for the court's inspection "a hand-written statement that Dickerson made while at the FBI Field Office in which Dickerson stated he 'was read [his] rights at 7:30 [p.m.].' " Dickerson added the additional statement that he "knew nothing [about] the bank robbery."

It seems obvious on its face that Dickerson was still denying his involvement in the bank robbery after he acknowledged receiving the *Miranda* warnings. He wrote out and signed a statement to that effect at the FBI field office. *Ipso facto,* Dickerson's confession came *after* he acknowledged receiving the *Miranda* warning.

A footnote states that according to the evidence, the 7:30 p.m. time may have been inaccurate—"Detective Durkin explained in his affidavit that when Dickerson wrote 7:30 p.m., he 'specifically recall[ed] thinking that Dickerson had no idea what time it was.' "

To anyone but a defense lawyer, that would seem to be irrelevant: the statement does corroborate the sequence of events and the fact that Dickerson's handwritten statement still denied any involvement with the bank robbery *after* he acknowledged that he received his *Miranda* rights.

It seems apparent from the documentary evidence that when he finally did confess, it was after receiving the warnings. But the United States Supreme Court, bent on preserving its power and affirming that Congress had no power over the Court, chose not to see it that way.

According to the evidence, it was only after he learned that the officers were executing the search of his apartment, and had found a "bait bill" there, that Dickerson admitted to his part in the crime.

All of this is consistent with Agent Lawlor's testimony that the defendant continued to deny his involvement in the robbery for some time after he signed the waiver of rights. However, the district court chose to believe the defendant rather than the FBI agent, so the confession was suppressed. If one reads between the lines, there may also have been an element of the district judge wanting to punish Agent Lawlor for what the judge perceived as overzealousness on the part of the agent.

Judges have wide discretion in ruling on what evidence to admit. If a lawyer or witness makes the judge angry, he can expect to get some unfavorable rulings as a result. Judges are human, too.

The government appealed the trial court's decision to the Fourth Circuit Court of Appeals. The Fourth Circuit Court looked at all the evidence, and in particular, the trial court finding of fact that the confession was voluntary. The court then relied on a law passed by Congress, 18 U.S.C.A. § 3501, which restored the voluntariness test two years after *Miranda* was decided in 1966.

Janet Reno's Justice Department, consistent with its announced policy, refused to invoke § 3501 but the Fourth Circuit Court ordered the issue briefed anyway.

The Fourth Circuit overturned the lower court and remanded the case for trial in *United States v. Dickerson*.[134] Judge Williams, writing for the court, stated that "without his confession it is possible, if not probable, that he will be acquitted." He continued:

> In response to the Supreme Court's decision in *Miranda v. Arizona*, 384 U.S. 436 (1966), the Congress of the United States enacted 18 U.S.C.A. § 3501 with the clear intent of restoring voluntariness as the test for admitting confessions in federal court. Although duly enacted by the United States Congress and signed into law by the president, the Department of Justice has steadfastly refused to enforce the provision. In fact, after initially "taking the Fifth" on the statute's constitutionality, the Department of Justice has now asserted, without explanation, that the provision is unconstitutional. With the issue squarely presented, we hold that Congress, pursuant to its power to establish the rules of evidence and procedure in the federal courts, acted well within its authority in enacting § 3501. As a consequence, § 3501, rather than *Miranda*, governs the admissibility of confessions in federal court. Accordingly, the district court erred in suppressing Dickerson's voluntary confession on the grounds that it was obtained in technical violation of *Miranda*.

After his conviction in the trial court, using the confession, the defendant appealed his case to the United States Supreme Court in *Dickerson v. United States*.

In writing the majority opinion for that appeal, Chief Justice Rehnquist clearly stated the conflict when he said, "We agree with the Court of Appeals that Congress intended by its enactment [of § 3501] to overrule *Miranda* .... Because of the obvious conflict between our decision in *Miranda* and § 3501, we must address whether Congress has constitutional authority to thus supersede *Miranda*."

To state the problem is to decide the outcome. There is no way the Supreme Court is going to acknowledge that Congress has the power to overturn a decision of the Court. The Court won't do anything to diminish its own power. However, the *Dickerson* decision goes directly against the United States Constitution, which gives Congress the authority to set limits on the Court's appellate jurisdiction and to pass laws establishing the way the Court works. Article III of the Constitution states, in part:

> [Clause 2]: In all Cases affecting Ambassadors, other public Ministers and Consuls, and those in which a State shall be Party, the supreme Court shall have original Jurisdiction. In all the other Cases before mentioned, the Supreme Court shall have appellate Jurisdiction, both as to Law and Fact, *with such Exceptions, and under such Regulations as the Congress shall make.* [Emphasis added; capitalization as in original.]

Dickerson appealed his case from a lower court, so the Supreme Court was hearing it under its *appellate* jurisdiction. The Constitution states explicitly that Congress has the constitutional authority to regulate the Court's jurisdiction and rules under those circumstances, and the Congress can make "such Exceptions" as it wills, which will modify the Court's jurisdiction.

The Rehnquist Court played semantic games with the prior rulings of the Court on *Miranda* issues. Some justices who are on record as believing that *Miranda* is not a constitutional requirement voted to make it one so that the *Dickerson* decision could trump Congress's attempt to restore reason by enacting 18 U.S.C. § 3501.

The Necessity of Amending the Constitution

If the Supreme Court followed the Constitution, it would not be necessary to have a constitutional amendment explicitly giving Congress the power to override the Supreme Court in order to reign in the otherwise omnipotent Court. Unfortunately, the Supreme Court does not follow the Constitution. It follows its own inclinations and what *it* says the Constitution says.

It may be desirable not just to give Congress the power but also to specifically rebuke the Supreme Court for overreaching in its power grab.

The people need to declare emphatically "government of the people, by the people, for the people, shall not perish from the earth."[135] By any definition, the United States Supreme Court is not the "people" of the United States, and the Supreme Court should not be able to "trump" the laws made by the lawfully elected representatives of the people of the United States.

Chapter 6: Taxation AND Legislation Without Representation

The candid citizen must confess that if the policy of the government, upon vital questions affecting the whole people, is to be irrevocably fixed by decisions of the Supreme Court, the instant they are made, in ordinary litigation between parties in personal actions, the people will have ceased to be their own rulers.[136] —President Abraham Lincoln, First Inaugural Address.

On December 16, 1773, a group of American colonists, dressed as Indians, boarded three British ships in Boston Harbor. They dumped 342 chests of tea into the harbor as a protest against a tax placed on the tea by the English Parliament.[137] Both the small tax and the reaction to it were mostly symbolic—Parliament had repealed the despised Townshend Acts, for the most part, leaving only the token tax on tea as evidence of Parliament's power to tax the colonists.

For their part, the colonists were having no part of it. They wanted their taxes, if any, levied by their own colonial legislatures.

The action in Boston Harbor was the culmination of a simmering decade-old dispute between England and its colonies in America, growing out of a unanimous vote in the House of Commons in March of 1763 whereby the English Parliament asserted its right to tax its citizens in the colonies. The tax was justified in British minds because the Crown had spent enormous sums in fighting the French and Indian War, and the English believed the colonists should help pay for their own defense.

The reaction in America, however, was swift and defiant. The Massachusetts Assembly, which happened to be in session, passed a resolution:

> That the sole right of giving and granting the money of the people of this province is vested in them, as the legal representatives; and that the imposition of taxes and duties by the Parliament of Great Britain upon a people who are not represented in the House of Commons, is absolutely irreconcilable with their rights. That no man can justly take the property of another without his consent; upon which principle the right of representation in the same body which exercises the power of making laws for levying taxes, one of the main pillars of the British Constitution, is evidently founded.[138]

When the three tea-laden ships arrived in Boston, the local citizens would not permit them to unload; the royal governor of Massachusetts would not let the ships return to England until the tax was paid, and so the stage was set for what came to be known in history as the Boston Tea Party.

History credits James Otis, a Boston politician, with coining the phrase "taxation without representation is tyranny,"[139] and the seeds of the American Revolution were a giant step closer to germinating. The English Parliament retaliated against the Americans by imposing the "Intolerable Acts" in 1774,[140] and the Revolution began a year later.

Today we are faced with a strikingly similar situation wherein the United States Supreme Court, unelected and unaccountable, with no one on the Court elected to represent the people, can authorize lower courts to levy taxes directly or, as is more common, to order legislators to take actions which by their nature require the raising of taxes.

Although the legislatures are not exercising independent judgment in this class of cases, it is the politicians who feel the people's wrath—which translates to higher approval ratings for the courts than for legislators when the courts are really the culprit.

The Court can override laws made by elected representatives as Congress carries out its constitutionally mandated duties.

Some would argue that only the legislature can impose a tax, the Court cannot. However, if the federal district court, with the encouragement and support of the United States Supreme Court, can order the city of Boston to transport children across school district lines to achieve racial balance—at an estimated cost of thirty million dollars per year to the taxpayers, it is the Court that has imposed the tax burden upon the citizens of Boston.

To restate the obvious, the Boston City Council that actually drafted the tax bill was merely translating the Court's order into a local tax ordinance. The city government gave up its legislative function and acted as agent—drafting the tax bill for its principal, the Court, and thereby carrying out the Court's imposition of the tax.

This may be particularly repugnant in Boston where the Massachusetts Assembly said, "That no man can justly take the property of another without his consent; upon which principle the right of representation in the same body which exercises the power of making laws for levying taxes, one of the main pillars of [government] is evidently founded."[141]

After all the money spent, we learn from *South Boston Online*: "It is now recognized that forced busing has been a failure…. Boston's racial problems aren't as bad as they once were, but Boston is still segregated. The huge number of students who had their education ruined by busing is hard to imagine."[142]

A more scholarly examination of the busing problem in a different city reaches the same conclusion. Dr. Thomas Bier, testifying before a congressional hearing, said of busing:

I believe busing for the purpose of racial balance has hurt the city of Cleveland because it has contributed to the economic and social weakening of its resident population. It has done that by pushing people to move out of the city to suburbs—many of whom have been the kind of residents that every community needs; people with good incomes and who value education....

The jurisdictional boundary between city and suburbs is a massive open door. Through that door, annually, a steady stream of parents who did not want their children bused has moved out.... I believe about half of the 100,000 households that have left Cleveland since 1977 did so at least in part because of busing.[143]

"Men Of Zeal, Well-Meaning But Without Understanding"[144]

Once again, men with the best of intentions have focused on the narrow issue before them without any consideration of unintended consequences or the long-term effect of their ruling. The unintended result of a court ruling was much worse in the Kansas City desegregation case, discussed in chapter 7.

The justices of the United States Supreme Court should not be making the laws because they are lawyers. That sounds self-contradictory but it's not. First, it will help if the reader understands how laws came about in the first place.

Webster defines morality as "conformity to ideals of right human conduct." But what is "right" human conduct? How do you know what is right?

In casual conversation, the author posed the question to his wife: "How do you know what's right?"

She said, "My mommy taught me."

He then asked, "How did she know what was right?"

"Her mommy taught her."

"And how did her mommy know what was right?"

"I guess her mommy taught her."

If you trace that back far enough, all sense of what mommy said is right, as we know it today, comes from or was filtered through somebody's religion. The ancient Hebrews believed if you did not do "right," you would be estranged from God, whose protection you needed to fend off enemies. The Babylonians came and carried off the Jews into captivity because the Jews had strayed from God's teachings and therefore lost his protection.[145]

In ancient Greece, failure to do right brought down the wrath of the gods, sometimes in the form of a lightning bolt flung by Zeus.

In the Judeo-Christian tradition, the rules came from God handed down through the Pentateuch—the first five books of Moses and, in particular, the Ten Commandments.

If one is an evolutionist, the rules developed somewhere back in prehistory and satisfied the need for order in society. When man's ancestors started walking upright and living in small family, and later tribal groups, they quickly learned that some things were very disruptive to the peace and good order of their family or tribal unit. If you killed somebody, the relatives of that person were likely to retaliate against the killer and his family. So one can imagine their making up a rule: "Don't kill people."

If you stole another man's wife, that man was likely to gather up all his male relatives, and they would come looking for her and the kidnapper, possibly leading to his death and war between villages. So they might have made up another rule: "Don't covet your neighbor's wife."

If you stole another person's property, if that person was big enough and strong enough, one was likely to get pummeled or even killed when the person came to take his property back. Stealing also made enemies who would try to do the thief and his tribe harm whenever they have the opportunity. Another rule was: "Don't steal."

As the rules became more numerous and more complex, the weaker members of the tribe, often the mothers and their children, discovered they needed the protection of the rules more than the bigger and stronger members of the tribe. The big guys could take care of themselves. So how did the weaker get the stronger to follow the rules? By playing to their superstitions.

From the time the children were born, for the most part it was the mothers who taught them to follow the rules and, eventually, that "God'll *'gitcha'* " if you don't follow the rules.

So even for the tiny minority of Americans that doesn't believe in God, the reality is that the moral code evolved symbiotically with the religious. Morality and religion were virtually indistinguishable until the middle of the twentieth century.

The concept of natural law comes from the belief that somewhere in time, there was some innate goodness and honesty of man before he was "corrupted" by greed, selfishness, and violence. The common law developed out of the belief that judges could discern this natural law and "do the right thing." That theory is bogus unless you also accept the creation story and the Garden of Eden. If you accept the Garden of Eden concept, then the rules come from God to Moses on Mount Sinai, and that is the end of that discussion.

But assume for the sake of argument that one believes in the theory of evolution. Try if you can to visualize Lucy (*Australopithecus Afarensis*) sitting around the cave with a strange man, with whom she just copulated, saying, "You know, I've got to tell my husband about this because we are all honest and good and uncorrupted here—well, maybe a little corrupted now—but still honest."

Not likely.

For the evolutionists, and given the animal nature of man's origins, it is highly unlikely that man ever lived in that ideal state from which natural law is said to emanate. If one believes in God, man was corrupted in the Garden of Eden, and God has been trying to get him back on the straight and narrow ever since. In the Western tradition, certainly by the time of the Romans—and before Charles Darwin made his now-famous voyage on the *Beagle*—natural law held sway.

Natural Law

Natural Law grew out of a Stoic concept, "According to nature," which:

> rested upon the purely supposititious existence, in primitive times, of a 'state of nature;' that is, a condition of society in which men universally were governed solely by a rational and consistent obedience to the needs, impulses, and promptings of their true nature, such nature being as yet undefaced by dishonesty, falsehood, or indulgence of the baser passions.[146]

If you accept Darwin's theory of evolution, it is difficult to imagine such a state ever existed; if natural law still exists at all, it must have come from something other than man's uncorrupted nature. In fact, early man probably came down from the trees corrupted and animal-like in every sense of that word. (Again, if you don't believe Darwin's theory, then the laws came from God, and that ends the argument.)

At the time of the American Revolution, almost everyone accepted that natural law came from, in the words of Thomas Jefferson, "Nature and Nature's God." From a "Creator" who endowed us with certain "inalienable rights."[147]

Intellectuals, professors, and philosophers separate morality from religion, but the average person who doesn't have too many deep philosophical thoughts doesn't even try. If it is morally right, it must have come from religion; if not now, at least somewhere in the dim, murky past.

So what does all this have to do with the Supreme Court?

In the mother country, England, there was a body of law made by judges and gathered together in books and called the "common law." Common law filled in the gaps left between the king's command and the Acts of Parliament.

Common law in its earliest form developed to fill a need left by conquering Norman armies in Anglo-Saxon England more interested in plunder and taxation than in ruling. Communications between king and subjects were poor, and the peasants in the countryside often had to settle the purely local disputes between themselves without benefit of any government structure.

The office of sheriff existed to collect taxes and to punish treason against the king. If the sheriff occasionally kept the peasants from killing each other, it was only to preserve the king's property and tax base, not to show compassion for the peasants.

As time passed and the peasants tired of killing (and being killed by) each other while the Norman lords enjoyed the fruits of their labor, the peasants began calling upon "wise" men to mediate disputes. These wise men—often clergy—after a while began to notice that the same kinds of disputes kept coming up again and again, both in the local village and across the country. The wise men started to write down their decisions and share them with other "wise men" of similar stature in other villages. As the decisions circulated, they became the "common law."

Common law depended for its authority on "natural law," law which could be discerned by the intellect of wise men, as opposed to "positive law," which was willfully made by man—the king, and later the Parliament.

Since the earliest mediators of disputes often were clergy, the unlearned illiterate peasants probably assumed, rightly so I suspect, that the mediators were following some rules, which even these primitive mediators themselves believed were handed down by God. When the disputes became more complex and the solutions became more complicated and subtle, it became necessary to go beyond purely religious teachings and get into interpretation of those teachings in ways the Bible never quite anticipated; thus the resort to "natural" law.

This evolution of the law also gave rise to employment of advocates who knew these "laws" and could advocate for a particular point of view, often making very fine distinctions between the facts of the settled case and the present case under adjudication.

That creates an interesting paradox for the modern court: decisions of the court in a post-Darwin world, and particularly after *Atkins v. Virginia,* depend now on the Court's superior "intuitions" and "feelings" rather than the Constitution, which had been the foundation—in theory, at least—of all American law. So where does the Court get its superior intuitions and feelings?

Where Does the Court Get Its *Moral* Authority?

Are the justices individually or collectively smarter than all of the rest of us?

Probably not. Not every lawyer who has a high IQ and graduates from a top law school can be on the Supreme Court. There are only nine seats up there behind that big bench. It would get awfully crowded. So there are other lawyers who are just as smart or smarter, and just as well educated as the current crop of Supreme Court justices. So what makes the Court smarter than the rest of us?

The answer, of course, is nothing. The justices who serve on the Supreme Court are not smarter or better educated or more moral, nor do they have more insight than many of the rest of us. They just have more power. Power which was given to them by mere appointment and then expanded by stealth. Not power that comes from being elected by the people. Power originally based on natural law and the belief that judges—for example, the king's chancellor, who often was a priest—had some superior claim on knowing what "natural law" was.

But that was before Darwin, and now we know that man probably never lived in that ideal natural state before he was "corrupted." So if there is no natural-law goodness that is innate in man, and the Supreme Court has taken God and religion out of the public discourse, what gives the Supreme Court the "moral authority" to make life-changing decisions for the rest of us?

The answer, of course, is the 101st Airborne Division.

For the benefit of those not old enough to remember, following the 1954 Supreme Court decision in *Brown v. Board of Education*,[148] holding that separate schools were inherently unequal, many people still resisted integrating schools. Anticipating the first day of the school year in 1957, when integration was finally to come to Little Rock, Arkansas, Governor Orval Faubus claimed he had information that activists from around the country were converging on Little Rock to make trouble for the black students planning to integrate the white high school there.

Faubus called out the Arkansas National Guard to "maintain order" and prevent the black students from entering the all-white school or white students from entering the all-black school.

Army National Guard troops in all states have a dual mission: the guard is available to each state's governor to maintain order in case of natural disaster or civil disorder, and it has a federal mission as a reserve component of the United States Army. If there is both a state and national crisis, the federal mission takes precedent.

As tensions grew and disobedience of federal court orders mounted, President Dwight D. Eisenhower called the Arkansas National Guard to federal service and placed the guard under United States Army command. Just to make sure that the guard obeyed its new federal commanders, Eisenhower also had one thousand regular army troops of the 101st Airborne Division flown into Little Rock to "stand by" in case the guard needed help maintaining order—or persuasion, if the Guard continued to follow the orders of Governor Faubus instead of its U.S. Army commanders.[149]

But is having the enforcement power of the United States Army at your disposal enough to give the Supreme Court the *moral* authority to make laws for the country? Of course it doesn't give the Court moral authority. It just gives it the raw power.

The author believes the Court, by ignoring the will of the people—and the Constitution—in favor of foreign laws and the justices' own feelings and intuitions, has forfeited its moral authority to make laws; it has only the *power* so to do.

Apart from the illegitimate power being asserted by an oligarchic Court, are judges the best people to make life-changing decisions for all of us? In the end, how is that oligarchy different from dictatorship?

In his first inaugural address, President Abraham Lincoln said:

> The candid citizen must confess that if the policy of the government, upon vital questions affecting the whole people, is to be irrevocably fixed by decisions of the Supreme Court, the instant they are made, in ordinary litigation between parties in personal actions, the people will have ceased to be their own rulers.[150]

Temperamentally and educationally, judges are not the best people to be running the country. In fact, they may be the absolute worst. There is a considerable body of published research which suggests that lawyers are different. That is not a value judgment. It does not suggest that they are better or worse than everyone else, just different.

"Professional schools are highly invasive institutions which exert intense control by purposely influencing beliefs, values and personality characteristics of students; and law schools appear to be the most invasive among all graduate education."[151]

Existentially you become what you think. Sigmund Freud, the father of psychoanalysis, thought that if you could change a person's thoughts you would necessarily change the way they behave. B. F. Skinner, experimenting with behavior modification, came to the opposite opinion; he believed if you changed a person's behavior, you would change the way they thought.

Having been trained in sociology and psychology as an undergraduate, with postgraduate work in guidance and counseling—and having working as a mental health counselor for years before enrolling in law school—the author believes they were both right. Thoughts, feelings, and behavior are so inextricably connected that if you change any one you necessarily change the other two. So thoughts are very powerful things. They influence in profound ways how one feels and behaves.

All Judges Are Lawyers First

Almost all jurisdictions require that judges first be lawyers before they can become judges.[152] Lawyers' training makes them narrowly focused, fact-specific analysts who look at detail and nitpick over slight factual differences. The cliché "can't see the forest for the trees" must first have been used to describe lawyers. Of all professions, lawyers are the absolute worst when it comes to looking at the "big picture" because they are so busy focusing on trees they don't even know they are *in* a forest.

The author's proofreader, who also is his wife of twenty years, read that last sentence and corrected it. She said, "Lawyers don't even look at the trees. They look at the leaves on the trees." She then corrected herself. "No, they look at the *veins* in the leaves on the trees."

A lawyer's idea of the big picture is making sure she has examined all the witness' statements, all the evidence, the controlling law, and all the contingencies so that she is fully prepared to meet whatever argument the other side throws at her in the case she is trying in court at the moment. There is zero thought or consideration for how the outcome may affect other people not parties to the suit.

This has implications not just for how judges make law, focusing on narrow, specific issues and not the big picture, but even issues of our national security. When you have a criminal defendant, who has constitutional rights, judges are superb at protecting those rights, even at the expense of victims of crime (think *Miranda*); we accept that because we have a deeply ingrained belief in America that "better a guilty person go free than an innocent one go to prison for something he didn't do."

Some Americans are even saying, in effect, "Let that terrorist who came here to kill us go free. The FBI forgot to read him his *Miranda* rights." There are a large number of people among the liberal and "progressive" left who still believe the war on terror is a law enforcement problem. Many Democrats have gone so far as to say, "The world would be better off if the United States loses the war in Iraq."[153]

Unfortunately, judges bring the same mind-set to the courtroom whether they are hearing criminal cases or cases involving national security issues. U.S. district court Judge Robert Doumar said in *Hamdi v. Rumsfeld,* "We must protect the freedoms of even those who hate us."[154] Many judges and lawyers want to extend the same constitutional protections that we afford criminal defendants to those individuals who are terrorists, mercenaries, or members of a foreign army at war with the United States and who are quite candid about what they want to do: they want to kill us.

Doumar ordered the government to give the defendant classified information pertaining to the national security of the United States. The Fourth Circuit reversed, stressing that "because it was undisputed that Hamdi was captured in an active combat zone, no factual inquiry or evidentiary hearing allowing Hamdi to be heard or to rebut the government's assertions was necessary or proper."

The United States Supreme Court reversed the Fourth Circuit. Now, enemy combatants do have a right to some kind of judicial review.[155] And after *Rasul v. Bush,*[156] terrorists now have the right to challenge their detention by filing a writ of habeas corpus in U.S. federal courts.

To put that in perspective, some older readers might remember the capture of the German-American citizens who returned to Germany and were trained by the Nazis as spies. They were put ashore on Long Island during World War II to commit sabotage in this country.

In today's court system, many judges and civil rights lawyers would insist we let those saboteurs go free, even if it meant they might still carry out their plans for sabotage, because the FBI agents did not read them their *Miranda* rights and tell them they have a right to consult with the German consulate before being interrogated.

Suffice it to say at this point that whether Americans live or die at the hands of a terrorist rests right now in the hands of federal judges who have no clue about the stakes in the decisions they make. Such judges focus, as they are trained to do, on the merits of the case before them and do not look at the unintended consequences of the decisions they make. Such judges are prime examples of Justice Brandeis's "men of zeal, well-meaning but without understanding." Specific-issue oriented. Not "big picture" guys.

This should be of particular concern to citizens living in high-value target areas like New York or Washington, D.C., or Los Angeles. Or Keokuk, Iowa (Keokuk would be considered to be pretty high value to the people who live there).

It should be of concern because by their nature, reinforced by rigorous training, lawyers, and therefore judges—even the Supreme Court justices—are not "big picture" guys. Franklin D. Roosevelt was a "big picture" guy. Ronald Reagan was a "big picture" guy. Lawyers (and judges) are nitpickers who get the actual job done after "big picture" guys figure out what the job is.

How does the author know this? Because he is a lawyer. How come he see this when other lawyers apparently do not? First of all, other lawyers do see this; they just don't talk about it in public. There is tremendous peer pressure for lawyers not to criticize judges. Secondly, because the author has not always been a lawyer. And finally, it is a function of age. The author graduated from high school the same year President Eisenhower appointed Earl Warren to be chief justice of the Supreme Court of the United States.

The author was forty-nine years old when he enrolled in law school. He had had a life; he had lived in the real world, and he had watched the Warren Court make a joke of what was once "settled law." The "brainwashing" of law school didn't fully "take." He is a hybrid species—the intellect and education of a lawyer but with the heart of the mental health counselor he once was before going to law school.

To help nonlawyers better understand how lawyers are trained to think, a first-person account of a law school experience of the author may be helpful. Allow me to quote at length from a letter written to a friend at the time the incident occurred:

> I remember well my own epiphany when I first realized I was starting to think like a lawyer: To fully appreciate the change in the way I think, compare this with what I've told you about being a mental health counselor, a profession that emphasizes trust, empathy, understanding of others but above all else, that trust thing.

At the time I went to law school I was (and am) married to a social worker who still works in the mental health profession. The letter continued:

> One day I had a movie scheduled in the Moot Courtroom in place of our regular class. There was no other activity scheduled for the room so when I was the first student to arrive outside the closed door of the room, I didn't even break stride. I just flung the door open and strode into the room before I realized a different professor than the one who taught our ethics class had moved his class into the Moot Court Room without telling anyone. Apparently, he had some problem with the A/C in his own classroom.
> The trespassing professor told me they were just about to finish up in time for us to see the movie. I excused myself and backed out into the hallway to wait.

The students in my ethics class were required to attend a showing of a movie, *To Kill a Mockingbird*. We could invite guests to see the movie with us.

By coincidence, the second student to arrive happened to be [a good friend] Brad. I told Brad we couldn't go in yet, there was another class in there. He went on up to the door, opened it, looked in, said "excuse me" to the professor and backed out. He then entered into the casual conversation I was having with Bredga [my wife]. A third student arrived at the closed door. Same ritual.

Now both Brad and I told student #3 as she approached the door that we could not go in yet, etc. etc. Student #3 dutifully opened the door to see for herself, said "excuse me" to the professor and backed out. She and the friend who came with her joined the conversation with Brad and Bredga and me.

Now we were beginning to be a small crowd. The fourth student arrived. Again, the same ritual. After hearing a chorus of fellow students say, "We can't go in yet," the newly arriving student had to see for himself. Bredga, ever the social worker, started to laugh out loud.

I didn't see the humor. I asked her what was so funny. She said: "You people don't trust each other."

With a perfectly straight face and without any sense of irony, I asked her, "What's your point?" And then it hit me! We didn't trust each other. We weren't supposed to.

We had been taught to be skeptical of what we were told, purely analytical in our thought process, to independently verify facts and to focus on specifics and not to generalize. "We can't go in there yet" wasn't specific enough and it didn't fit the template—none of us were expecting there to be another class using the room so "there's another class in there" was something each of us was compelled to confirm for ourselves.

Lawyers [And Judges] Are Different—Not Better or Worse, Just Different

A well-researched examination of the professional literature, and commentary on how lawyers think, was documented by Mark C. Miller's paper on how legal training influences the decision-making process of lawyers and, in particular, lawyers serving in Congress.[157]

From time to time, the author's wife will say to him, "Will you send Mr. Spock home, and let me talk to my husband?" The reference is to Leonard Nimoy's character on the *Star Trek* TV series. It is a cue that he is in "lawyer mode"; that is to say, being too analytical and fact specific, not attending to feelings.

Most social scientists suggest your basic personality traits are determined by the time you are four years old. After that you continue to change and grow, to adjust, and to compensate by new learning and experience. But your basic "map" of the world is pretty well laid out. The overwhelming majority of people do not change their "map," and the few who do change do so only after some profound life-changing event—a religious conversion, for example, or an accident leading to a near-death experience. The author's personality changed during law school.

Now that you know how lawyers (and Supreme Court justices) think, are these the kind of people you want to hold dictatorial power over the lawmaking process in this country? It's not just the decisions of the Supreme Court itself: the Supreme Court sets the tone and supervises the lower federal courts. Whatever the Supreme Court decides, that's what the lower courts, where the bulk of the work gets done, also do.

Even given the best-written laws of Congress, the court system—including trial courts and the various appellate courts up the line—profoundly affects policy in this country by interpreting and implementing those laws, often in ways that bear little resemblance to the laws Congress thought it passed. By training and by inclination, the lawyers who make up the court system are characteristically incapable of seeing the "big picture." They are detail guys.

There is an even darker, sinister side to the court. Former federal appellate Judge Robert Bork wrote in *Coercing Virtue*[158] that hostility toward religion, destruction of moral standards, the invention of the right to abortion, and secular humanism have spread across national boundaries; it is a two-way flow with the attempt to have liberal views adopted abroad then reimported through judges in this country sympathetic to the liberal agenda.

The justices who depend on foreign law instead of our own Constitution are willing accomplices in that importation. Five of the nine justices (six before O'Connor retired), a majority on the Court, have already demonstrated that they are receptive to importing the ideas of foreign courts to help them interpret the United States Constitution. Expect Obama's nominee, Elena Kagan to be of that same mold.

Justices Stevens and Sandra Day O'Connor, in decisions cited herein, have expressed their affinity for the guidance of foreign courts in deciding American domestic cases, as have Kennedy, Souter, Ginsberg, and Breyer. All look to international law and custom to help them decide cases here.

That process has encouraged the International Court of Justice (ICJ), created by the United Nations, to believe it can interfere with the decision of a Texas court in a purely domestic case brought under state law. After some U.S. legal experts protested the ruling, and over the objections of President George W. Bush, who wanted the ICJ ruling to stand, the United States Supreme Court finally drew the line:

"While a treaty may constitute an international commitment, it is not binding domestic law unless Congress has enacted statutes implementing it or the treaty itself conveys an intention that it be 'self-executing' and is ratified on that basis." *Medellin v. Texas,* 06-948 (decided March 25, 2008).

It is always dangerous to have fact-oriented, narrowly focused, nitpicking specialists looking to foreign laws and customs for guidance on how to decide purely domestic American law issues, precisely because they cannot see the "big picture."

Nor do they have a moral compass based on Judeo-Christian teaching and values. At least not when they are deciding law cases.

That is as true of the U.N. court as it is with domestic courts in the United States. They want desperately to do the right thing but without a real understanding of what the right thing is for America. Having ruled against religion and morality in public life, the U.S. Supreme Court has lost its own moral compass, and so it exhausts every avenue of inquiry.[159] It looks at all the options; it looks at what solutions others have found—even others who live in foreign lands with un-American values—because it wants to "be fair" and "do the right thing."

But life isn't fair. God "makes his sun rise on the evil and on the good, and sends rain on the just and on the unjust." Sometimes innocent children are afflicted with terrible diseases; sometimes you have to choose between the lesser of two evils and there is no good choice.

We elect representatives to debate those issues, thoroughly study the probable consequences, and vote on the best choice. The people elect those representatives— hundreds of them, and they come from all parts of the country and represent many different cultures and interests and points of view.

What gave Sandra Day O'Connor the right to think her personal judgment is superior to the combined judgment of all the elected representatives? What makes O'Connor think her judgment is so superior to all of the other Supreme Court justices who ever served on the Court that she could substitute her judgment for theirs?

With O'Connor's retirement, it is now Justice Kennedy who decides all of the important cases. That will continue until some justice dies or retires and a new justice is appointed who could possibly change the balance—or until we the people tell the Supreme Court that "nobody died and made you God. We want our country back!"

Chapter 7: The End of Representative Government

The opinion which gives to the judges the right to decide what laws are constitutional and what are not, not only for themselves in their own sphere of action, but for the Legislative and Executive also in their spheres, would make the judiciary a despotic branch.— Thomas Jefferson, letter to Abigail Adams, September 11, 1804.[160]

Thomas Jefferson believed that allowing the federal judiciary to seize power by deciding which laws are constitutional and which are not would lead eventually to the end of representative democracy. History is proving him right.

President Jefferson's concern came from the Supreme Court case in 1803, *Marbury v. Madison,* in which Chief Justice John Marshall claimed for the Court, without any constitutional authority, the right of "judicial review."

Marshall asserted the absurd claim (now generally accepted as gospel among lawyers) that for purposes of judicial review, the Constitution was of the same kind and character as ordinary laws of the kind passed by Congress: "In some cases then, the Constitution must be looked into by the judges. And if they can open it at all, what part of it are they forbidden to read or obey?"[161]

Or, one might add, "to change!"

If the Constitution is of the same kind and character as ordinary laws of the kind passed by Congress, and if the Court can override an act of Congress, why then should the Court not be able to change the Constitution? And in fact, the modern Court does change the Constitution—fairly regularly.

According to Marshall, the Court had the right to interpret the meaning of the document rather than rely on its plain wording. In Jefferson's letter to Abigail Adams quoted at the beginning of this chapter, he told her that allowing the Court to decide how the other two branches shall comport their actions to the Constitution "would make the judiciary a despotic branch."

Judicial review, as practiced in the twenty-first century, has certainly achieved that. There is no practical limit on what the Supreme Court can do. The Court in theory is constrained by the Constitution, but in fact, it is not. A theme repeated throughout this book: the Constitution has become what any five of the nine judges, voting together on any particular day, say it is.

Jefferson, still reflecting on the potential of the *Marbury* decision, feared the encroachment by the Supreme Court, and he resisted expanding the powers of the federal government generally. In a letter to Mr. Hammond in 1821, he wrote:

> The germ of dissolution of our federal government is in...the federal judiciary;
> an irresponsible body (for impeachment is merely a scare-crow) working like
> gravity by night and by day, gaining a little today and a little tomorrow, and
> advancing its noiseless step like a thief, over the field of jurisdiction, until all
> shall be usurped from the States.[162]

Notice Jefferson's concern was about the Court encroaching on the powers reserved to the States—which it certainly has; however, the idea that the Court would
challenge Congress for the federal lawmaking power would have been so absurd to
the Founding Fathers that no one even thought of it.

The "bad seed" of *Marbury*, which would lead to the encroachment of the Supreme Court on the power of the States, would really begin to germinate after the
American Civil War. The Fourteenth Amendment became the instrument that allowed the Supreme Court to rule on matters which heretofore had been strictly
reserved to the States and to the people. The concept is known as federalism.

The first section of the Fourteenth Amendment declared that:

> No State shall make or enforce any law which shall abridge the privileges or im-
> munities of citizens of the United States; nor shall any State deprive any person
> of life, liberty, or property, without due process of law; nor deny to any person
> within its jurisdiction the equal protection of the laws.

The amendment was not well thought-out: it did admirably what it was intended to do—give full citizenship to the freed slaves—but it went far beyond that.
It gave virtually unlimited power to the federal government in its relationship with
the States.

The Northern states would learn soon enough that they had ceded much of
their own autonomy to the federal government, and they, along with the South,
would feel the heavy hand of this new federal government power. Those pesky, unintended consequences again.

It could have been worse: the author of the Fourteenth Amendment had proposed a similar amendment a year earlier that would have given the federal government the power to legislate prohibitions on individual as well as state behavior.

The Joint Committee on Reconstruction recommended passage of an earlier
amendment, but Congress did not accept it. The earlier version too would have had
the practical effect of repealing the Ninth and Tenth amendments of the Bill of
Rights, thereby gutting the concept of federalism.

The Court's power to encroach on the constitutional powers of the other two
branches of the federal government, however, would not gain "legitimacy" until the
latter half of the twentieth century.

The punitive action taken by the central government during Reconstruction was joyfully embraced by the victorious Northerners. They wanted to punish the South and to make the South feel the pain that it had inflicted on the nation.

Thaddeus Stevens advocated for treating the Southern states as if they were a foreign country, conquered in war, and now entirely subjugated to the victors.[163] Stevens was a radical Republican and the chairman of the Ways and Means Committee in the U.S. Congress. He also chaired the floor managers during the impeachment of President Andrew Johnson.

Stevens was born in Vermont with a clubfoot.[164] In light of today's increased knowledge of psychology and human behavior, it is reasonable to infer that due to his physical handicap he probably was teased by his peers and made the butt of jokes. He probably would have experienced some impairment in his ability to engage in rough and tumble play with his peers. History does record that Stevens suffered many hardships and grew up bitter and vindictive.[165]

His father was an alcoholic and had difficulty maintaining employment, so the family was poor. His father died in the War of 1812. Once he gained power, Stevens used that power and influence to spearhead many of the harshest policies of Reconstruction.

Few Northerners realized at the time that by encouraging the federal government to exercise its power in order to gain supremacy over and punish the rebellious Confederate states, the central government was growing stronger in direct proportion to the diminution of federalism generally. Gradually, Northerners too would experience the overweening power of the national government and the subjugation of the states—including the Northern states.

The Curse of the Fourteenth

The Fourteenth Amendment became a perfect vehicle for the Supreme Court to expand the power of judicial review unlawfully seized in 1803. At first, the import of the *Marbury* decision seems to have been lost on all but Jefferson and some of his political allies.

Any new power gained by the Court was exercised with restraint and good faith—probably because Justice Samuel Chase was impeached, and Chief Justice John Marshall thought he would be, following the *Marbury* decision[166]—but as time passed, the Court regained its confidence and expanded its power gradually, insidiously, over the states but with little obvious encroachment on the powers of the other two branches of government.

The Court was too well aware that Congress held the purse strings, and the president commanded the army, navy, and marines. Any enforcement of a Court order necessarily had to depend on another branch of government. Still, the Fourteenth Amendment became a powerful weapon for expanding the Court's reach over the states.

No one at the time saw the danger of allowing the Supreme Court of the United States to radically interfere with federalism—the balance of power not just between the three branches of the federal government but also the balance between the United States government and the governments of the several states.

Certainly, the people of the United States did not realize what they were asking for when they encouraged their elected representatives during the emotionally inflammatory, vindictive aftermath of the Civil War to ratify the Fourteenth Amendment, giving the federal government expansive power over the states far beyond its announced intent to grant full citizenship to the former slaves.

Anyone who understands the exercise of power will recognize the fact that when there is a balance of power, and that balance is upset, the stronger party will try to expand and consolidate its power in order to protect its advantage. If the United States Supreme Court can gain power over the states, it is inevitable that it will, at some point, test its newfound power over its coequal branches within the federal government.

As the people and their state governments accept that the Supreme Court has power over them, it is more difficult to resist, or even recognize, that that Court is now expanding its power over the other two branches in Washington.

Pastor Martin Niemöller said of the Nazis:

First they came for the Communists, but I was not a Communist, so I said nothing. Then they came for the Social Democrats, but I was not a Social Democrat, so I did nothing. Then they came for the trade unionists, but I was not a trade unionist. And then they came for the Jews, but I was not a Jew, so I did little. Then when they came for me, there was no one left to stand up for me.[167]

Such is the state of the several states when they deal with the federal government; and so it is with any person or group, such as the Supreme Court, seeking to expand their power. This is not to suggest the Supreme Court, or any part of the federal government, is akin to the Nazis.

Quite the contrary, it is the author's personal belief that the Court is a left-leaning oligarchy trying to gradually eliminate all free religious expression in public and to impose a Socialist agenda on the country. (Come to think of it, wasn't that among the goals of the National *Socialist* German Workers' Party [NAZIs]?)

The analogy is to what happened when the Congress and the president facilitated the Supreme Court's usurpation of power from the states. The two coordinate branches then found no defense in federalism when the Supreme Court begins to encroach on their constitutional powers.

Still, more than a hundred years after the Constitution was adopted, and eighty-two years after the *Marbury* decision, the Supreme Court still expressed, in a 1895 case, its belief that "we are bound to interpret the constitution in light of the law as it existed at the time it was adopted, not as reaching out for new guaranties of the rights of citizens, but as securing to every individual such as he already possessed."[168]

A few years later, President Theodore Roosevelt reinforced that proper role of the Court when he said, "It is the people, and not the judges, who are entitled to say what their constitution means, for the constitution is theirs, it belongs to them and not to their servants in office—any other theory is incompatible with the foundation principles of our government."[169] The year 1947 saw a continuation of the Court's power grab, begun in *Marbury* when the Court assumed in *Everson v. Board of Education*[170] the right to rule on religious issues.

While that assumption of power was a radical departure from the traditional understanding of religious freedom, the decision itself seemed rather benign at the time. After all, the Court did not overrule the New Jersey Supreme Court.

But the Court had assumed the power to rule to uphold a particular state court decision on religious freedom; so *ipso facto*, if the Court has the power to grant religious freedom, it must also have the power to take that religious freedom away! That was the whole point of Jefferson's letter to the Danbury Baptist Association. (See *post*).

It is worth repeating: the First Amendment prohibited the federal government from making any law "respecting an establishment of religion, or prohibiting the free exercise thereof." At the time the first ten amendments were ratified, they were understood to be a restraint on *federal government* power and were not applicable to the states. Therefore, according to the plain words of the First Amendment, the Supreme Court did not have jurisdiction to rule on the New Jersey court's decision and should have declined to accept the case for review.

Cumulatively that case, and the ones which followed its precedent, led judicial activists to accelerate exponentially their attack on religion in the latter half of the twentieth century. "Judicial activism" means courts which take on, without clear constitutional authority, the power to make laws, a power the Constitution gave exclusively to Congress.

As Judge Robert Bork put it: "Activist judges are those who decide cases in ways that have no plausible connection to the law they purport to be applying, or who stretch or even contradict the meaning of the law."[171]

Activist Courts

The Court's activist decisions touch on, among other things, the criminal law, a woman's right to an abortion, banning voluntary school prayers, ordering legislative bodies to raise taxes, and prohibiting the display of religious symbols on public property. The Court has ruled that desecrating the flag is a form of "speech" and has blocked school vouchers, which would give parents a better chance to get their children out of failing schools and give them a chance at a good education.

The Court gave underage female children the right to have an abortion without the parents' knowledge or consent by ruling that a state law may not insist on parental notification *unless* the law also contains a "judicial override." That allows an advocate for the child (like Planned Parenthood, for example) to petition the court to rule that the child, notwithstanding her age, may give "informed consent," thereby negating the need for parental consent.

The Court's animus toward religion was introduced in chapter 2.

This chapter will also touch on some of those same cases. It happens to track that group of religious freedom cases because that is the area of law which lies at the heart of the Supreme Court's modern assault on the balance of powers.

The cases here are not about religion per se. rather, they represent a change in the attitude and belief among the justices about what power the Supreme Court has.

Following World War II, the Court, made bold by its success in overturning many of President Roosevelt's New Deal policies, felt strong enough to challenge the Constitution itself. In *Everson*, the Court ruled that "[t]he First Amendment has erected a wall between church and state. That wall must be kept high and impregnable"[172]

There's just one problem with that. *NOWHERE* in the Constitution is there anything about "a wall of separation"! Not in the Constitution itself, not in the First Amendment, not in any of the debates leading up to adoption of the Constitution or the First Amendment.

A close examination of the debates and discussions in the *Congressional Record* during the period June to September 1789, when Congress considered the First Amendment, will find no mention in any form about the "wall of separation between church and state." As stated elsewhere in this work, all thirteen of the original American colonies had some kind of government support for the Protestant Christian religion; some states did not disestablish their religion until after the American Civil War.

Obviously, the founders did not object to establishing a religion at the state level, just not a *national* established religion. Imagine the fight that would break out if the Congress tried to establish a single religion.

The five Anglican or Church of England states, mostly in the South (but also New York), would have expected their religion to be the one established. The three New England-established congregational churches and the states that did not have an established religion per se (these latter states did support churches with their tax dollars) would have said, "No way!" and the Civil War may have been fought simultaneously with the Revolution.

In 1802, fourteen years after the passage of the First Amendment, President Jefferson wrote a letter to the Baptist Association of Danbury, Connecticut.

The Danbury Baptists worried that the First Amendment might be interpreted by some as giving them their religious freedom. The Baptists believed if the government, rather than "natural law," gave them their religious freedom, then the government also would have the power to take it away.

Almost a century and a half later, the U.S. Supreme Court did exactly what the Baptists feared. In the *Everson* case, it gave itself the power to rule on issues of religious freedom, and in subsequent cases, the Court voted to substantially restrict religious freedom. The Supreme Court, in defiance of the plain wording of the First Amendment, has made laws *prohibiting* the free exercise of religion.

President Jefferson told the association in his letter that the free exercise of religion was a "natural right." In the Declaration of Independence, Jefferson had cited the "Laws of Nature and Nature's God." He also used the phrase, "unalienable rights endowed by the Creator."

Jefferson was assuring the Baptists that a "wall of separation" between church and state prevented the government from even addressing the issue of religion one way or the other:

> Believing with you that religion is a matter which lies solely between man and his God; that he owes account to none other for his faith or his worship; that the legislative powers of government reach actions only and not opinions, I contemplate with sovereign reverence that act of the whole American people which declared that their legislature should 'make no law respecting an establishment of religion or prohibiting the free exercise thereof,' *thus building a wall of separation between Church and State.*[173] (Emphasis added.)

Seen in this context, Jefferson's remarks had the opposite meaning to that of the Supreme Court's interpretation in *Everson*. In Jefferson's understanding of the Constitution, the *government*, including the Supreme Court, had no jurisdiction in religious matters. It could not interfere on behalf of religion, nor could it restrict religion in any way. It had no jurisdiction to rule *unless* Congress passed some law either establishing an official government-sponsored religion or interfering with a citizen's religious freedom.

The modern Court, in asserting that the First Amendment "erected a wall between church and state," and assuming for itself the right to rule on religious issues, was being disingenuous. By taking Jefferson's words out of context, it stood his idea on its head.

An earlier Court acknowledged the phrase comes from President Thomas Jefferson, not the Constitution. The earliest reference to the "wall of separation" this writer has found in law was in a 1785 case, *Reynolds v. United States*, which quoted Jefferson's letter to the Danbury Baptists then added,

> Coming as this does from an acknowledged leader of the advocates of the measure, it may be accepted almost as an authoritative declaration of the scope and effect of the amendment thus secured. Congress was deprived of all legislative

power over mere opinion, but was left free to reach actions which were in violation of social duties or subversive of good order.[174]

Congress could enact laws to regulate behavior that was harmful but had no
authority to make any laws regulating thoughts and the physical expression of those
thoughts about religion through, ceremony, and public expressions of faith.

Where Did "Separation of Church and State" Come From?

The *Reynolds* court properly attributed the phrase "wall of separation between
church and state" to Thomas Jefferson's letter to the Danbury Baptists. In *Everson*,
the justices acknowledged Jefferson's authorship of the phrase[175] but glossed over
the fact that the phrase was contained in a letter to a private group and not from
the Constitution itself. The *Everson* court would go on to state boldly, "The First
Amendment has erected a wall between church and state. That wall must be kept
high and impregnable. We could not approve the slightest breach."[176]

The *Everson* court, without actually saying so, leaves the casual reader with
the impression that Jefferson's words were written into the First Amendment. And
indeed that is how later generations would interpret it.

Unless one is an astute student of history and the Supreme Court, most readers probably would not ascribe any significance to footnote 4 of *Everson*. The note
cites *Reynolds* (without *Reynolds*'s clear attribution of the true origin of the phrase to
Jefferson's letter) and another case with a vague reference to the history of the religious atmosphere at the time the country adopted the First Amendment.

One could reasonably infer that the Court wanted to disguise the origin of
the phrase. It wanted anyone reading the case to believe it came straight from the
Constitution. This gave the "wall of separation" more authority and provided the
precedent for the antireligious rulings that would follow. It "set up" the Court's own
assault on religious freedom.

Judges, when writing opinions, tend to be very technical and meticulous in
their use of words. As Lincoln said, "Words are the tools of the lawyer's trade"; lawyers who become judges become very good at crafting opinions out of mere words.
They also carefully document and cite the precedents they rely on in reaching their
decision.

It is inconceivable that the justices *carelessly* disguised the actual source for
what would become the most important part of the *Everson* case: the "separation"
phrase by which they seized the power to rule on religious issues. Modern jurists are
still struggling with the effects.

Justice Rehnquist was sharply critical of the *Everson* decision. After reviewing the history of the debates in Congress leading up to the adoption of the Bill of
Rights, he wrote in *Wallace v. Jaffree*:

It seems indisputable from these glimpses of Madison's thinking, as reflected by actions on the floor of the House in 1789, that he saw the [First] Amendment as designed to prohibit the establishment of a national religion, and perhaps to prevent discrimination among sects. He did not see it as requiring neutrality on the part of government between religion and irreligion. Thus, the Court's opinion in Everson [that there must be a total separation of church and state] is deliberately wrong to suggest that Madison carried these views onto the floor of the United States House of Representatives when he proposed the language that would ultimately become the Bill of Rights.[177]...

State establishments were prevalent throughout the late 18th and early 19th centuries. See Mass. Const. of 1780, Part 1, Art. III; N. H. Const. of 1784, Art. VI; Md. Declaration of Rights of 1776, Art. XXXIII; R. I. Charter of 1633 (superseded 1842)."[178]...

In *Abington School District v. Schempp*, the Court made the truly remarkable statement that 'the views of Madison and Jefferson, preceded by Roger Williams, came to be incorporated not only in the Federal Constitution but likewise in those of most of our States' [footnote omitted]. Based on what evidence we have, this statement is demonstrably incorrect as a matter of history. And its repetition in varying forms in succeeding opinions of the Court can give it no more authority than it possesses as a matter of fact; stare decisis may bind courts as to matters of law, but it cannot bind them as to matters of history.[179]

As Rehnquist points out, depending on Madison's statements to support a claim that the First Amendment requires a strict separation of church and state is bogus. In this author's opinion, deliberately so. Lawyers have a talent for twisting words or choosing the perfect word from a number of words seemingly identical in meaning in order to state the exact nuanced idea they want to convey, usually to the detriment of someone else.

Rehnquist continues:

It is impossible to build sound constitutional doctrine upon a mistaken understanding of constitutional history, but unfortunately the Establishment Clause has been expressly freighted with Jefferson's misleading metaphor for nearly 40 years. Thomas Jefferson was of course in France at the time the constitutional Amendments known as the Bill of Rights were passed by Congress and ratified by the States. His letter to the Danbury Baptist Association was a short note of courtesy, written 14 years after the Amendments were passed by Congress. He would seem to any detached observer as a less than ideal source of contemporary history as to the meaning of the Religion Clauses of the First Amendment.[180]

The author, who has been an admirer of William Rehnquist and his work on the Supreme Court, must respectfully disagree with the late chief justices' characterization of the separation of church and state phrase being "expressly freighted" with Jefferson's words. The author also disagrees that a detached observer might find Jefferson "a less than ideal source of contemporary history as the meaning of the Religious Clauses of the First Amendment."

To address the second point first, Jefferson had always been a strong advocate of religious freedom. He paid tribute to God, and man's natural rights emanating from God, in the Declaration of Independence. He was author of the Virginia Statute for Religious Freedom (1786), which became the source for the religious freedom language in the First Amendment, adopted in 1791.

It is true that Jefferson was in France when the First Amendment was adopted, but it's not like he was a tourist. He was the American ambassador to France and kept in close touch with his new government in America through his official dispatches and personal letters. Jefferson began the Virginia Statute for Religious Freedom this way:

> Whereas Almighty God hath created the mind free; that all attempts to influence it by temporal punishments or burdens, or by civil incapacitations, tend only to beget habits of hypocrisy and meanness, and are a departure from the plan of the Holy author of our religion, who being Lord both of body and mind, yet chose not to propagate it by coercions on either, as it was in his Almighty power to do.[181]
>
> And though we well know that this assembly elected by the people for the ordinary purposes of legislation only, have no power to restrain the acts of succeeding assemblies, constituted with powers equal to our own, and that therefore to declare this act to be irrevocable would be of no effect in law; yet we are free to declare, and do declare, that the rights hereby asserted are of the natural rights of mankind, and that if any act shall be hereafter passed to repeal the present, or to narrow its operation, such act shall be an infringement of natural right.[182]

The Statute for Religious Freedom

It was Madison who was instrumental in getting Jefferson's Statute for Religious Freedom adopted by the Virginia legislature. The two shared the same views about religious freedom and worked closely together in a common cause; Madison played a similar role in getting Jefferson's ideas (as well as his own) about religious freedom into the federal Constitution.

The two corresponded on a regular basis, and you can be sure that Madison was thoroughly conversant with Jefferson's views on religious freedom. It was Madison who argued in Congress for including the religious freedom language in the First Amendment.

The author's disagreement with Rehnquist as to Jefferson as a source of history on the First Amendment notwithstanding, the author believes the chief justice is preaching to the choir. Our society is deeply divided between "a highly secularized cultural elite and a general population that continues to be deeply religious."[183] "Attitudes toward religion and the place of religion in society are a key determinant of who stands where in the conflict [between the two]."[184]

Syndicated columnist Dennis Prager is even more specific:

> If you want to predict on which side an American will line up in the Culture War wracking America, virtually all you have to do is get an answer to this question: Does the person believe in the divinity and authority of the Five Books of Moses, the first five books of the Bible, known as the Torah?...
> Name the issue: same-sex marriage; the morality of medically unnecessary abortions; capital punishment for murder; the willingness to label certain actions, regimes, even people "evil"; skepticism regarding the United Nations and the World Court; strong support for Israel...belief in a G-d-based authority of the Torah is as close to a predictable dividing line as exists.[185]

The cultural elite, what Judge Bork calls the "New Class," if it is listening to Rehnquist at all, will not accept his argument, and the religious majority is already convinced. What the majority needs is someone to tell it how to "fix it."

There are two references in the Constitution to religion: Article VI states, "No religious test shall ever be required as a qualification to any office or public trust under the United States." That is consistent with the idea of separation of church and state, but it does not prohibit one holding office from exercising his or her religious freedom, or does it forbid, for example, a student from saying a prayer at a football game. Secondly, the First Amendment states, "Congress shall make no law respecting an establishment of religion, *or prohibiting the free exercise thereof*" (emphasis added).

It is important to understand that the First Amendment—or the Second, or any of the others—does not convey any rights on the citizens of the United States of America. Look at the language again: "Congress shall make no law respecting an establishment of religion, or prohibiting the free exercise thereof."

That was the whole point of Jefferson's letter to the Danbury Baptists. The government didn't *give* people religious freedom, they already had religious freedom, given by God. The amendment prohibited the government from taking away the freedoms the people already had.

That is why the Supreme Court has no authority to take away religious freedom. People should start a campaign of civil disobedience by speaking to and about God whenever and wherever they please. I personally believe God expects nothing less of us. But I digress.

The Court always emphasizes the separation language, rarely acknowledging the free exercise clause, which appears in the same sentence.

So where did the Supreme Court get the power to prohibit any religious expression in any public forum? From us. We get the government we deserve. By staying home on Election Day, by acquiescing in decisions we don't like, by passively assuming we have no power to stop it, we have allowed the Supreme Court to take over the governance of the country. The perception then becomes the reality. We *believe* the Supreme Court has the power, so it does, in fact, have the power.

People comport their behavior to what they *believe* to be true. With regard to behavior, actual, empirical truth is irrelevant.

Consider this: if one staged a demonstration wherein a coconspirator injected a whiff of smoke (not tobacco smoke—think of burning rags) into a room filled with people, and one then yelled "fire," the occupants of the room would behave *exactly* as if the building was on fire. There is no fire, of course; it was a mere staged demonstration with no actual danger to the occupants of the room. Nonetheless, at such a time one would not want to stand between the occupants and the exit!

It is the president who calls out the 101st Airborne[186] Division to ensure compliance with Court orders. But because we believe the Supreme Court's illegitimately seized power is real, the result of the president's refusal to send the 101st Airborne to enforce a Court order would create an outcry in the country calling for his impeachment. We have been brainwashed to believe the Court's orders must be obeyed or the republic will fall!

President Andrew Jackson thought otherwise. He is credited with saying, "Mr. Marshall has made his decision. Now let him enforce it." Although that statement sounds like something Jackson would say, it is probably apocryphal. History records that Jackson actually said, "The decision of the supreme court has fell stillborn, and they find that it cannot coerce Georgia to yield to its mandate." (Not nearly as poetic as "let him enforce it.")

A more recent defiance of the Court came in 1969 when the House of Representatives voted to expel eleven-term Harlem Congressman Adam Clayton Powell for corruption. Powell sued the Speaker of the House, John McCormick, to overturn his expulsion, and the Supreme Court upheld Powell's position and awarded him back wages.

The speaker ignored the Court's order; Powell went on to win reelection. This time Powell was seated, but without his seniority—as if elected for the first time.[187]

❖   ❖   ❖

The American people could choose to behave as if we believed what Jefferson said about religion: that the government shall be neutral toward religion. People could talk about religion and pray where and when we want. Jefferson, like most of his contemporaries, routinely invoked the name of God in his personal as well as professional life. He prayed at each of his inaugurations.

Praying in Public: the New Civil Disobedience

Jefferson's idea is that the government should in all respects be neutral toward religion, and he freely expressed his own beliefs that there should be no interference whatsoever by the federal government. He believed that the government did not give the people religious freedom, and the government (read "Supreme Court") had no power to take away anyone's religious freedom, including the freedom to express one's religious beliefs in the public square and at public events.

But the Supreme Court has set itself up as the single tribunal that ultimately determines all American law. Any lingering doubt was put to rest by the Warren Court, which held:

> Article VI of the Constitution makes the Constitution the "supreme Law of the Land." In 1803, Chief Justice Marshall, speaking for a unanimous Court, referring to the Constitution as "the fundamental and paramount law of the nation," declared in the notable case of Marbury v. Madison, 1 Cranch 137, 177, that "It is emphatically the province and duty of the judicial department to say what the law is."[188]

Within the lifetime of this writer, the Supreme Court has gone from being the least dangerous branch to the most oppressive. Throughout our nation's history, there has been pretty much of a balance between the three branches of government. For example, within six years after the United States Supreme Court handed down the *Dred Scott*[189] decision, holding that people of African ancestry, even those born in the United States, were mere property and "[were] not citizens and could not be a citizen," President Abraham Lincoln ignored the ruling of the Court and issued the Emancipation Proclamation.

By a stroke of his pen, President Lincoln nullified the Supreme Court decision that African-Americans were "property." Persons of African descent were no longer property, but free people in the eyes of the law by virtue of a presidential order.

Now. Imagine, hypothetically, that you, the reader, are a newly freed slave in 1864 America, a year after the Emancipation Proclamation. Last year, when President Lincoln declared the slaves free, slave owners decided they would sue Lincoln in order to protect their property rights.

The court system expedited the appeal because of its political importance; it has now worked its way up through the system to the United States Supreme Court.

The Court rules, "We hold that *Dred Scott*, being a constitutional decision of this Court, may not be in effect overruled by the president...the president may not supersede this Court's decisions interpreting and applying the Constitution."

The slave owner now has the legal authority to track you down, lay hands on you, and drag you back to Mississippi in chains. Absurd? Not really. Not by the standards of the modern Supreme Court.

Change the name of the case name from *Dred Scott* to *Miranda*, and change "the president" to "Congress," and the remaining language is taken verbatim from *Dickerson v. United States*.[190]

As it happened, in the real world, President Lincoln had thrown down the gauntlet in his first inaugural address, putting the Supreme Court on notice that he did not consider it to be the final word on law or the power of the presidency:

> I do not forget the position, assumed by some, that Constitutional questions are to be decided by the Supreme Court; nor do I deny that such decisions must be binding, in any case, upon the parties to a suit, as to the object of that suit, while they are also entitled to very high respect and consideration in all parallel cases by all other departments of the government. And while it is obviously possible that such decision may be erroneous in any given case, still the evil effect following it, being limited to that particular case, with the chance that it may be overruled and never become a precedent for other cases, can better be borne than could the evils of a different practice. At the same time, the candid citizen must confess that if the policy of the government, upon vital questions affecting the whole people, is to be irrevocably fixed by decisions of the Supreme Court, the instant they are made, in ordinary litigation between parties in personal actions, the people will have ceased to be their own rulers, having to that extent practically resigned their government into the hands of that eminent tribunal.[191]

Following the president's lead, Congress overruled the Court by adopting the Fourteenth Amendment to the Constitution granting citizenship to African-Americans and once and for all nullifying the *Dred Scott* decision. Congress had the power to override the Court then, and it can override the Court now—but given the accretion of more and more power to the Court, it will now require amending the Constitution.

The Effect of a Living Constitution

Because of the invention of a "Living Constitution," the Supreme Court of the United States no longer lives or works in the real world that we ordinary mortals recognize. Fast forward to 1973:

> The Constitution does not explicitly mention any right of privacy. In a line of decisions, however, the Court has recognized that a right of personal privacy, or a guarantee of certain areas or zones of privacy, does exist under the Constitution. In varying contexts, the Court or individual Justices have, indeed, found at least the roots of that right in the First Amendment, in the penumbras of the Bill of Rights, in the Ninth Amendment or in the concept of liberty guaranteed by the first section of the Fourteenth Amendment. These decisions make it clear that only personal rights that can be deemed "fundamental" or "implicit in the concept of ordered liberty" are included in this guarantee of personal privacy. (Citations omitted.)

That convoluted logic is from *Roe v. Wade*. The Court admits that it can find no right of *privacy* in the Constitution; certainly, the word *abortion* does not appear in the Constitution. Justice Blackmun did not have any legitimate precedent or law to support his position. In other words, he just made it up.

The Court could not even find any specific language or even nuances in its own prior rulings that extended a "right of privacy." Justice Blackmun had to resort to a mushy amalgam of unnamed prior decisions, some nebulous "penumbra of the Bill of Rights" (whatever that means), and the common law to find the "right of privacy." From that shaky springboard, the Court leaped to the right of a woman to have an abortion.

In other words, the Court "passed" a new law, declaring that the Constitution guarantees a woman's right to abort her fetus. It *amended* the Constitution.

As disturbing as the decision itself is the fact that Justice Blackmun's law clerks, rather than the justice himself, wrote most of the decision. Blackmun was "a justice who ceded to his law clerks much greater control over his official work than did any of the other 15 justices from the last half-century whose papers are publicly available."[192]

Again, the author expresses no opinion on *Roe v. Wade* or a woman's right to choose. Nor should the reader be distracted by the merits of *Roe* or any of the other Court decisions discussed herein.

The thesis of this book is that the Court routinely oversteps its legitimate authority and creates new law; that is, the Court has acted as a legislative body in an area which belongs exclusively to a separate and independent deliberative body—the Congress. It gets worse. The Court amends the Constitution without the benefit of Article V, which is the *only legitimate way* to amend the Constitution. Therefore, any decision of the Court that changes the Constitution is *ipso facto* illegitimate.

The effect of the *Roe* decision was to split and polarize the country as few other things have and probably more than any single factor since the Civil War.

The Supreme Court moved further toward becoming the supreme legislature when it first ruled to restrict religious freedom, then overturned an act of Congress intended to restore a certain amount of religious freedom.

Prior to 1990, the Court had applied a "balancing test" requiring a "compelling interest" on the part of the state before the state could restrict religious freedom. Justice O'Connor, in a concurring judgment in a 1990 case, wrote:

> As the Court recognizes...the "free exercise" of religion often, if not invariably, requires the performance of (or abstention from) certain acts.... Because the First Amendment does not distinguish between religious belief and religious conduct, *conduct* motivated by sincere religious belief, like the belief itself, *must be at least presumptively protected by the Free Exercise Clause*.[193] [Emphasis added.]

In 1990, the Court ruled against a Native American religious ceremony, holding that the use of peyote by Native Americans was not exempt from the general laws prohibiting the use of controlled substances without a prescription.

Contrast that ruling with the laws during Prohibition, which allowed the continued use of alcohol by Christians for Communion. Maybe Native Americans don't vote in the same numbers as Catholics.

If *Everson* was the beginning of the attack on religious freedom the *Smith* case was the culmination.

Congress responded to the Court's further encroachment on religious freedom by passing the Religious Freedom Restoration Act of 1993 (RFRA).[194] RFRA did not purport to limit the Court's power of judicial review. Congress restrained itself to merely rolling back the standard of review to that which the Court had used continuously for almost two hundred years—from the beginning of the republic until the *Smith* case in 1990. In *Smith,* the Court arbitrarily abandoned its own precedent to establish one it liked better.

This arguably fell into Congress's power to regulate the Court under Article III of the Constitution. Apparently the Court didn't like that part of the Constitution, so it did what the Court always does when it finds something in the Constitution it doesn't like. It ignored it. In 1997, in *City of Boerne*,[195] the Court overturned RFRA.

In *Olmstead v. United States*, Justice Louis Brandeis said:

> Experience should teach us to be most on our guard to protect liberty when the government's purposes are beneficent. Men born to freedom are naturally alert to repel invasion of their liberty by evil-minded rulers. The greatest dangers to liberty lurk in insidious encroachment by men of zeal, well meaning but without understanding.[196]

Noah Webster stated it more simply:

> Good intentions will always be pleaded for every assumption of authority. It is hardly too strong to say that the Constitution was made to guard the people against the dangers of good intentions. There are men in all ages who mean to govern well, but they mean to govern. They promise to be good masters, but they mean to be masters.[197]

From the beginning of the republic until the middle of the twentieth century, and well within the living memory of this author, a balance existed which kept the all-powerful federal government, and especially the Supreme Court, confined within some reasonable boundaries and prevented an oligarchy, unchecked, from dictating laws for the people.

The Supreme Court has now gained supremacy among the three branches of government. That does not bode well for the future of elected, representative government.

Chapter 8: Marbury v. Madison: How the Imperious Court Got That Way

It is emphatically the province and duty of the judicial department to say what the law is. Those who apply the rule to particular cases, must of necessity expound and interpret that rule.—Chief Justice John Marshall in *Marbury v. Madison*.[198]

The present-day news "junkie," who follows the political bickering in Washington, D.C., would have felt very much at home reading about John Marshall's judicial *coup d'état* when Marshall foisted off judicial review on the country. The maneuver had everything to do with partisan politics and would profoundly influence how the courts operated in the future.

The concept of judicial review had been considered—and rejected—by the framers of the Constitution. It was such a controversial and nondemocratic idea that if it had been included in the Constitution, it probably would have been impossible to get that document ratified. Alexander Hamilton, a shrewd and calculating political operative, wrote, "The judiciary is beyond comparison the weakest of the three departments of power."

He argued in favor of judicial review and disdained the view of others who opposed it. "Some perplexity respecting the rights of the courts to pronounce legislative acts void, because contrary to the Constitution, has arisen from an imagination that the doctrine would imply a superiority of the judiciary to the legislative power."

Sadly, history has vindicated Hamilton's critics. The modern Court obviously believes its judgment, and its power is superior to that of the legislative branch as demonstrated by Justice Stevens' plain words in *Atkins v. Virginia*, "Our own judgment 'is brought to bear'...by asking whether there is a reason to disagree with the judgment reached by the citizenry and its legislatures." If the Court does not agree with the citizenry and the legislature, the Court changes the law. It's as simple as that.

One of the very first cases, if not the first case, every first-year law student learns about is *Marbury v. Madison* and the concept of "judicial review," which flows from it.

It is introduced in the opening days of law school, I suspect, for two reasons: (1) it is the concept which defines how modern courts operate and where they get their power; and (2) law school professors want to begin the "brainwashing" of their students before their students learn enough law to be able to say, "Wait a minute,

Marshall can't do that! He has no authority—but what he does have is a conflict of interest. Oh, and by the way, didn't Marshall, while he was serving in Congress, vote *for* that law he just overturned?"

In the election of 1800 the Federalist president, John Adams, and his cohorts in Congress were soundly defeated by Thomas Jefferson and his Republican allies as the presidency and both houses of Congress came under Republican rule. The Federalists would never again exercise power over the national government.

Do not confuse the word *Republican* with the modern Republican Party; the Jeffersonians (modern-day democrats) took the name *Republican* because they supported a republican form of government with much of the power diffused through the states, as opposed to the Federalists, who wanted a strong central government with all power concentrated in the federal government.

Ironically, it is the modern Democratic Party which traces its roots to the Jeffersonian Republicans, but modern Democrats are closer philosophically to John Adams's Federalists.

They believe that the federal government should be all-powerful and watch over us like a benevolent father, spending our money for us and telling us how to live. Jefferson and James Madison, who would become his secretary of state, were both vehemently anti-Federalist.

They anonymously composed resolutions for Virginia and Kentucky in 1798, specifically asserting the rights of the states to interpose themselves between the citizens of those states and the federal government in order to defeat the purpose of the Alien and Sedition Acts.

The anti-Federalists believed that the act was a Federalist attempt to wipe out the Federalists' political opponents by branding them as criminal.

Hard-Ball Politics

After Jefferson was elected president, but a month before he was sworn into office, the Federalist Congress passed the Judiciary Act, creating fifty-eight new judges. Two weeks later, Congress created forty-two new justices of the peace. The lame duck president, John Adams, signed the new bills into law, then proceeded to pack the judiciary with Federalist judges and justices in a blatant attempt to preserve Federalist power after the party had lost the election.

President Adams also attempted to fill a vacancy on the Supreme Court by reappointing John Jay, who had been the first chief justice, to become the fourth. When Jay declined, Adams, still determined to fill the vacancy with a Federalist, nominated John Marshall, his secretary of state, as chief justice of the United States Supreme Court. The Senate confirmed the appointment on January 27, 1801.

Notwithstanding his new job as chief justice, John Marshall continued to serve as secretary of state throughout the remainder of President Adams's term, which ended when Jefferson was sworn in as president on March 4, 1801.

The Judiciary Act further provided that upon the first vacancy to occur on the Supreme Court, the number of justices would be reduced from six to five, thereby denying President Jefferson his first opportunity to appoint someone from his political party to the Court.

In a race against the clock, Adams appointed party loyalists and instructed Marshall to get the commissions evidencing the appointments sealed and delivered before Jefferson took office. Wearing his secretary of state hat, Marshall dutifully carried out Adams's order. He prepared the commissions, presented them for President Adams's signature, then affixed the great seal upon the appointments to judicial office.

Marshall delivered the commissions for the judges in a timely manner, but because of the time difference between the act creating the new judgeships and the second act creating new justices of the peace, many of the latter did not win Senate confirmation until March 3, 1801, the eve of Jefferson's inauguration. In spite of having only a day left in his term of office, Marshall managed to deliver many of the appointments, but a few, including that of William Marbury, could not be delivered in time.

Jefferson instructed his new secretary of state, James Madison, to withhold delivery of the commissions. Marbury filed a suit in the Supreme Court, seeking a writ of mandamus to compel Madison to give him his certificate evidencing his appointment.

Marbury's contention was his appointment was complete when the Senate confirmed him, President Adams signed his commission, and Secretary of State Marshall affixed the seal of the United States. Jefferson said he was not a justice of the peace until the document was delivered into his hands.

Marshall, when *Marbury v. Madison* came before the Court, was in the awkward position of presiding over a Court that would rule on the legality of his (Marshall's) own actions when he was secretary of state. Short of accepting bribes to rule a certain way, there is no more egregious conflict of interest in law.

To put that in a modern context, when he was secretary of defense, Donald Rumsfeld held Yaser Esam Hamdi as an enemy combatant. Hamdi sued Rumsfeld, charging unlawful detention.

One can imagine the screams of outrage if Rumsfeld had been appointed by President Bush to be the new chief justice of the Supreme Court while Hamdi's case was still pending.

Rumsfeld would then get to preside over the Court and rule on whether his actions as secretary of defense were proper in holding Hamdi without a judicial hearing. Would Rumsfeld's conflict of interest be any more outrageous than Marshall's presiding over a case about something he did when he was secretary of state?

That is not a perfect analogy—Marshall was not a named defendant in *Marbury v. Madison*. However, the principle is precisely the same: can a Supreme Court chief justice fairly and impartially rule on a controversy that came about because the chief justice, while serving as a Cabinet officer and carrying out the president's orders, *performed an act which is now the subject of the case before the Court?*

If anything, Marshall's conflict is far more blatant than the Rumsfeld hypothetical, because Marshall had already been appointed, confirmed, and was *serving as the chief justice*, as well as still carrying out his duties as the secretary of state, when he performed the act that led to the suit.

So Marshall, while chief justice of the Supreme Court *and* secretary of state, *personally* committed the act which became the basis of the suit that Chief Justice Marshall now had before him in the Supreme Court—MARSHALL WAS JUDGING HIMSELF.

Marshall had another problem: he was very much aware that without the backing of the executive branch, the Court had no enforcement powers. He also was aware that Thomas Jefferson and his former boss, John Adams, were bitter political rivals and Jefferson was none too fond of Marshall. Therefore, Marshall had to face the reality that if the Court issued a writ of mandamus ordering the new secretary of state, James Madison, to deliver Marbury's commission, the president would likely instruct Madison to ignore it, further diminishing the Court's power and prestige.

Marshall, ever the shrewd lawyer, decided to make a virtue out of necessity. He would give the Jeffersonians what they wanted—he would not issue the mandamus—but he would do it in a way that grabbed more power for the Court. He would invent "judicial review."

The Genesis of Judicial Review

Arguably, some earlier Courts had hinted at the possibility of judicial review. In a 1796 case,[199] the Court ruled to uphold a federal tax, which assumed that it had the jurisdiction to rule on such matters, and by implicit extension, if it had the power to rule on the issue, it must have the power to overturn the law.

But as noted earlier, the Court had no practical method to enforce its rulings absent favorable action by the executive; therefore, to entertain the open challenge to the president by way of mandamus action was a bold move on the part of Marshall and the Court.

Marshall was by no means stupid. He could take the case, but he knew going in that he could not rule against the president. In the first place, he had no jurisdiction until he created it. Equally important, the judges were mostly Federalists who were bitterly opposed to the politics of Jefferson and his Republicans, and the enmity was mutual.

Therefore, he needed to figure out a way to rule in such a fashion as would not challenge the president's power but would give the Court a precedent saying it had the jurisdiction to rule on such matters, including the authority to overturn an act of Congress.

Ruling on the constitutionality of the law was not necessary to the outcome of the case. Marshall could simply have said that with the separation of powers and the checks and balances specifically enumerated in the Constitution, he had no power in mandamus to compel the president to do anything. While honest, that would not have served his purposes—to expand the power of the Court and metaphorically jab a sharp stick in Jefferson's eye.

In drafting the opinion, Marshall said he must answer three questions: "(1) Has the applicant a right to the commission he demands? (2) If he has a right, and that right has been violated, do the laws of his country afford him a remedy? (3) If they do afford him a remedy is it a *mandamus* issuing from this court?"[200]

In finding that Marbury had a right to his commission, Marshall said President Adams's "signature is a warrant for affixing the great seal to the commission; and the great seal is only to be affixed to an instrument which is complete."

Marshall also answered the second question in the affirmative; Marbury had the right to his commission because the appointment by Adams was for a term of years and was not revocable. The laws of the country, therefore, afford him a remedy. It was in the answer to the third part of the question that Marshall got tricky.

By misdirection that would make David Copperfield feel proud, Marshall began by citing a precedent that did not exist: he appears to have referred to a "case," which was in fact a blend of several cases. Even taken together, however, the cases ("case") did not exactly give him the authority he was claiming. But he said it did.

The "case," which he never names, did give him part of what he wanted as a precedent, but it or they also had some insurmountable problems that would have been counterproductive to his cause. Marshall took what he wanted and, like many modern Supreme Court justices, conveniently ignored the parts he didn't like.

Marshall never named the case because in all probability it was not a single case, but a group of Court actions known as the pension cases.

Having determined that there was a right to the commission, and the laws afforded Marbury a remedy, was the remedy a writ of mandamus from the Supreme Court? Marshall then goes into a very selective reading of the Constitution's grant of power to the Court, finding nothing in the Constitution itself granting the Court the power to issue a writ of mandamus under its *original* jurisdiction.

Marshall further noted that Congress has power to set rules and regulations for the Court's *appellate* jurisdiction; Marshall said the Judiciary Act, giving the Court mandamus power under its original jurisdiction, was, therefore, unconstitutional. This is not altogether unreasonable—except that the Court in several earlier rulings had accepted the validity of the act and issued rulings using the Judiciary Act as authority for its action.

This was a masterstroke of clever lawyering. Marshall was saying in effect that to avoid a writ of mandamus directed to the president—which Marshall knew the Court could not have enforced anyway—the Court had to find the law passed by

Congress and signed by the previous president was beyond the Congress's power. That is, the Constitution granted the Court no such power, so a law that attempted to grant that power was in violation of the Constitution, i.e., "unconstitutional."

This was quite a novel idea, and more than a little disingenuous. The federal courts, including the Supreme Court, had been accepting the authority of the act and issuing mandamus under its authority for the past ten years—but not to the president.

It was Machiavellian in another way: This same Marshall who condemns the Judicial Act was a member of Congress when the act passed, and at that time, he was a supporter of the act. Now he wanted to grab power for the Court. The law hadn't changed, but Marshall's agenda had.

Marshall also totally disregarded the fact that the pension "case" that he had just relied on in his mandamus discussion appeared to raise the same jurisdictional problem he faced in *Marbury*. Whichever mandamus action one considers, whether the one brought by Attorney General Randolph or the one brought by the veteran Chandler, it was an original motion in the Supreme Court seeking a writ of mandamus directed to an executive official. The Court accepted those cases and issued a ruling.

Marshall could not have been ignorant of the fact that the jurisdictional posture in those cases seemed to be identical to the one in *Marbury*.

Jefferson was furious. But he was in no position to appeal the decision or ask for a rehearing. After all, he was the winner and not aggrieved by the decision. Legally there was no basis for an appeal. Moreover, philosophically, how do you protest a decision that says you don't have to do something that you didn't want to do, and did not intend to do, anyway?

Jefferson saw the danger in allowing the Court to have the power of "judicial review" of laws passed by Congress. Jefferson knew that there was no constitutional authority for the Court to override an act of Congress. Again, those who wrote the Constitution had rejected judicial review.

Judicial Review Unnecessary, Marshall Admits

In fact, Marshall himself essentially admitted that judicial review was not necessary under our system of law. When Marshall's fellow Supreme Court Justice Samuel Chase was impeached, during the ongoing political wars between the Federalist judges and the Jeffersonian Republicans in Congress, Marshall suggested that Congress could just repass any law the Court found unconstitutional.[201]

Marshall also offered to abandon judicial review altogether if Congress would give its pledge not to impeach him.

Congress wouldn't agree because it already had Marshall in its sights once it dispensed with Chase; however, while a sizable majority of senators wanted to impeach Chase, they could not muster the necessary two-thirds vote. Marshall calculated that now they couldn't remove him from office either, so he withdrew his offer to give up judicial review.

Anyone who believes the Supreme Court is "nonpolitical" must have been reading the press releases from the Court's "spin doctor," not what the Court is actually saying in its opinions—then and now.

President Jefferson pledged to fight what he considered a dangerous power assumed by the Court, but there would be no further use of judicial review during his lifetime, so he never had an opportunity to try to overturn the doctrine in court.

Among lawyers, judicial review became gospel. But many scholars throughout the nation's history, and even today, criticized Marshall's decision. It may not matter. The Court is writing a new Constitution more to its own liking, and it does not give a damn about what scholars, or a substantial majority of Americans, think about it.

A sizeable minority of citizens like what the Court is doing. It advances its own socialist agenda. Robert Bork wrote, "Courts in general have enlisted on the liberal side of the culture war. They are infected, as is the New Class to which judges belong and to which they respond, with the socialist impulse."[202]

It also has seized dictatorial power, including the power to tax, in order to carry out its agenda. In a 1964 school desegregation case in Virginia, the United States Supreme Court said:

> The District Court may...require the Supervisors to exercise the power that is theirs to levy taxes to raise funds adequate to reopen, operate, and maintain without racial discrimination a public school system in Prince Edward County like that operated in other counties in Virginia.[203]

Think about that for a moment: if you have a legislative body with taxing power which flatly refuses to fund a particular program, and the Supreme Court comes along and forces that legislative body to raise taxes to pay for the program, isn't that the same thing as the Supreme Court imposing the tax to support the program?

Using that precedent, in 1990, a federal court in Missouri, without waiting for the legislative body to raise taxes, directly levied taxes on the citizens of Kansas City to carry out the most ambitious school desegregation scheme yet devised.

The Kansas City Missouri School District (KCMSD) desegregation case began in 1977. The district, which had been three-fourths white, now has more than 68 percent black, 12 percent Hispanic, and just under 17 percent white. White flight to the suburbs following *Brown v. Board of Education*[204] aggravated the racial divide originally created by state laws requiring separate schools for blacks. Enrollment dropped from seventy thousand to thirty-six thousand. Now, poverty and geography maintained a de facto segregation.

The district court, after hearing many arguments in multiple trips by the litigants to district court, interspersed with over twenty appeals to the Eighth Circuit Court of Appeals and three appeals heard by the United States Supreme Court,[205] ordered an expenditure of some two billion dollars[206] for capital improvements, increased teachers' salaries, equipment, and material to create magnet schools, which would attract white students back into the inner city.

Court Causes Chaos

It didn't work. It did create chaos.

Arguably, in some respects, the case that caused all the "chaos in KC" may not even have been a real case or controversy as required by law. It was a setup! Some history may help understand what lawyers mean by a "case or controversy." The Supreme Court ruled in *Muskrat v. United States*[207] that it could only entertain "cases" and "controversies." "That judicial power, as we have seen, is the right to determine actual controversies arising between adverse litigants duly instituted in courts of proper jurisdiction."

Muskrat was a case between Native Americans, friendly to each other, who had a common interest in determining whether an act of Congress giving them title to certain lands was constitutional. So they agreed among themselves that one would sue the other in order to test their land ownership in the Court of Claims and then in the Supreme Court. The Court made very clear it would not hear "friendly suits."

In the Kansas City case, the plaintiffs, Jenkins and the Kansas City Missouri School District (KCMSD), together decided to sue the state of Missouri to try to squeeze out more money to assist in the integration of Kansas City public schools. The federal judge hearing the case thought it would make a better (more sympathetic?) case and meet the "case or controversy" requirement if Jenkins was the only plaintiff, and if she sued both the state and KCMSD.

The judge realigned the case to reflect his view of who should be the parties, and the case went forward with the plaintiff Jenkins and one of the defendants, the KCMSD, having a common interest in going after the state—in other words, a friendly suit as between Jenkins and KCMSD, and KCMSD was still sympathetic toward Jenkins.

In any suit the codefendants must cooperate with each other and share information; they also need to agree on a strategy for defending the case. The state of Missouri had no chance—the "cooperating" codefendant KCMSD was in effect a mole for the plaintiff, Jenkins.

In the end, KCMSD was "hoist by its own petard." Having started out in a friendly suit as a co plaintiff suing the state for more money for schools, KCMSD, now an inadvertent *codefendant*, could not pay the judgment rendered against it because of a state law that prohibited raising local taxes above a level set by the state.

The district court ordered taxes raised from $2.05 per $100 of value to $4.00 then $4.96 per $100 [208] in spite of the state law, and the state appealed. On hearing the appeal, the circuit court reversed that part of the district court order directly raising taxes. It ruled that the court should have voided the state law prohibiting KCMSD from raising taxes and allowed the school district itself to levy the tax.

The Supreme Court ruled, among other things:

The District Court abused its discretion in imposing the tax increase, which contravened the principles of comity. Although that court believed that it had no alternative to imposing the tax itself, it, in fact, had the very alternative outlined by the Court of Appeals:

> Authorizing and directing local government institutions to devise and implement remedies not only protects the function of those institutions but, to the extent possible, also places the responsibility for solutions to the problems of segregation upon those who have themselves created the problems. While a district court should not grant local government carte blanche, local officials should at least have the opportunity to devise their own solutions to such problems. Here, KCMSD was ready, willing, and, but for the operation of state law, able to remedy the deprivation of constitutional rights itself.[209]

The Supreme Court approved the Court of Appeals solution:

> The Court of Appeals' order does not exceed the judicial power under Article III. A court can direct a local government body to levy its own taxes' where, as here, the local government was willing so to do but for a state law which prohibited it raising taxes above limits set by the state.[210]

Nonetheless, the Supreme Court made clear that as a last resort, directly levying taxes is not beyond the court's authority: "It is therefore clear that a local government with taxing authority may be ordered to levy taxes in excess of the limit set by state statute where there is reason, based in the Constitution, for not observing the statutory limitation."[211] It is well to keep in mind that being "in the Constitution" as used by the Supreme Court does not mean what is *written* in the Constitution. It means whatever the Supreme Court *says* is in the Constitution.

Therefore, the Supreme Court can rule on anything that five justices agree to rule on; then the Court can use its own ruling as the constitutional basis for ordering a legislative body to raise taxes—a ruling the authority for which is manifestly not in the Constitution.

Furthermore, the Court left open the possibility that if both local and state government were to refuse to raise taxes, the district court's equity power would allow the court to levy taxes directly upon the citizens of Missouri and Kansas City. Look at that opinion again: "[W]hile a district court should not grant local government carte blanche, local officials should at least have the *opportunity* to devise their own solutions to such problems." (Emphasis added.)

The clear implication, picked up by every lawyer who read that case, is that if you have a recalcitrant defendant who resists a federal court's order to raise taxes, the district court itself can directly levy taxes on the citizens under its jurisdiction.

Justice Kennedy, while concurring in the judgment in that particular case, took issue with giving the federal courts direct taxing authority. In a concurrence— which read more like a dissent—he said, "Today's casual embrace of taxation imposed by the unelected, life-tenured Federal Judiciary disregards fundamental precepts for the democratic control of public institutions."[212]

How has the experiment into court-controlled schools worked? According to a Cato Institute Policy Analysis, not well:

> For decades critics of the public schools have been saying, "You can't solve educational problems by throwing money at them." The education establishment and its supporters have replied, "No one's ever tried." In Kansas City, they tried.
>
> To improve the education of black students and encourage desegregation, a federal judge invited the Kansas City, Missouri, School District to come up with a cost-is-no-object educational plan and ordered local and state taxpayers to find the money to pay for it.
>
> Kansas City spent as much as $11,700 per pupil—more money per pupil, on a cost of living adjusted basis, than any other of the 280 largest districts in the country. The money bought higher teachers' salaries, 15 new schools, and such amenities as an Olympic-sized swimming pool with an underwater viewing room, television and animation studios, a robotics lab, a 25-acre wildlife sanctuary, a zoo, a model United Nations with simultaneous translation capability, and field trips to Mexico and Senegal. The student-teacher ratio was 12 or 13 to 1, the lowest of any major school district in the country.
>
> The results were dismal. Test scores did not rise; the black-white gap did not diminish; and there was less, not greater, integration.[213]

The Outcome Was Predictable

The results are not unlike the outcome in Cleveland and Boston set out in chapter 5.

In the end, how well did the judge do in Kansas City? Judge Clark's stated goal was to build magnet schools that would attract suburban students back into the city. He ordered large enough schools built to accommodate up to ten thousand suburban students but at its peak never more than fifteen hundred enrolled at any one time, and virtually all attended for only a single year.

After spending two billion dollars in an attempt to achieve integration and a 60 percent black, 40 percent white ratio by the 1996-1997 school year, only 387 students bused (or brought by taxi at government expense) from the suburbs attended school in the KCMSD. "Given that the district's annual desegregation budget was approximately $200 million, the cost of attracting those suburban students was half a million dollars per year per child."[214]

The bad result should not have come as a surprise: A massive sociological study, encompassing thirty-one years of research, and several scholars working to replicate the original Coleman Report, found no significant correlation between money spent and the achievement of students. In spite of a massive attempt by other academics and educators to debunk the study, the announcement of a conference at New York University in 2001 said:

> Almost 35 years ago, James Coleman and his co-authors issued their controversial report on inequality in schooling (Coleman et al. 1966). The document—which later came to be known as the Coleman Report—reached the troubling conclusion that the strongest predictor of academic performance was *not* school-based dynamics, but rather was the student's family background—as measured by household income, parental socio-economic status, etc. While for minority students some school characteristics had minor to moderate effects, these were largely school composition effects (only for Southern blacks did expenditures seem to matter). The most shocking and important lesson of this report is that the indicators that we focus our educational policy debate upon—per pupil expenditures and student-to-teacher ratios—did not appear to matter much.[215]

This seems counterintuitive until one understands that the schools which appear to do better because they have more money are the same schools that have better, more stable, crime-free neighborhoods, more involved parents, better supervision at home, and higher expectations by parents and community leaders that the students will achieve. The scientific data seem to indicate that *money is the least important* of those factors. In spite of the evidence:

> [G]overnment school officials consistently assert that it is a lack of funding that has prevented schools from being effective. Between 1970 and 1997, however, total revenues for public schools increased from $44.5 billion to $305 billion, yet scores on the SAT actually dropped by 27 points at the same time."[216]

Chapter 9: The Court Empowers Terrorists

There is danger that, if the Court does not temper its doctrinaire logic with a little practical wisdom, it will convert the constitutional Bill of Rights into a suicide pact.—Justice Jackson dissenting in *Terminiello v. City of Chicago.*[217]

At the founding of the Republic, the three branches of the federal government were created equal. However, James Madison believed if there was a branch that should take the lead in setting policy it should be the legislature—who had the sole lawmaking power; in addition, the Members of the House of Representative had to stand for election every two years so they were closer to the people. Like siblings everywhere, each branch began almost immediately trying to gain superiority over the other two branches.

The Supreme Court's grab for power began in 1803 with the decision in *Marbury v. Madison* discussed in the previous chapter. Presidents from time to time have tried to interpret the Constitution to give more power to the executive. Still, there can be no doubt today the Supreme Court can overrule Congress or the president any time five justices vote so to do.

Constitutional Rights for Terrorists vs. National Defense

In a recent series of cases involving foreign terrorists—and one American citizen—the Court has provided constitutional rights to foreign citizens fighting on foreign battlefields if they come into the control of U.S. military authorities.

What effect will that have on our own national security? We won't know for a while. What is immediately apparent, however, is the fact that the United States Supreme Court is so narrowly focused on individual rights—even the rights of those religious fanatics from foreign countries who are trying to kill us—that it handcuffs the president, who has the constitutional duty to keep us safe from foreign invaders.

Would anyone question whether the hijackers of 9/11 were foreign invaders? They attacked us on U.S. soil. They were not members of any nation's armed forces; but they claimed to be part of an organization which has declared *war* against the United States of America. Members have committed overt acts in furtherance of the goal of destroying America and Americans. The declaration of war appears from the evidence to be genuine and should not be dismissed as a mere figure of speech—like the "war on poverty."

If a bully says to you, "I'm gonna' punch you in the mouth" and then follows the words with the action of punching you in the mouth wouldn't you take him seriously the next time he threatened to punch you in the mouth?

The loose organization called al Qaeda is not a sovereign government; however, its members carry out attacks on America *as if* it were an invading army. Suppose for sake of argument one of the 9/11 highjackers had survived the crash and was transported to Guantanamo. How would they be treated?

This is new territory because all prior armed invasions have been by foreign armies covered by the traditional laws of war and more recently by the Geneva Convention—well, there was that Pancho Villa thing, but General Pershing never caught him so we don't know what his legal status might have been.

This is not the kind of new ground the unelected and unaccountable Supreme Court should be plowing. This is a job for Superhero, *Elected Man!* (i.e., Congress and the President). Why, then, are we treating terrorists like ordinary street criminals? Because the Supreme Court in its majestic ignorance says we must.

A good illustration of the vast gulf between the knowledge of the executive compared to knowledge of judges is the José Padilla case.[218] *Padilla* demonstrates the Court's disdain for government institutions other than the Court, its reluctance to give credence to executive branch witnesses, and its abysmal lack of knowledge about what motivates individuals—specifically, the whole field of psychology and in particular the Stockholm syndrome.

Keep in mind what the judge hears in the courtroom is strictly limited by the rules of evidence; and in nearly all cases becomes a part of the public record as soon as the testimony in court is spoken. The president must protect his spies in the field; he must maintain secrecy of any information that would compromise the national defense and provide actionable intelligence to foreign enemies.

Judge Mukasey vs. Attorney General Mukasey—Same Guy, Different View

The Islamic faith, according to the FBI, is actively recruiting in U.S. prisons for alienated, angry prisoners who are prone to violence.[219]

José Padilla had converted to Islam while in a Florida jail. In addition, Richard Reid, who pleaded guilty to trying to blow up a jetliner with a bomb in his shoe, converted to an extreme form of Islam while in prison in London.[220] Some in the FBI believe the recruitment primarily is an attempt to build up a support network to facilitate al-Qaida operations rather than trying to recruit the next generation of suicide bombers and terrorists per se.

In papers filed in the Padilla case, the Jacoby Declaration describes the Defense Intelligence Agency's (DIA) interrogation technique:

> DIA's approach to interrogation is largely dependent upon creating an atmosphere of dependency and trust between the subject and the interrogator. Developing the kind of relationship of trust and dependency necessary for effective interrogations is a process that can take a significant amount of time. There are numerous examples of situations where interrogators have been unable to obtain valuable intelligence from a subject until months, or even years, after the interrogation process began. Anything that threatens the perceived

dependency and trust between the subject and interrogator directly threatens the value of interrogation as an intelligence-gathering tool. (Jacoby Decl. at 4-5)

Admiral Jacoby...concludes that Padilla "could potentially provide information" on about a dozen subjects, including not only the so-called 'dirty bomb' plot in which Padilla is alleged to have been involved, but also more general subjects such as al Qaeda training, planning, recruitment, methods and operations in several countries, including the United States. (Id. at 7-8)...The Sealed Jacoby Declaration sets forth in greater detail information linking Padilla to al Qaeda, and thereby confirms the nature of the information Padilla could provide to interrogators. (Sealed Jacoby Decl. at 8-10)

The Jacoby Declaration and the Sealed Jacoby Declaration contain the following assessment of the "Potential Impact of Granting Padilla Access to Counsel": Permitting Padilla any access to counsel may substantially harm our national security interests. As with most detainees, Padilla is unlikely to cooperate if he believes that an attorney will intercede in his detention. DIA's assessment is that Padilla is even more inclined to resist interrogation than most detainees. DIA is aware that Padilla has had extensive experience in the United States criminal justice system and had access to counsel when he was being held as a material witness. These experiences have likely heightened his expectations that counsel will assist him in the interrogation process. Only after such time as Padilla has perceived that help is not on the way can the United States reasonably expect to obtain all possible intelligence information from Padilla....

Additionally, permitting Padilla's counsel to learn what information Padilla may have provided to interrogators, and what information the interrogators may have provided Padilla, unnecessarily risks disclosure of the intelligence sources and methods being employed in the War on Terrorism. (Jacoby Decl. at 8-9; Sealed Jacoby Decl. at 12-13)

Judge Mukasey criticized the government's supporting documentation, saying both the Jacoby Declaration and the Sealed Jacoby Declaration:

[A]re silent on the following two subjects: (i) the particulars of Padilla's actual interrogation thus far, and what they suggest about the prospect of obtaining additional information from him, and (ii) when, if at all, intelligence personnel have ever experienced effects of an interruption in interrogation like the effects predicted in both of the excerpts from the Jacoby Declaration quoted above.[221]...

Although I would not be so bold as to substitute my own judgment for Admiral Jacoby's on any of the numerous intelligence-related topics in his declaration, including the importance of intelligence gathered from al Qaeda prisoners and the proper technique for conducting an interrogation, when it comes to his forecast about how Padilla might react to even a brief interruption in his interrogation, it is important to recognize that that forecast is speculative—as is clear from repeated use of such words as "might" and "could"—absent any information about either Padilla's actual interrogation or information about interruptions in past interrogations that would suffice to show whether they are truly analogous to the case at hand. Moreover, the forecast speculates not about an intelligence-related matter, in which Admiral Jacoby is expert, but about a matter of human nature—Padilla's in particular—in which, most respectfully, there are no true experts.

The judge is wrong. By meddling in, and restricting, what well-established methods are available to the executive branch to protect us against foreign terrorists, he may be deadly wrong!

Psychology can be very good at understanding human nature; a naval intelligence officer of Admiral Jacoby's rank and some thirty years experience will have had extensive training and practice in psychology and what motivates people under stress. He will have studied the "brainwashing" techniques used by the North Koreans and the Chinese on our prisoners of war during the Korean conflict; he would have more than a passing familiarity with the Stockholm syndrome:

> On August 23rd, 1973 two machine-gun carrying criminals entered a bank in Stockholm, Sweden. Blasting their guns, one prison escapee named Jan-Erik Olsson announced to the terrified bank employees 'The party has just begun!' The two bank robbers held four hostages, three women and one man, for the next 131 hours. The hostages were strapped with dynamite and held in a bank vault until finally rescued on August 28th.
> After their rescue...it was clear that they supported their captors and actually feared law enforcement personnel who came to their rescue. The hostages had begun to feel the captors were actually protecting them from the police...[222]

The techniques have been considerably refined and improved since 1973 and have many applications such as, for example, the "good cop/bad cop" routine seen on crime shows on TV when the protagonists are interrogating criminal suspects.

There is also a whole new body of science growing out of science fiction writer Isaac Asimov's "psychohistory," introduced in the *Foundation* novels. Studied, quantified, and moved into mainstream science, psychohistory is defined as "the science of historical motivation,"[223] the "why" of history discerned by the "systematic application of the findings and methods of the science of psychology to help explain individual and group behavior, past and present." A study of "psychohistory" is, in fact, a study of the individuals who made that history.

Asimov inspired other fields of inquiry, such as the use of experiments in such disciplines as "sociophysics" and the study of networks and "contagion theory."

Steven Schultz interviewed Jonathan Cohen, a professor of psychology at Princeton University and director of the university's newly established Center for

the Study of Brain, Mind, and Behavior, which seeks to combine the methods of cognitive psychology with neuroscience:
Measuring Behavior

> "Measuring people's behavior has served psychology well for many years and will continue to do so, but now that approach is augmented by a completely new set of tools," said Cohen. Brain imaging allows scientists to build a catalog of brain areas and their function, which can then be cross-referenced with behaviors that employ the same processes. Eventually, this combination of behavioral analysis and biological neuroscience could inform questions in fields from philosophy to economics.[224]

It is manifest that Judge Michael B. Mukasey is not up to speed on advances in the understanding of human nature and human behavior. It is presumptuous and a graphic demonstration of his ignorance of things other than the law, for him to say what Admiral Jacoby could or could not predict about human nature and specifically, about Padilla's responses to the CIA's interrogation methods. *Judge Mukasey doesn't even know how much he doesn't know!*

[Author's Note: This chapter was written during the original draft of this book in 2004. After his retirement as a judge, Mukasey went on to become the U.S. attorney general. (See "Bush Picks Another Underqualified Lawyer for Attorney General" by syndicated columnist Robert Novak, September 27, 2007.) After serving in the executive branch and listening to the national security briefings, "Mr. Mukasey said, 'It is way beyond—way beyond anything that I knew or believed. So, if I was picked for the level of my knowledge...that was a massive piece of false advertising.' "[225]]

But then, that's the hazard of judges having so much power—power which they use to settle the fact-specific, narrow issue before them with no consideration for the "big picture" or the unintended consequences of their decisions. In the *Padilla* case, Mukasey continued:

> Even before Padilla achieved his current status as a suspected terrorist, he was a criminal, and criminals are people with whom this court has at least as much experience as does Admiral Jacoby and perhaps more.
> The Jacoby Declaration is none too subtle in cautioning this court against going too far in the protection of this detainee's rights, suggesting at one point that permitting Padilla to consult with a lawyer "risks that plans for future attacks will go undetected." (Jacoby Decl. at 9) More than a match for that are passages in the amicus curiae submissions in this case, where lawyers raise the specter of Korematsu v. United States, 323 U.S. 212 (1944), and call Padilla's detention "a repudiation of the Magna Charta", Supplemental Br. of Amici Curiae N.Y. State Ass'n of Criminal Defense Lawyers at 8, 25, thereby suggesting that if Padilla does not receive the full panoply of protections afforded defendants in

criminal cases, a dictatorship will be upon us, the tanks will have rolled. Those to whom images of catastrophe come that easily might take comfort in recalling that it is a year and a half since September 11, 2001, and Padilla's is not only the first, but also the only case of its kind. There is every reason not only to hope, but also to expect that this case will be just another of the isolated cases, like *Quirin*, that deal with isolated events and have limited application.

Let's hope that judges will now make better choices when dealing with terrorists. But let's not bet our life on it!

Chapter 10: The "Living Constitution"

Our peculiar security is in the possession of a written Constitution. Let us not make it a blank paper by construction.[226] —Thomas Jefferson.

The United States Constitution *has* become a blank paper. It no longer binds judges—and in particular, it does not bind the justices of the Supreme Court—they do pretty much what they want to do and the Constitution be damned!

If five Supreme Court justices can look in the Constitution and see what they want to see, and that becomes the law, why have the document? Why not end the charade and just say we are ruled by the diktat of the Supreme Court and have done with it?

Ultraliberal (for his time) Felix Frankfurter, who would later become a Supreme Court justice, reportedly told President Roosevelt, "Constitutional law often has little to do with the Constitution and much to do with the views of judges."[227] Often what the Court *says* the Constitution says bears no resemblance to what the Constitution says!

The Constitution was a grant of power, in trust, by the people to the government to be exercised in accordance with the mandate of the people. But now the Constitution has been commandeered by lawyers (remember *all* federal judges are lawyers first before they became judges) who use their legal skills to twist the simple words of that venerated document into a parody of the framer's intent. The Supreme Court with its "Living Constitution" are like vandals with spray cans spraying graffiti on the venerated document we call the Constitution.

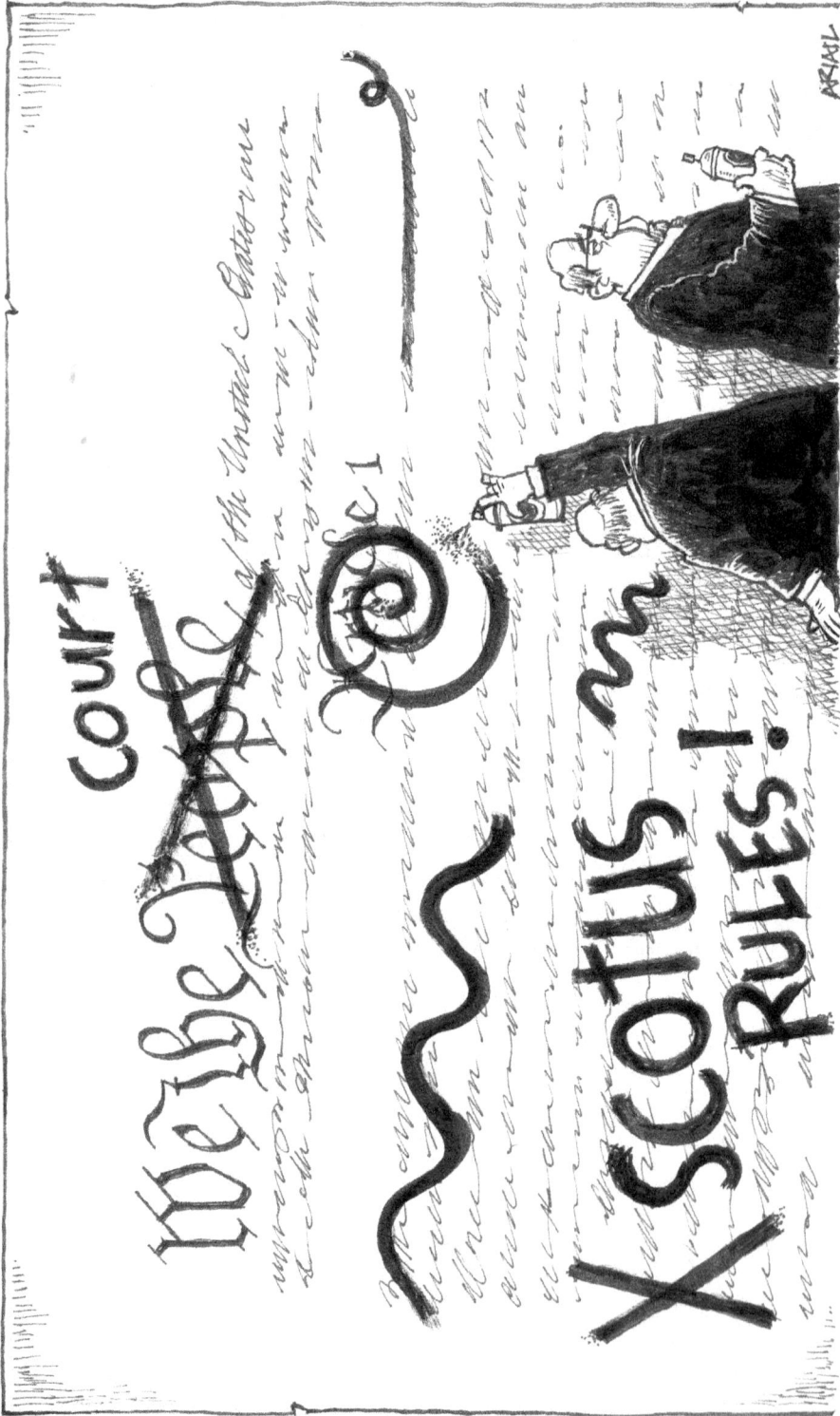

Robert Nagel, a constitutional scholar for over twenty years, in an appearance before the House Subcommittee on the Constitution, said, "[Two recent Court] decisions are clear illustrations of how far the specialized and ingrown thinking of lawyers has come to depart from common sense and general experience. They are to constitutional law what the O. J. Simpson trial is to criminal procedure."[228]

One of the reasons the confirmation battles for federal judges have become so bitter and divisive comes directly from the U.S. senators' knowledge that the Supreme Court is the real policymaker for the country. Senator Orin Hatch put it this way: "The battle over judicial appointments today is a battle over how much power judges should have in our system of government. If judges are masters over the charter they have sworn to protect, then 'we the people' are not."[229]

That has raised the stakes in the Senate's duty to "advise and consent" for the president's nominees to the federal courts and, in particular, the circuit courts and the Supreme Court.

The Heritage Foundation's Todd Gaziano, appearing before the House Judiciary Committee on October 10, 2002, charged, "Ten senators are currently dictating the composition of the federal bench. Even a filibuster by a minority of the Senate would be less cowardly than the current practice."[230] Gaziano was referring to the Senate committee that was refusing to allow President Bush's judicial nominees to go to the Senate floor for an up or down vote.

The Democrats on the Senate Judiciary Committee know that most, if not all, of the nominees, all of whom are rated "qualified" or "well-qualified" by the American Bar Association, would easily win approval if voted on. Therefore, their strategy is to prevent a vote. Gaziano presented to the committee a graphic demonstration of the increasing delays in getting federal judges appointed:

Confirmation of President Reagan's first eleven appointees to the courts of appeals took thirty-nine days and all were confirmed.

G. H. W. Bush (41) saw his first eleven nominees average ninety-five days to confirmation, but all were eventually confirmed; Bill Clinton's nominees waited an average of 115 days before being confirmed, but all were confirmed.

By contrast, only 27 percent of George W. Bush's (43) first eleven nominees to the appellate courts had been confirmed after four hundred days; looking at the two-year average for judicial confirmations over the past four administrations, only 53 percent of the circuit court nominations submitted by President Bush had been confirmed by the end of Bush's second year in office compared to 86 percent for President Clinton, and 96 percent for Bush 41. District Judge Terrence Boyle was nominated to the 4th Circuit by Bush 41, renominated by Bush 43, but was never confirmed in 15 years. Among other nominees, Richard A. Griffin was nominated to sit on the Sixth Circuit Court of Appeals on June 26, 2002; the Senate held his nomination in limbo for three years (until June 5, 2005). When he did finally get a vote on the Senate floor, he was confirmed by a vote of ninety-five-zero with five senators not voting. David W. McKeague was nominated to be a federal district court judge in 1991.

Because of a critical shortage of appeals judges in the Sixth Circuit Court of Appeals, vacancies on that court were deemed "judicial emergencies." McKeague was nominated to serve on the Sixth Circuit in November 2001, during the judicial emergency, but his nomination was held until June 2004, at which time the nomination came up for a vote.

A filibuster followed, and on July 22, 2004, a cloture motion failed; he continued to serve as a district judge.[231] Democrats accused him of misconduct; the Republicans accused the Democrats of unfair partisan politics.

McKeague was renominated in February 2005 and won confirmation in June of that year. The vote was ninety-six-zero with four senators not voting. Byron York, writing in *National Review Online*:

> Bush picks for the Sixth Circuit [were] *blocked* by Michigan Senators Carl Levin and Debbie Stabenow, not because of any ideological objections but because Levin and Stabenow are angry that two Democratic nominees for the Sixth Circuit were not confirmed by the Republican-controlled Senate during the Clinton years. Levin is said to be especially angry because one of those Clinton nominees, Helene White, is the wife of one of Levin's cousins.[232]

Does Character Assassination Ever Become Misconduct? What *Is* Misconduct Among Lawyers?

Susan Bieke Neilson was also nominated to the Sixth Circuit in November 2001. Her nomination was held until late October 2005, but when she did finally get a vote, she was confirmed ninety-seven-zero. Henry W. Saad, the first Arab-American to be appointed to a Circuit Court of Appeals (Sixth Circuit), failed to win confirmation. The Republican National Lawyers Association charged that Saad was:

> "[T]hrown over the boat" by the unprincipled Senate compromise that avoided the Constitutional Option in May 2005. In violation of Senate ethics, Democrats Harry Reid and others have introduced a new and insidious tactic to suggest that there is something untoward in Judge Saad's FBI file to justify their obstruction. There is nothing.

The Sixth Circuit vacancies are particularly troubling because of unlawful and unethical behavior charged against one of the attorneys for a defendant (University of Michigan Law School) who was cocounsel on an affirmative action case before that court of appeals. The charge stems from an alleged conspiracy between the lawyer, who, while the case was still pending before the Sixth Circuit Court of Appeals, went to work for Senator Edward Kennedy.

The lawyer, in cooperation with her former cocounsel, approached Senator Kennedy and asked him to delay confirmation of a judge appointed to the Sixth Circuit. She believed the judge was too conservative, and she wanted to delay his confirmation to the Sixth Circuit Court of Appeals until the affirmative action case was decided by that Court. Nor was that the only misconduct in the Sixth Circuit. More about that after we examine the behavior of the chief judge of the Sixth Circuit Court of Appeals.

The case began in 1967 when Barbara Grutter applied to the University of Michigan Law School. Ms. Grutter had a GPA of 3.8; her LSAT score was 161. In spite of the good numbers, Ms. Grutter was denied admission. She said it was because she was white.

The law school conceded that if a black applicant had that same GPA and LSAT scores, the black applicant would have been offered admission. The U.S. district court agreed and said the Michigan practice constituted unlawful racial discrimination.

The Sixth Circuit Court of Appeals, en banc[233], reversed, stating that the law school's desire to have a diverse student body was sufficient reason to discriminate against white people. The Supreme Court affirmed in *Grutter v. Bollinger*, 539 U.S. 306 (2003).

So far, this sounds like just another variation and extension of the *Bakke* case. (See chapter 3, *ante*.) But on closer inspection, arguably, the facts were different, the racial discrimination was blatant—the University of Michigan Law School used race not just as a factor to be considered, but as the dominant factor to be considered—and it did not follow the *Bakke* precedent. In other words, the outcome should have been different; however, to focus on the merits of the case is a distraction from what really is important about *Grutter*.

For that story, we need to look both inside and outside the published cases and examine the behind-the-scenes maneuvering, and the irregularities, that led to the decision.

There were two parallel lines of misconduct in that case, which cried out for an investigation by an ethics panel. One ethics complaint was actually filed. A separate breach of ethical rules involved the chief judge of the Sixth Circuit Court of Appeals. To date no formal ethics complaint has been filed against the chief judge. (What mere mortal has the *chutzpah* to file an ethics complaint against a chief federal appeals court judge?)

Judge Danny Boggs, one of the dissenting judges, did take the extraordinary step of filing a "procedural appendix" with his opinion. The irregularities, of which Judge Boggs complained, illustrates how the hubris of the Supreme Court has filtered down to the lower courts who exhibit the same contempt for the Constitution *and their own rules*:

1. The panel, which heard the case, was not properly constituted in accordance with long-standing Sixth Circuit rules.

2. The request for a hearing *en banc* was not circulated to the most members of the court for five months. This was highly irregular. (Note: During the time Judge Boggs has been on the court [sixteen years], every other request for an *en banc* hearing was circulated within two days.)

3. The case was not assigned to a randomly selected panel as required by Sixth Circuit rules and traditional practice.

4. A three-judge panel had heard procedural challenges in the case and remanded the case back to the district court; therefore, the rules required that the initial assignment when the case came back on appeal would go to the same panel who would then decide if the case should have an *en banc* hearing.

5. The chief judge improperly interjected himself into the three-judge panel, rather than randomly drawing a judge from all active Sixth Circuit judges while the panel was hearing interlocutory appeals during trial at the district court.

6. The failure to circulate the petition for an *en banc* hearing for five months appears to have been calculated by the chief judge to allow two of the more conservative judges, Norris (senior status: July 1, 2001) and Suhrheinrich (senior status: August 15, 2001), to take senior status. They then would not be eligible to vote and thus affect the outcome. The petition for *en banc* hearing, received May 14, 2001, was finally circulated to all the Sixth Circuit judges in mid-October, five months after it was filed with the court.

The other ethical breach involved a lawyer, Olantunde C. A. Johnson, former cocounsel in the *Grutter* case, who went to work for Massachusetts Senator Ted Kennedy. A complaint filed with the New York State Bar charges:

> Ms. Johnson violated both the spirit and the letter of the ethical rules and obligations she was bound to uphold when she intentionally acted to manipulate and influence an impartial tribunal that was then in the deliberative process of considering and deciding a high-profile constitutional case in which she had represented one of the parties as co-counsel.[234]

After Ms. Johnson resigned as cocounsel to go to work for Senator Kennedy, but while the Sixth Circuit was still considering how to rule on *Grutter,* "she received a telephone call from her former supervisor and co-counsel, Elaine R. Jones, Esq., President and Director-Counsel of the NAACP Legal Defense and Educational Fund, Inc.," instructing Ms. Johnson to have Senator Kennedy delay confirmation of any nominees to the Sixth Circuit.[235] There seemed to be particular concern about Judge Julia Gibbons, who was not a controversial nominee and was expected to win easy Senate confirmation.

Ms. Jones, according to Ms. Johnson, believed the *en banc* Sixth Circuit "will sustain the affirmative action program, but if a new judge with conservative views is confirmed before the case is decided, that new judge will be able, under 6th Circuit rules, to review the case and vote on it."[236] Ms. Jones further believed that a Bush appointee with conservative views would tip the balance on the [ethically challenged] Sixth Circuit Court of Appeals and do the right thing: uphold the district court ruling that Ms. Grutter was the victim of unlawful racial discrimination.

The Ethical Complaint Against Ms. Johnson

> The ethical ramifications of Ms. Jones' request and conduct were not lost on Ms. Johnson. After all Ms. Jones was intentionally attempting to influence the outcome of a pending case in which she was counsel by covertly seeking to manipulate the composition of a federal appellate court. Ms. Johnson explicitly noted these ethical concerns in her Memorandum to Senator Kennedy, and was even joined by the Senator's Chief Counsel, Melody Barnes, Esq., herself a lawyer licensed in the State of New York, in questioning the propriety of delaying hearings to affect the outcome of a particular case. Ms. Johnson wrote in her Memorandum to Senator Kennedy that, "Melody and I are a little concerned about the propriety of scheduling hearings based on the resolution of a particular case." Nevertheless, Ms. Johnson along with Ms. Barnes, disregarded these ethical concerns, and "recommend[ed] that [Judge Julia Smith] Gibbons be scheduled for a later hearing [because] the Michigan case is important."[237]

A footnote on page 3 of the ethical complaint charges, "The Memorandum to Senator Kennedy written by Ms. Johnson taken by itself, wholly encapsulates Ms. Johnson's clear ethical violations...[as well as] consciousness of guilt, detailing the fact that she knowingly ignored her ethical obligations." (NOTE: For additional details, the author recommends that you Google "Democrat Memogate: In the Eye of the Scandal.")

Neither the New York State Bar nor the Virginia State Bar took any disciplinary action against the lawyers involved. (Don't *ever* confuse legal ethics with morality.)

The example of the Sixth Circuit Court of Appeals is not intended to diminish trust in the courts; rather, it is intended to convey to citizens the need to pay attention to *all* branches of government. The unethical actions in that Sixth Circuit case cannot be attributed to the United States Supreme Court; however, it should put everyone on notice that judges, in exercising their power, are not different from the rest of us.

The historian Lord Acton once said, "Power tends to corrupt, and absolute power corrupts absolutely." Please keep that in mind as you think about the ultimate lawmaking power the Supreme Court has usurped from Congress.

Obviously, not all the problems in our dysfunctional government come from the Supreme Court. But getting the Supreme Court under control is the essential first step in beginning to treat the dysfunction. Since the Supreme Court has seized and consolidated its supremacy over the other two branches of government, it is futile to try to reform Congress or the presidency until the Supreme Court is forced to obey the Constitution.

President Theodore Roosevelt said, "It is the people, and not the judges, who are entitled to say what their constitution means, for the constitution is theirs, it belongs to them and not to their servants in office—any other theory is incompatible with the foundation principles of our government."[238]

President Theodore Roosevelt was a forceful, active president who believed what he was saying. In all probability, a substantial majority of present-day American citizens and voters believe what he said. But that doesn't matter.

What matters is what the judges think about what President Roosevelt was saying; and the truth is, they don't think about it at all—they just go on overriding presidents, people, precedents, and principles laid down by the Constitution. And they get by with it because most people (1) don't know any better, (2) don't care, or (3) both.

Again, quoting Pastor Niemöller's comment on the Nazis:

> First they came for the Communists, but I was not a Communist, so I said nothing. Then they came for the Social Democrats, but I was not a Social Democrat, so I did nothing. Then they came for the trade unionists, but I was not a trade unionist. And then they came for the Jews, but I was not a Jew, so I did little. Then when they came for me, there was no one left to stand up for me.[239]

To paraphrase: the United States Supreme Court *came after the States*—the Court used the Fourteenth Amendment to essentially repeal the Ninth and Tenth amendments. That destroyed much of the federalism the Founding Fathers put in place to prevent an all-powerful federal government—*and we did nothing*; the Court *told a farmer that he could not grow wheat for his own use* because that interfered with interstate commerce. *And we did nothing.* The Court ruled:

> Hence, marketing quotas not only embrace all that may be sold without penalty but also what may be consumed on the premises. Wheat produced on excess acreage is designated as "available for marketing" as so defined and the penalty is imposed thereon. Penalties do not depend upon whether any part of the wheat either within or without the quota is sold or intended to be sold.[240] (Emphasis added.)

Again *we did nothing*. In *Missouri v. Jenkins*, the Supreme Court *gave the lower federal courts the power to levy taxes*—a power the Constitution gave exclusively to the legislative branch—and *still we did nothing*. The Court *extended the power of eminent domain* to take private property from a person to give to another private party who would pay higher taxes (*Kelo v. New London*[241]). But *we did nothing.* There are many more examples, but you get the idea.

The author is not comparing the U.S. Supreme Court to the Nazis; however, the quotation from Pastor Niemöller is a graphic example of how bad things happen when good people stand by and do nothing: how bad, repressive government grows out of the disinterest of free people who are too busy with living their ordinary, frantic lives to become fully engaged in their society. When free citizens become too lazy or too disinterested in exercising their franchise to get out and vote, it is easy for the demagogues to take over.

According to the United States Census Bureau, fewer than six out of ten eligible voters cast their vote in the 2000 presidential election. Meanwhile, while citizens are preoccupied with their own problems and not paying attention, Associate Justice Brennan, in a 1980 case, wrote a separate opinion concurring in the judgment of a case involving Richmond Newspapers:

> Under our system, judges are not mere umpires, but, in their own sphere, lawmakers—a coordinate branch of government. While individual cases turn upon the controversies between parties, or involve particular prosecutions, court rulings impose official and practical consequences upon members of society at large.[242]

From the Horse's Mouth

There. A judge finally said it out loud—judges are LAWMAKERS; COURT RULINGS IMPOSE OFFICIAL AND PRACTICAL CONSEQUENCES UPON MEMBERS OF OUR SOCIETY AT LARGE. (So, by the way, do the decrees of kings and dictators!)

Common law judges have always been lawmakers to some degree. The difference is that common law judges, at the time the U.S. Constitution was written, just ruled in the interstices—i.e., filled in the blanks—where the legitimate lawmaker, the king or Parliament, had not yet made law. Contrast the *Richmond Newspapers* ruling with the words in the first inaugural address of President Lincoln:

> The candid citizen must confess that if the policy of the government, upon vital questions affecting the whole people, is to be irrevocably fixed by decisions of the Supreme Court, the instant they are made, in ordinary litigation between parties in personal actions, the people will have ceased to be their own rulers.

The modern U.S. Supreme Court *overturns* laws legitimately made by Congress and signed by the president; then the Court substitutes its own. The Court believes it has superior wisdom and insight; therefore, it feels free to make law even where Congress, acting pursuant to its constitutional power, believes it *has* made law. Actually, the way the system works today, Congress makes *tentative* law. If the Court doesn't object to (overrule) the congressional act, it is indeed the law.

But the Court holds a veto power over any act of Congress it doesn't like—not just laws that are actually unconstitutional—the Court merely has to say a new law passed by Congress is "unconstitutional" and, ipso facto, the law is unconstitutional. The Court relies on its own "intuitions" and "feelings" about what the law should be, then it rules. Except the Court rarely comes right out and says that.

The rare exception is Justice Brennan's slip of the pen in the *Richmond Newspapers* case cited in this chapter. The Court considers itself the final arbiter, the supreme law*maker*, Congress and the people be damned. And since the people acquiesce, the Supreme Court *is* the final arbiter, the supreme lawmaker.

Justice Scalia probably said it best:

> What secret knowledge, one must wonder, is breathed into lawyers when they become Justices of this Court, that enables them to discern that a practice which the text of the Constitution does not clearly proscribe, and which our people have regarded as constitutional for 200 years, is in fact unconstitutional?[243]

It was a rhetorical question, which no one at that time answered. But here is one: the obvious answer to Justice Scalia's question, "It's not secret knowledge, it is hubris!" Hubris of the members of the Court, coupled with a lack of understanding on the part of most citizens of how the Court works, exacerbated by the apathy of many others who don't *care* how the Court works.

So we have ceased to be our own rulers. Justice Brennan spelled it out for us in *Richmond Newspapers*. That may not bother some people. Some would suggest that democracy and representative government is "too messy" and too likely to lead to "tyranny of the majority." So we have come to accept the opposite—tyranny of the minority. A *tiny* minority. Five people.

Often those five people are goaded into action by another tiny minority, who are making great strides toward making atheism the *established* state religion. We have the tyranny of an oligarchy consisting of five unelected individuals, some in their dotage. "The history of the Court is replete with repeated instances of justices casting decisive votes or otherwise participating actively in the Court's work when their colleagues and/or families had serious doubts about their mental capacities" (Garrow, David, "Mental Decrepitude on the U. S. Supreme Court"[244]). They get together in secret conferences and decide that their collective judgment is superior to the judgment of more than two hundred years of history and tradition. If readers take only one thought away with them after reading this book, the author hopes it will be this: one supreme justice, on either side of the argument, is about as intelligent as another. Each of the nine is about equally well educated in the better law schools. All have extensive practical experience in the practice of law.

Therefore, when the vote on a particular issue is split five to four—and the same four or five justices repeatedly group together on one side or the other of an issue—you can be sure the split is not about the law. It's about politics. It's about an agenda.

That agenda is being set right now by Justice Kennedy—a blithe spirit who "likes to wander all over the constitutional law like an errant voyager." (See page 8.) Kennedy was Ronald Reagan's third choice to fill the vacancy left by the retirement of Justice Lewis Powell from the Supreme Court after Robert Bork had been "borked" and the nomination of Douglas Ginsburg failed because he admitted that he used marijuana.

"Described as unassuming and friendly, Kennedy has won the respect and admiration of his colleagues over the years. Kennedy often used his personality to win over allies and form unlikely coalitions."[45] Unfortunately, he uses those same traits to decide cases coming before the Supreme Court without much regard for the law or the Constitution.

He votes more often with the conservative block on many issues but is steadfastly liberal on such hot-button topics as gay rights, abortion, and school prayer. He also to likes to use foreign law to decide cases that are purely domestic—cases that should be decided solely with reference to the United States Constitution and laws.

Part II
What You Can Do

Chapter 11: Who Do You Trust?

We are under a Constitution, but the Constitution is what the judges say it is.[246]— Charles Evans Hughes, governor of New York (later, chief justice of the Supreme Court of the United States), 1907 speech.

Making changes to the massively intrusive federal government—and in particular the most malignant threat to individual liberty, the Supreme Court—will require some minimal understanding of the Supreme Court's role as authorized by the Constitution as opposed to the *real* Supreme Court role today under the so-called "Living Constitution."

Trial lawyers quickly learn a law—statute—passed by a legislative assembly is the law *only* until a judge has occasion to interpret that statute. Then the judge's interpretation is the law. Often, the court interpretation—the new law—cannot be altered by legislation. If the court interpreting the statute happens to be the United States Supreme Court, Congress cannot overrule the Supreme Court by passing another law. The Supreme Court's ruling is final.

To change the relationship between the Supreme Court and the other two branches of the federal government and to restore the sovereignty of the states as a check and balance to a bloated federal government, which has unlawfully accreted more power to itself, will require altering the Constitution.

Over time, the Supreme Court has learned to ignore the written Constitution we have and substitute its own "interpretations." The result is today's "Living Constitution," which allows five justices, voting together on a given day, to change the law and even the Constitution itself. To change that relationship, however, will require you to *believe* you can make the change. And it will require that you be willing to *do* something instead of complaining over what is not getting done.

In our family we have a tradition: "If you don't vote, you lose your bitchin' rights." If you don't do something positive to promote good government—you forfeit your right to bitch about what government is doing to you. In President Ronald Reagan's first inaugural address, he said, "In this present crisis, government is not the solution to our problem; government is the problem." I will show you how you can achieve the change you seek.

❖　❖　❖

The changes to the Constitution proposed herein are for the sole purpose of restoring the Constitution to the status quo ante—a return to the representative republic that existed immediately after the Constitution was ratified and before the

Supreme Court gave itself the power to overrule an act of Congress and to write its own Constitution.

The other branches, for their part, seem to have forgotten that the president can ignore the Court when the Court makes an outlandish decision—as President Abraham Lincoln did when he freed the slaves in defiance of the *Dred Scott* decision; and the Congress can ignore the Court when the Court meddles unlawfully in Congress's internal affairs as it did in the Adam Clayton Powell case. If Congress and the president aren't willing to keep the "checks and balances" balanced, *We, the people* must!

The bold action by the Court in trumping an act of Congress in *Marbury* came a mere seventeen years after the constitutional convention considered and specifically rejected giving the Court that power. This usurpation of Congress's power "was accompanied by one of the great propaganda efforts in our history. Convincing people that judges appointed for life were an integral and independent part of America's democratic governments."[247]

How the modern American people feel about the Supreme Court as compared to the other branches of government is difficult to discern. If people knew more about the Court, their feelings and beliefs about the Court might be quite different. Congress is under scrutiny by the press; the Court works in secret and only announces its final decision, not how it got there. President Bush was vilified as no other modern president has been.

But few people outside the legal profession really know very much about the Court, or how the Court affects our daily life.

The author wants to change that: to paraphrase the Hans Christian Andersen fairy tale and say, "The Supreme Court has no clothes"—to publish the Court's own rulings and public statements of its justices and let the real Court stand naked in front of the people.

The author believes if the Court was exposed to the same intense scrutiny that the president and Congress endure every day, the people's perception of the Court would be radically different from what it now is.

Approval figures for the Supreme Court are difficult to compare directly with the well-documented disapproval for Congress and the president. In all of 2006, Gallup and FOX News/Opinion Dynamics did one poll each where they directly asked, "Do you approve or disapprove of the job the United States Supreme Court is doing?" Quinnipiac asked the question again in August 2007 and found that 45 percent of the people surveyed approved, 37 percent disapproved, and 17 percent didn't know.

The president's job approval numbers were sixteen points lower, with Congress's approval lower still. By the summer of 2008, the approval rating for Congress was in single digits. No branch of the federal government enjoys the approval of a majority of the people surveyed.

Most of the Supreme Court polling that was done focused more on whether the Senate should approve a particular justice (Harriett Myers, Samuel Alito, and John Roberts) or whether *Roe v. Wade* should be overturned. The few numbers available, however, which ask the "approve or disapprove" questions about the Supreme Court, are higher than those for the president and Congress.

The author contends this is so because few nonlawyers really know much about the Supreme Court and how it works, and the lawyers aren't talking.

It is essential, if we are to have representative government, that we reign in the Supreme Court and prevent it from making more unilateral, unauthorized, and clandestine amendments to the United States Constitution. In order to do that, we need to give Congress the stature and legal authority to be what the founders intended it to be. James Madison's words are worth repeating:

> If men were angels, no government would be necessary. If angels were to govern men, neither external nor internal controls on government would be necessary. In framing a government which is to be administered by men over men, the great difficulty lies in this: you must first enable the government to control the governed; and in the next place oblige it to control itself. A dependence on the people is, no doubt, the primary control on the government; but experience has taught mankind the necessity of auxiliary precautions...In republican government, the legislative authority necessarily predominates.[248]

In modern America, the legislative branch does not predominate. There are two problems acting in concert to diminish American self-government: first, the federal government, with the help of the Fourteenth Amendment, has usurped much of the legitimate role of the states and essentially emasculated the states' ability to maintain the balance in a republican form of government.

The states brought that catastrophe upon themselves when some of them decided to sever their ties with the Union States and ended up fighting—and losing—a civil war.

The federal government's power to preempt state government functions expanded exponentially after the American Civil War. Originally, the term *states' rights* referred to "[r]ights not conferred on the federal government or forbidden to the States according to the 10th Amendment, U.S. Constitution"[249] and therefore retained by the states.

That the federal government was a government of limited (delegated) powers was axiomatic to the founders. "States' rights" was a concept embraced and enthusiastically advanced by the founders as an important check on excesses by, and indeed prevention of, a strong federal government.

Down with "States' Rights," Up with the Federal Power Grab

Unfortunately, during the run-up to the Civil War, "states' rights" became a code word for supporting slavery; therefore, the phrase became discredited as a legitimate assertion of the rights retained by the states. After the war and the adoption of the Fourteenth Amendment, the Ninth and Tenth amendments to the Bill of Rights became, in effect, a nullity.

The result was that now there are no practical limits on the federal government's power. There are some *theoretical* limits, but who can enforce them?

The second part of the problem is the Supreme Court. Again, *theoretically*, the Supreme Court could have restrained the overreaching by the federal government, but instead it went the other way—not just permitting the federal legislature and the president to grab more power for themselves, but then going beyond that and usurping that power grab, accreting more power to the Court in the process.

The Supreme Court began ordering certain actions by state and local governments—i.e., busing children to achieve school integration, requiring *all* jurisdictions to modernize, or build new jails—the Court assumed it had the "necessary and proper" authority to see that its orders were carried out.

There is a necessary and proper clause in the Constitution ("Congress shall have Power To...make all Laws which shall be necessary and proper for carrying into Execution the foregoing [§ 8] Powers," U.S. Const. Art. I, sec. 8). But it is in Article I describing *legislative* powers. The Supreme Court, created by Article III, has no *necessary and proper* powers because the Court is not authorized to promulgate legislation.

This led inevitably to the outcome in *Jenkins v. Kansas City Missouri School District* case and the federal courts' power to levy taxes directly upon the people, completely bypassing the legislative process if necessary. Justice Kennedy, concurring in *Missouri v. Jenkins*, wrote, "Today's casual embrace of taxation imposed by the unelected, life-tenured federal judiciary disregards fundamental precepts for the democratic control of public institutions."[250]

How Do We Fix It?

When one begins to examine how to bring about reform, the resistance to overcome in order to give Congress override power over bad Supreme Court decisions is that, at this point, the American people trust Congress even less than they trust the Supreme Court.

The approval rating of Congress in early 2007 was just over a third (34.3 percent) while more than half (52.2 percent) disapproved of the way Congress was doing its job.[251] By June 2007, when the new Democratic Congress had been in power for six months, the Rasmussen poll showed only 19 percent of Americans thought Congress was doing a good or excellent job; and only "8% of Americans say it's Very Likely that Congress will seriously address the important issues facing the nation this year."[252]

By late July, the number was down from 19 percent to 14 percent of people believing Congress was doing a good or excellent job.[253] By August 2007, it was back up to 20 percent in other polls, still a dismal showing.

An April 26, 2007, Harris poll, published in the *Wall Street Journal*, showed only 28 percent of people approved of President Bush; Congress's approval stood at 27 percent.[254]

An e-mail to Senator Arlen Specter, dated June 30, 2007, citing another Rasmussen report, read:

> We live in a world where most Americans believe that most Members of Congress will sell their vote for cash or a campaign contribution. Only 16% believe the legislators' votes are not for sale. By a nearly 5-to-1 margin, voters believe that Members of Congress are more interested in their own careers and agenda rather than the public good.[255]

People perceive the Court to be less threatening to their civil liberties than either Congress or the president when the opposite is true, if only because we have Congress and the president under closer scrutiny and hold them more accountable. The Court, meanwhile, continues on its stealthy path amending the Constitution at will and inflicting the personal values of the individual justices, rather than the law, on the American people.

If we are to be a country that believes in the "rule of law," the people need to know what the law is. They should be able to read it, understand it, and therefore be in a position to follow it. They should not have to conform to the *ex post facto laws* of the United States Supreme Court. Nor should they be required to get a crystal ball or a Ouija board to discern what the law is.

Every Court decision that changes the law comes after someone has acted in good faith to conform his conduct to what he thinks is compliance with the law; the Supreme Court then says, "Not so fast, that is not really what that law says." Then the Court writes its own law in the place of the one Congress passed and which the person relied on.

Lawyers (remember, all judges *are* lawyers before—and after—they become judges) perverted the words of the Constitution to make them mean what the lawyers—and federal judges—want those words to mean.

As recently as 1931, the Supreme Court ruled, "The Constitution was written to be understood by the voters; its words and phrases were used in their normal and ordinary as distinguished from technical meaning; where the intention is clear there is no room for construction and no excuse for interpolation or addition."[256] That principle prevailed from the beginning of the republic until the mid-twentieth century.

Requiring the Court to obey the Constitution is simple in concept. It is relatively more difficult, but not impossible, in the execution. Article V of the Constitution contains the mechanism for the people to take back what once was—but no longer is—"government of the people, by the people and for the people."[257] Now it has become government unfairly influenced by whoever can afford to hire the best lobbyists and the best lawyers—or who gave the largest campaign contribution!

The mechanism for the people to take back their government is in the Constitution itself. The only practical means to regain control of the federal government is for the states to demand a convention for offering amendments to the Constitution.

The author suggested that proposed solution to a friend—who was the Senate president of the West Virginia state legislature—and he appeared horrified at the idea. His immediate response was, "Oh no! Who would you trust to write the amendments?"

Uh—the American people, maybe?

The senator's exclamation pretty much sums up the problem: no one trusts politicians, not even the politicians themselves! This was the first clue on how to solve this problem: *trust the American people*. They did a pretty good job of writing the first one. It is only when the Supreme Court started to "interpret" the document that the carefully crafted balance of power between the branches of government, and between the federal government and the states, began to unravel.

President Abraham Lincoln, on the subject of amending the constitution, said:

> I will venture to add that to me the convention mode seems preferable, in that it allows amendments to originate with the people themselves, instead of only permitting them to take or reject propositions originated by others, not especially chosen for the purpose, and which might not be precisely such as they would wish to either accept or refuse.[258]

What a great idea. The American people writing their own Constitution—just like the people who wrote the one we have now. Except that, modern people could not write a new Constitution. They can only offer amendments to the one we have. Article V of the 1787 Constitution, which permits calling "a Convention for proposing Amendments," continues in the same sentence to limit the authority of the convention: amendments so proposed and ratified shall be a "Part of this Constitution." There is no authority to write a whole *new* Constitution.

The Constitution's Built-in Safety Net

Look. It requires a supermajority of the people acting through their elected legislators to change the Constitution—unless you are the United States Supreme Court, in which case it takes only five people voting together for the change. Whether Congress puts forward the amendment or the states demand a convention, it takes a two-thirds majority to get the process started and *three-fourths* of the states to ratify. That's a pretty good safety net.

To get that kind of majorities would require that there be widespread agreement in all parts of the country. Properly—and lawfully—amending the Constitution is a burdensome process. It was intended to be; amending the Constitution is serious business. This is why it is so dangerous to have the Supreme Court amending that document any time any five of the justices think it ought to say something that it does not.

Chapter 12: Restoring the Balance

What do we mean when we say that first of all we seek liberty? I often wonder whether we do not rest our hopes too much upon constitutions, upon laws, and upon courts. These are false hopes; believe me, these are false hopes. Liberty lies in the hearts of men and women; when it dies there, no constitution, no law, no court can save it; no constitution, no law, no court can even do much to help it.—Judge Learned Hand, *The Spirit of Liberty.*[259]

The author's generation, born before World War II, will be the last to remember the American Republic as it was before the United States Supreme Court usurped Congress' power and corrupted, perhaps forever, the democratic process—unless *you* do something about it. Americans who came of age during or after the tenure of Chief Justice Earl Warren (1953-1969) will have no personal memory of what it was like to *elect* representatives who made the laws we live under.

They will know that we elect representatives to Congress, but they will also know that the Supreme Court trumps Congress any time there is a dispute about the law's meaning and effect. The politically correct public school system isn't helping.

A survey of seventy-six high school students in the nation's capital and nearby Virginia and Maryland found one student who made a B in history who could not name a single general (Eisenhower, Patton, Bradley, Sir Bernard Montgomery, Rommel), battle, (Pearl Harbor, Battle of Midway, Battle of El Alamein, Battle of the Bulge) or the president of the United States (FDR) during World War II. She did know about the Japanese-Americans thought to be a war risk held in "concentration camps" on the West Coast.[260]

No mention that the camps, often integrated, also held Italian-Americans, German-Americans, and Latin-Americans. Apparently, the schools can make a better case for *racial* prejudice if they confine the list to the Japanese.

Oh. She did know about Rosie the Riveter.

Only one-third of her contemporaries could name a general from that war; only about half could name a battle. Nor did college students do much better. A civic literacy test found half of incoming freshmen missing half of the 60 question multiple-choice test; seniors did little better at 54% correct.

Nor will they understand FDRs power grab, which drastically increased the size and influence of the federal government. In the case of Roosevelt, they just saw someone who would "save" them from the Great Depression.

Exacerbating the Supreme Court's stealthy lust for power was the Administrative Procedures Act (APA),[261] which had its roots in the New Deal legislation promoted by President Franklin Delano Roosevelt. The APA in the form we know it now was passed in 1946 (after FDR's death) to try to clean up the chaos of all the new federal agencies created by the New Deal Congress at the insistence of Roosevelt.

The APA ratified the president's power to make laws—historically, the power to make law rested solely with the legislative branch of government.

The authority for the president to make laws appears nowhere in the Constitution. In fact, it is a blatant violation of the Constitution, but it has become a fact of life because the people have allowed it to happen, and the younger generation, inadequately educated in what we used to call "civics class," believes that is the way is it supposed to be. Therefore, the president has the de facto power to make his own laws.

Compare that with Thomas Payne's view that:

> A constitution is not the act of a government, but of a people constituting a government; and government without a constitution is power without a right. All power exercised over a nation, must have some beginning. It must be either delegated, or assumed. There are not other sources. All delegated power is trust, and all assumed power is usurpation. Time does not alter the nature and quality of either.[262]

So the Constitution belongs to the people, not to the lawyers who happen to sit on the Supreme Court right now. Nor the president—whose laws exceed in volume and shelf space than those passed by Congress. Unfortunately, too many people think the Constitution is written in "legalese" and too complex for ordinary citizens to understand.

But that clearly was not the case. The Constitution uses the language of the people, and the people could read and understand it.[263]

The body of Supreme Court "interpretations" that most people equate with the "Constitution" certainly is written in "legalese" because the lawyers and the Supreme Court want it that way. It's called job security. If the Constitution and laws can be made so complicated and esoteric that only lawyers can understand them, well, duh! Lawyers will always have a job.

Numerous references cited herein reaffirm the obvious: until the mid-twentieth century, everyone, including the Supreme Court, agreed that the Constitution was written in the language of the people and the people understood it.

Most of us learned in school that Congress makes our laws, the president enforces them, and the Supreme Court decides disputes about the laws and the way they are enforced. And that was true—once upon a time.

The separation of powers taught to an older generation in school has largely become a fairy tale now. It is used primarily to keep the partisan bickering going and create campaign issues. Each of the three branches is always trying to extend their power over the other two.

So *How* Do We Restore the Balance?

> *The Congress...on the Application of the Legislatures of two thirds of the several States, shall call a Convention for proposing Amendments, which, in either Case, shall be valid to all Intents and Purposes, as Part of this Constitution, when ratified by the Legislatures of three fourths of the several States, or by Conventions in three fourths thereof, as the one or the other Mode of Ratification may be proposed by the Congress.*—U.S. Constitution Article V

A simple majority vote of the legislatures of two-thirds of the states is enough to call a convention to offer amendments to the Constitution. There is no mechanism in the Constitution which would permit the states to call for a *general* convention where everything is on the table; however, the states have every right to call for a convention to propose amendments to the Constitution. The states could set the agenda by what is contained within the call for the convention.

A convention thus called would be limited to what was in the "call" for the convention. A general convention is out of the question for several reasons: the most important one is the Constitution is not "broken" and doesn't really need to be "fixed." The United States Supreme Court has "bent" the Constitution almost beyond recognition in some areas, but we don't have to rewrite it.

We just need to nudge it back on track—install mechanisms to ensure that the present government officials actually read what the Constitution says and follow it as opposed to listening to what the Supreme Court *says* it says.

Assurances To Restore Trust

Another reason is that there is so much distrust in the country today that if it were possible to call a general convention where everything is on the table, no one would ever agree to have one.

In 1992, the Congress, in the process of raising its members' own salary, was stunned when an amendment, originally offered in 1789 as a part of the original Bill of Rights, and which had been sitting in limbo for over two hundred years, was ratified as the Twenty-seventh Amendment to the Constitution. That Twenty-seventh Amendment prohibited Congress from raising salaries for elected officials during the session of Congress that voted for the raise; an election cycle had to pass.

Congress was angry; it was also fearful of what else might be out there waiting to be ratified. It took steps to ensure that none of the other amendments in limbo could be brought up for ratification, and it began putting time limits on any new proposed amendments.

❖   ❖   ❖

A substantial majority of average citizens are frustrated with the career politicians in Washington who disregard the will of the people and their own oath, taken upon entering office that they will protect and defend the Constitution. Only 17 percent of Americans think the government follows the will of the people.

Many of the people in the middle and from the "center-left" and the "center-right" feel disenfranchised because they have so little control of the government and what government leaders do. Much of that frustration stems from feeling that the Supreme Court is also the supreme lawgiver.

If the "spirit of liberty" (see heading paragraph for this chapter) is dead in the hearts of the American people changing the Constitution, even if possible, would be futile. If, on the other hand, the spirit still lives, then the people can take back their government.

This writer believes that the spirit of liberty is not dead. If it were, there would not be so much angst about a government that is out of touch with the people. People would just accept their fate. The people yearn to express their spirit of liberty and just need to know what they can do to return that spirit to the American government.

When Franklin D. Roosevelt was elected to his fourth term as president, there was fear among many that he was becoming "president for life." Which, as it turned out, he was! Roosevelt died in office. Most Americans living at that time (the author was one of them) thought that FDR probably would have been elected to a fifth term had he lived to see the successful conclusion of World War II.

To prevent another "president for life" the people, through their elected representatives, adopted the Twenty-Second Amendment to the Constitution (1951) in order to prevent that ever happening again.

Legislators for Life

That same two-term limit should be applied to senators; members of the House might be limited to three or four terms (six to eight years).

Much of the corruption in Washington today comes from the fact that most who serve in Congress are career politicians who know that they will not have to go back home when their term is over and live with the laws they pass.

Furthermore, being elected to Congress also seems to confer a certain de facto immunity from obeying the laws the rest of us have to obey. Not just in the laws that legislators specifically exempt themselves from obeying, but the criminal laws that are not applied equally to those in power.

Stories abound about young police officers who are so bold as to try to arrest a member of Congress or a senator for drunk driving, or some other criminal charge, only to be dressed down by their superiors and then told to "un-arrest" the dignitary and drive him home so he doesn't hurt himself. (See, e.g., "Sen. Robert Byrd: Invoking an Ancient Rule to Avoid a Modern Law." The eighty-one-year-old Byrd invoked the immunity clause to prevent getting a ticket when he hit another vehicle from the rear while driving his own car.)[264]

We must term-limit Congress and get some new faces before anyone will trust the federal government enough to restore to Congress its legitimate constitutional power.

The term-limited Congress, now drawing more ordinary citizens and fewer professional politicians to its ranks, must have the power to override any decision of the Supreme Court which purports to declare an act of Congress "unconstitutional."

We should amend the Constitution to restore Congress's lawmaking power, granted under Article I, and truncated by the Supreme Court. This could be done in either of two ways:

1. Congress could be required to state with specificity the part of the Constitution that confers on Congress the power to make this particular law. Any bill passed which meets this condition would be *per se* constitutional, and the Supreme Court would not have the jurisdiction to consider whether the said law is constitutional.

2. In the alternative, Congress could reject any unlawful interference by the Court by overriding a Supreme Court decision that declares a law passed by Congress unconstitutional. That override power could be exercised in the same manner as overriding a presidential veto. (U.S. Const. Art. I, § 7, clause 2)

Overriding the Court could require a two-thirds majority of both houses of Congress and would not be subject to review by the Supreme Court; or the convention delegates may want to consider another formula for override. An override vote should not be subject to a presidential veto.

The Supreme Court has no jurisdiction to amend the Constitution. This should be self-evident but obviously is not. (See discussion about *Roe v. Wade.*) Through its "interpretations" over the years, the Supreme Court has evolved a way to circumvent that lack of jurisdiction implied in the Constitution. We need to explicitly spell out the prohibition against the Court making decisions which are de facto amendments.

With all the attention an Article V convention would generate, we should make clear that the people want to enforce the Ninth and Tenth amendments in the Bill of Rights. One would probably assume that we already enforce the Ninth and Tenth amendments, but the Supreme Court's "interpretation" of the "Living Constitution" has rendered those two amendments, for all practical purposes, null and void. (More about this in chapter 13: "The Rule of Law.")

In order to honor the Ninth and Tenth amendments, it may be necessary to repeal parts of the Fourteenth. Congress should not have the power to override the Constitution and the Bill of Rights by passing simple legislation.

The Founding Fathers anticipated the apportionment of power between the federal government and states. The concept of "states' rights," would enforce the limitations on federal power and would keep the federal government from seizing and centralizing more and more power unto itself.

The federal government is one of limited powers. Those two amendments are directed specifically to keeping the federal power limited: "The enumeration in the Constitution of certain rights shall not be construed to deny or disparage others retained by the people" (Amendment IX). And "the powers not delegated to the United States by the Constitution, nor prohibited by it to the States, are reserved to the States respectively, or to the people" (Amendment X). That should be the ideal we strive for.

"States' rights" was a great idea, and it worked—for a while—but since the words *states' rights* were tainted by the association with support for slavery, supporters of the idea behind the words will need to call it something else—like "restoration of the Ninth and Tenth Amendments" or "federalism." Not too many people have strong negative feelings about the word *federalism*. It sounds like—America!

The content of the Ninth and Tenth amendments could be enhanced and fortified using as a model President Ronald Reagan's Executive Order No. 12612 (October 30, 1987).

The convention could debate whether the executive order should be codified in the Constitution. An alternative method would be an amendment which specifies that the Ninth and Tenth amendments and the whole Bill of Rights were in the way of a condition precedent to getting the Constitution ratified. More on this subject is in chapter 13.

This would limit the power of Congress to override the Bill of Rights by mere legislation. The Fourteenth Amendment, giving Congress that power, has been controversial from the start. The very timing of the amendment made it suspect: it was a result of the American Civil War and was passed in the immediate aftermath of that war when the mood in the country was to punish the South.

Legitimate questions have been raised about whether there was the requisite number of senators voting to make up the two-thirds majority to send the amendment out to the states for ratification.

Eleven Southern states had been excluded from representation in Congress because they were "states in rebellion," and the powerful Senator Thaddeus Stevens even argued that they were in effect a foreign country under military occupation. Contrast that to President Abraham Lincoln's view that the Southern states did not need to be readmitted to the Union because they never left. The *attempt* to leave, thwarted by the Civil War, never came to fruition, according to Lincoln.

Lincoln's view did not prevail; however, the Southern States' belated seating in Congress came only after they had been forced to pledge that they would support passage of the Fourteenth Amendment.

If one ignores the passions of the day and just looks at the law, that should have been a fairly easy problem to solve:

An "Act of the Whole People, Sacredly Obligatory Upon All"

"The basis of our political systems is the right of the people to make and to alter their Constitutions of Government. But the Constitution which at any time exists, 'till changed by an explicit and authentic act *of the whole People*, is sacredly obligatory upon all" (George Washington, farewell address, 1796;[265] emphasis added). A decision of the Supreme Court is self-evidently *not* the act of the whole People!

The "all" upon whom the Constitution "is sacredly obligatory" obviously should include the United States Supreme Court—but of course it doesn't: the Court gets to write its own Constitution! Chief Justice Burger may have said it best: "We are the Supreme Court and we can do what we want."[266]

That is one of the unintended side effects of the Fourteenth Amendment adopted after the Civil War.

Scholars have debated the legal question about *whether* the Southern states ever left the Union. Again, President Lincoln believed that the states did not have the legal right to leave the Union, therefore they never left. Had he lived this would have had profound implications in the way Reconstruction would be applied. It also would have meant that Southerners, still loyal to the Union, could be seated in Congress as soon the shooting war stopped.

One can think of the Civil War as being, in Lincoln's eyes, a riot on steroids. If that were the case, there is no question the Southern states were committing an illegal act, but unless and until the rebellious *individuals* are tried and convicted in a court of law, they still enjoy all the rights of being an American citizen.

Had that view prevailed, all of the arguments about whether the Southern states could be coerced into ratifying the Fourteenth Amendment before being readmitted to the Union would be moot. In fact, the Fourteenth may not have been ratified at all. As it actually happened, the Fourteenth Amendment was not the act of the "whole people" (as George Washington stated), but rather an act of only half of them. But that argument is of purely academic interest. We must deal with the government we have, not with the one we might have had.

❖   ❖   ❖

James Madison, in extolling the virtues of the convention method of amending the Constitution chosen by the founders, said, "It guards equally against that extreme facility, which would render the Constitution too mutable; and that extreme difficulty, which might perpetuate its discovered faults." The Supreme Court, unilaterally, through interpretation, *has* rendered the Constitution mutable—now it just takes five votes.

None of the founders, in their wildest imagination, could have envisioned five old guys on the Supreme Court changing the Constitution at their mere whim.

Article V of the Constitution provides for a bypass mechanism whereby the people, through their elected state representatives, can get past an entrenched Congress—which is so arrogant it believes it can ignore the people—and propose their own amendments to the Constitution.

This is precisely the time in history that the founders anticipated: the "culture of corruption" in Washington appears to be the same under Democratic control as under Republican control. None of the current crop of candidates look like they will make much of a difference.

The late Strom Thurmond, the only senator to attain the age of 100 while still serving, and Senator Robert C. Byrd (D-WV) are but two examples of people elected "senator for life." Senator Kennedy also comes to mind. If one's reelection is virtually assured, there is no need to listen to the people.

Even as incumbents enjoy near-perfect job security, Congress in general is often held in contempt; for example, in one survey (2007), only 2 percent of Americans thought Congress is doing an "excellent" job while another 14 percent believe it is doing a "good" job. A meager 9 percent think it is "very likely" that "Congress will seriously address the most important problems facing our nation."[267] Again, only 17 percent believe that the whole *federal government* pays attention to the will of the American people.

One of the key advantages to the convention method for offering amendments would be working with your local state legislators who are closer to home, more attentive to their constituents' needs, and who probably would like to take back some of their power and freedom of action taken away by an ever-expanding federal government.

Many of the serving senators and representatives in Congress don't even live in their home district anymore. They live in Washington and have a "token" home "back home" where they can visit from time to time when Congress is in recess, or when they need to use the home as a base while campaigning for reelection.

Another prime reason for term limits is rules and traditions, which favor seniority. If people know their senator or representative has been in Washington for a long time and has seniority and powerful friends, they know he is in a position to bring home his state's "fair share" of the bacon. Even as they hold Congress as an institution in contempt, most approve of their own members of Congress.

But the flip side of having made powerful friends is that necessarily one is also making powerful enemies, so the Beltway bickering continues.

Calling the convention would be a matter of federal law.[268] State laws that require a supermajority to initiate amendments to their *state* constitution would not apply, and each state legislature would need only a majority vote to demand the convention.

The supermajority requirement to initiate the amendment process would be met in the federal context by the fact that two-thirds of all the states have to agree to call the convention; then three-fourths of the states must ratify each amendment in a separate action before it becomes a part of the Constitution.

Article V anticipates that amending the Constitution is entirely up to the people and the people's representatives in Congress. The president has no role. Justice Samuel Chase, writing for the Court in 1789, said, "The negative [veto] of the President applies only to the ordinary cases of legislation: He has nothing to do with the proposition, or adoption, of amendments to the Constitution."[269]

The wording of Article V gives "the Legislatures of two thirds of the several States" the authority to demand the convention. The words of Justice Chase in the preceding paragraph about the president having no role, therefore, would seem to apply equally to state governors.

The role of the people is to persuade their state representatives to call the convention; then they may seek election as a delegate and/or vote for delegates who will attend the convention as the agents of the people. The Supreme Court has ruled in *United States v. Sprague*[270] that the word *shall* in Article V means that if the state legislatures ask for the convention to offer amendments to the Constitution, Congress must call the convention.

Federal officeholders are not eligible to be delegates unless they resign their federal office. The convention delegates alone will have the authority to vote on proposed amendments. The prohibition against federal officeholders would not apply to state legislators who could keep their office while still running for convention delegate. From a practical standpoint, however, most state officials would know that the convention would take up too much of their time, and they might not be able to attend the convention and still be an effective legislator at home.

Once assembled in convention, the delegates would have the same power as Congress (and no more) to propose amendments to the Constitution. When convention delegates approve proposed amendments, Congress has the authority to determine if the ratification, which is a separate process, shall be by the state legislatures or by state convention.

Whichever Congress chooses will be binding on the states. We have it within our power to restore the balance.

But do we have the courage?

Chapter 13: The Rule of Law

The rule of law is a fundamental component of democratic society and is defined broadly as the principle that all members of society—both citizens and rulers—are bound by a set of clearly defined and universally accepted laws. In a democracy, the rule of law is manifested in an independent judiciary, a free press and a system of checks and balances on leaders through free elections and separation of powers among the branches of government.[271]

The paragraph heading this chapter is what the U.S. State Department tells the world about the rule of law. But is it the reality? At http://www.ruleoflaw.org/, we read, "Concerns centered on the rule of law are the consistency, predictability, and transparency of the law. Legal rules that are variable, intrusive, and unclear stand in the way of economic freedom and global progress."

The definition of the rule of law in *Black's Law Dictionary* states, "Decisions should be made by the application of known principles of laws without the intervention of discretion in their application." It is stated as a maxim. [Maxim: "a principle of law universally admitted as being a correct statement of the law or agreeable to reason."]

Are all members of American society subject to the same laws applied equally?

Uh—no.

Several laws exempt Congress and the entire United States government from having to obey them. The Occupational Safety and Health Act of 1970 plainly states that the definition of employer "does not include the United States."[272] The Freedom of Information Act does not apply to Congress. Discrimination laws do not apply to Congress, nor does the National Labor Relations Act. Congress has a very generous pension plan and, according to the National Taxpayers Union, stands to collect two to three times more in retirement than an executive earning a similar salary and retiring from private employment might expect to receive.

These are but a few of the laws Congress and the federal bureaucracy do not have to obey. And that does not even take into consideration the way laws are applied differently to those who can afford good lawyers and those who cannot.

Are decisions made by the application of known principles of laws without the intervention of discretion in their application?

Uh—no.

The United States Supreme Court has the absolute discretion to make the laws mean whatever any five justices, voting together on a given day, want the laws to mean.

Separation of powers is important to keep an intrusive and powerful government in check; however, the United States Supreme Court has clearly gained supremacy over the Congress and the president as well as the government of the several states. The Constitution does not confer any power of "judicial review" upon the Supreme Court. That's a power the Court seized, without any legal authority, in *Marbury v. Madison.*

And all branches of the United States government have gained supremacy over the states.

How "Sausages" Get Made[273]

Congressmen (and women) often do not read the legislation they vote on, and once a conference between the House and Senate works out a compromise on their separate versions of a bill, even if they get around to reading the bill, they have no power to change it. Each house votes up or down on the committee report: amendments are not permitted. A critical look at the lawmaking process will demonstrate how this works. The following exchange took place between Senator Armstrong (R-CO) and Senator Dole (R-KS), chairman of the Finance Committee.

> MR. ARMSTRONG: My question, which may take [the chairman of the Committee on Finance] by surprise, is this: Is it the intention of the chairman that the Internal Revenue Service and the Tax Court and other courts take guidance as to the intention of Congress from the committee report which accompanies this bill?
>
> MR. DOLE: I would certainly hope so.
>
> MR. ARMSTRONG: Mr. President, will the Senator tell me whether or not he wrote the committee report?
>
> MR. DOLE: Did I write the committee report?
>
> MR. ARMSTRONG: Yes.
>
> MR. DOLE: No; the Senator from Kansas did not write the committee report.
>
> MR. ARMSTRONG: Did any Senator write the committee report?
>
> MR. DOLE: I have to check.
>
> MR. ARMSTRONG: Does the Senator know of any Senator who wrote the committee report?
>
> MR. DOLE: I might be able to identify one, but I would have to search. I was here all during the time it was written, I might say, and worked carefully with the staff as they worked...
>
> MR. ARMSTRONG: Mr. President, has the Senator from Kansas, the chairman of the Finance Committee, read the committee report in its entirety?
>
> MR. DOLE: I am working on it. It is not a bestseller, but I am working on it.
>
> MR. ARMSTRONG: Mr. President, did members of the Finance Committee vote on the committee report?
>
> MR. DOLE: No.

MR. ARMSTRONG: Mr. President, the reason I raise the issue is not perhaps apparent on the surface, and let me just state it...The report is not considered by the Committee on Finance. It was not subject to amendment now by the Senate....

If there were matter within this report which was disagreed to by the Senator from Colorado or even by a majority of all Senators, there would be no way for us to change the report. I could not offer an amendment tonight to amend the committee report....

[F]or any jurist, administrator, bureaucrat, tax practitioner, or others who might chance upon the written record of this proceeding, let me just make the point that this is not the law, it was not voted on, it is not subject to amendment, and we should discipline ourselves to the task of expressing congressional intent in the statute.[274]

Since it is well known that courts rely on legislative history, congressmen often advance their own personal agenda by *creating* legislative history by inserting language during the floor debates or in the committee reports that did not have majority support and could not have been adopted if included in the actual written language of the bill to be voted on.

Congresspersons do this with the knowledge that their comments will become part of the legislative history, and that courts in the future may come to look at their comments as an authoritative statement of Congress's intent when it passed the bill—and why do the courts look for "congressional intent" when they could just read the statute?

As Justice Scalia put it, "It is less that the courts refer to legislative history because it exists than that legislative history exists because the courts refer to it."[275]

When one looks at the extent to which the will of Congress is being subverted by those who game the conference committee process, it becomes obvious that what goes on among the conference committee members and their staff goes far beyond reconciling language between two versions of a bill: individual members of Congress have also found that the use the conference committee is a wonderful, stealthy way to dole out pork. George Will wrote in his *Washington Post* column February 10, 2008 (*q.v.*):

On July 29, 2005, the House and Senate passed legislation granting Lee County, [Florida]'s. request for $10 million for "widening and improvements for I-75" to facilitate evacuations during hurricanes....

When the legislation reached the president on Aug. 10, 2005, the language about widening I-75 had been mysteriously deleted and replaced by "Coconut Rd. interchange I-75/Lee County." So $10 million was to be spent for a project that neither the House nor the Senate voted for, that Lee County did not want, and that someone unknown wrote into the legislation.

Congressman Don Young admitted that his staff made the unauthorized language change *after* the House and Senate versions of the bill passed—and a person who would have benefited greatly from the proposed interchange was Florida developer Daniel Aronoff, who owned four thousand acres along Coconut Road.

Is it just coincidence that a few months before the bill's passage, Aronoff had contributed money to Alaska's Congressman Don Young, chairman of the House Transportation and Infrastructure Committee? (Young is most remembered outside Alaska for his part in Alaska's famous "Bridge to Nowhere.")

The Senate has called for an FBI investigation; the House claims that would violate the speech and debate clause of the Constitution.[276]

Restoring Confidence

Let's begin by reforming Congress. Although reigning in the Supreme Court is the major thesis of this book, that will not be possible unless we can restore faith in government generally and in Congress in particular. Several things will be necessary before the people trust Congress enough to give it power to restrain a dictatorial Supreme Court.

The call for the Convention for Offering Amendments, in my opinion, should include a list of items that will be on the agenda. It is apparent if you read the Friends of Article V Convention Web site[277] submitting a call for a convention by several states over a long period of time is not effective.

Nor is individual states requesting individual amendments, even if in the aggregate—over time—you may have the requisite number of states. A good example is the Balanced Budget Amendment (BBA). Thirty-nine states have asked for an Article V convention to draft the BBA; the requests cover a period of forty-five years—beginning with Oklahoma's request in 1955 until the most recent request by Oregon in 2000.

If proposals for amendments trickle in from individual states over an extended period of time, it is not clear from the record that Congress even tabulates the proposals to see if the two-thirds requirement is met—and even if the petitions were tabulated, it is unclear whether, over such a long period of time, the petitions represent the will of a majority of people at any given time. For example, many of the people making the request in 1955 may have changed their mind, or died, before the request in 2000 comes into existence.

After considerable research and thought, it is my opinion that the best way to get Congress to fulfill its obligation to call a convention for offering amendments would be to have an organization that has a good relationship with all the state legislatures, The National Conference of State Legislators (NCSL), for example, draft a resolution and coordinate getting the state calls for a convention to Congress.

This would serve two major purposes: first, it would put Congress on notice that the voters are fed up and coordinated in their demands for relief (I think they have a hint with the 2010 midterm elections); and secondly, if a majority of states

agree to the plan, it will give the others a good reason to look at the proposal seriously. If voters are talking to their legislators in the mean time, this should be an
easy sell.

The Amendments

To anyone who reads the Constitution—the actual document and not a Supreme Court "interpretation" of it—two things are self-evidently true: (1) Congress
pays little regard to the Constitution or the will of the people; and (2) the Supreme
Court, while aiding and abetting Congress in its mockery of the Constitution, dis-
plays its own hubris in using the "Living Constitution" to do whatever the Court
wants, including overriding any laws of Congress it may disagree with..

When I began this manuscript I advocated term limits for all elected federal
officeholders. Over time, and after much thought and research, I believe I found
a better way; and so I reordered my priority list of amendments. In an ideal world,
amending the Constitution would not be necessary; however, when both the Court
and Congress have "interpreted" the original document, ratified by the founders,
out of all recognition draconian action becomes necessary. Therefore, it is essential we declare the will of the people that the federal government and each of its
branches follow the Constitution as written.

There is great fear among many that a convention for amending the Constitution could end up trashing the Constitution and writing a new one. If you read the
Constitution, that fear comes from ignorance of what the document actually says.
An amendment offered by an Article V "Convention for proposing Amendments"
will be subject to the same treatment as amendments proposed by the Congress—
no more and no less. The *proposed* amendments that come out of the convention
must meet the same ratification standard—three-fourths of the states—as if they
were proposed by Congress. The Constitution's Article V which authorizes the convention for offering amendments is here: http://www.archives.gov/exhibits/charters/
constitution_transcript.html. Go read it. Don't be mislead by demagogues who may
be ignorant of the facts—or worse, may be promoting their own hidden agenda.

The amendments I propose in priority order are:

1. End Gerrymandering.

If I was limited to one action to end the partisan bickering in Washington,
DC and get back to the nation's business, the choice would be easy—end gerrymandering. Gerrymandered congressional districts favor one party, ethnic, or racial
group to the exclusion of others; it appears on its face to violate "one man-one vote."
After all, voting is an individual, not a group right. However, the Supreme Court
has shown little enthusiasm for sorting out how to enforce the prohibition against
gerrymandering.

Congressional Districts drawn to include the most Democrats possible, or the
most Republicans possible, or the most of a particular ethnic or racial group possible, logically tend to elect people that are highly partisan and rigid in their ideol-

ogy—in other words, people who are like them and who share their views. Moderate candidates who run in gerrymandered districts have little chance of beating an ideologue who appeals to the group or groups the gerrymander intends to protect.

Good examples of gerrymandering are **Illinois' District 4** (Chicago and vicinity) which is actually two gerrymanders shaped roughly like tadpoles, joined together at the tail by a narrow strip of I-294, and **California's 23rd**, a narrow stretch of coastline some 200 miles long averaging about 5 miles wide.

Maps of Congressional Districts, in color, are available at a government website:

http://www.national atlas.gov/printable/congress.html

Congressional District 4

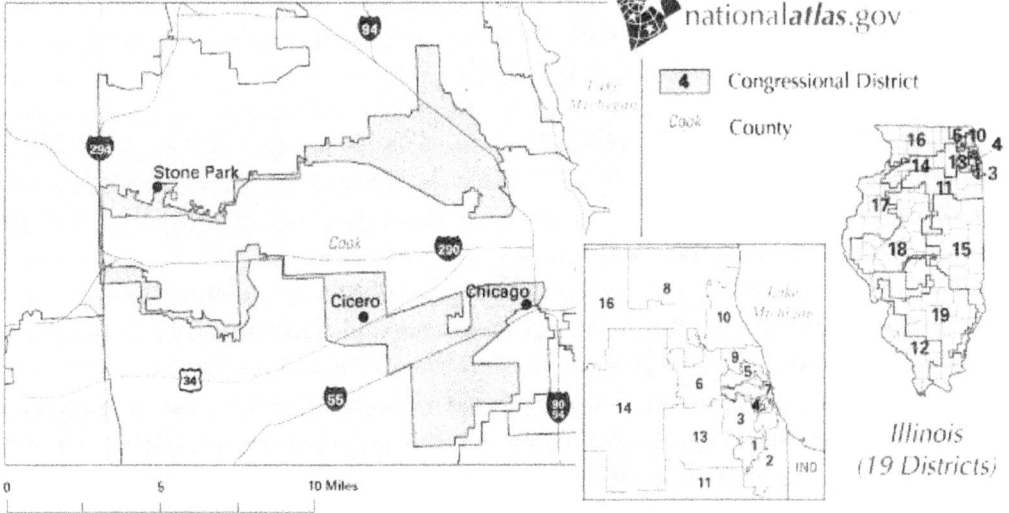

nationalatlas.gov

4 Congressional District
Cook County

Illinois (19 Districts)

Congressional District 23

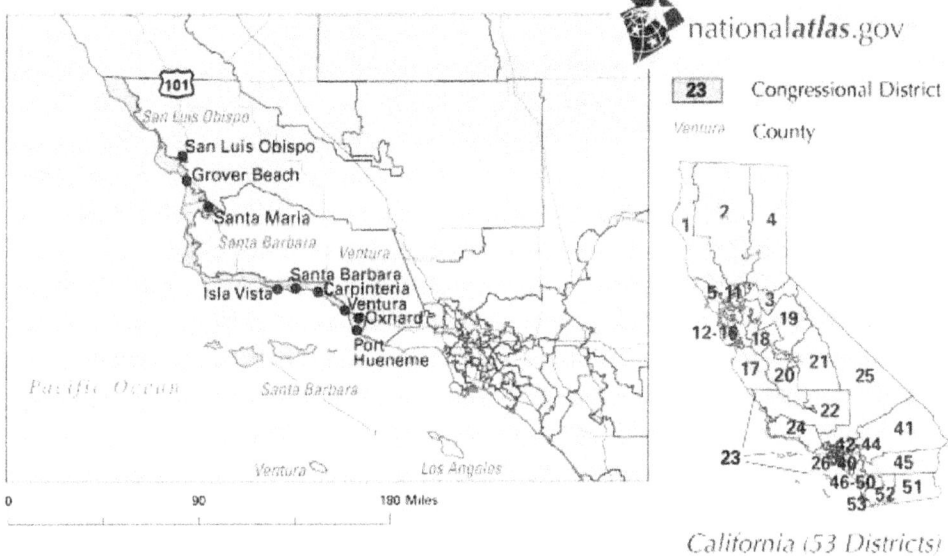

nationalatlas.gov

23 Congressional District
Ventura County

California (53 Districts)

The states redraw districts after each U.S. census; however, the Supreme Court has muddled redrawing the district maps by its one-man-one vote ruling and that minorities must be represented. Redrawing district boundaries has become a highly partisan and bitterly fought political battle. States have no power to change qualifications or the way representatives are elected but they can use very sophisticated redistricting to try to control the outcome of elections.

2. The Supreme Court of the United States (SCOTUS) Shall Interpret the Constitution According to Principles of Contract Law;

SCOTUS must consider only what is within the four corners of the document. Prior decisions of the Court in conflict with this amendment shall be void 180 days after the ratification of this amendment and new precedent shall be established that conforms in all regards to the provisions of this amendment.

SCOTUS ruled in *U. S. v. Sprague,* "The Constitution was written to be understood by the voters; its words and phrases were used in their normal and ordinary as distinguished from technical meaning; where the intention is clear, there is no room for construction and no excuse for interpolation or addition."[278] in all future decisions of the Court this shall be the standard of interpretation and such interpretations shall be written in standard English prose the average voter could be expected to understand.

In all future actions of the Court, SCOTUS has no jurisdiction to make common law except in the interstices where Congress has not yet acted. *See, also,* "Rules for Congress," paragraph 3, subparagraph 1

SCOTUS shall not extend any rights under the Constitution of the United States to combatants, lawful or unlawful, or to any terrorist committing an act of war against the United States of America, its possessions or territories, or its citizens wherever located. Persons committing such acts of war shall be given humane treatment and any benefits of the Geneva Convention, international treaties and the traditional laws of war.

This amendment is consistent with Congress being the sole legislative authority and the president's Article II power to negotiate treaties (requiring the advice and consent [approval] of two-thirds of the Senate). There is no constitutional authority for the Supreme Court to extend the benefits or obligations of a duly negotiated and approved treaty beyond its plain words.

As a guide to interpreting treaties, SCOTUS shall be guided by the actions of the president and the Congress that negotiated and ratified the treaty, not by "modern sensibilities" or what the Court thinks the treaty should mean.

Much of this book has focused on the Supreme Court and its "Living Constitution." A living constitution is an oxymoron. Either you have a Constitution or you don't. A government can function without a Constitution—the English Parliament comes to mind—but if you have agreed to live under a *written* Constitution, the Supreme Court has no jurisdiction to change it. The only valid way to change the

United States Constitution is through the procedure in Article V of that Constitution.

3. Rules for Congress;

Congress is the sole and exclusive lawmaking body identified in the Constitution of the United States of America.

Article I contains no authority for Congress to delegate its legislative power; therefore, neither SCOTUS nor the President of the United States shall have authority to enact law contrary to those passed by Congress. Present Administrative Rules, which have the force and effect of law, shall expire at the end of five years after ratification of this amendment unless enacted by Congress in the normal course of business;

Administrative agencies in the Executive Branch may investigate matters within their jurisdiction and make recommendations to Congress, but said agencies shall have no authority to issue binding regulations.

Congress shall cite with specificity the part of Article I, section 7 or section 8 which gives it authority to enact the legislation being considered.

The necessary and proper clause shall be narrowly construed to mean "those things necessary and proper, *without which* the power delegated by the several States to Congress could not be effectuated."

When an amendment to the Constitution specifies, "Congress shall have power to enforce, by appropriate legislation, the provisions of this article," the grant of power is limited to carrying into effect that amendment. That section of the amendment shall not be construed as a broad grant of power to Congress to legislate regarding areas of the law, which are only peripherally related to the intent of the Amendment.

The Commerce Clause in Article I, section 8, ("Congress shall have Power To...Regulate Commerce with foreign Nations, and among the several States, and with the Indian Tribes") shall be construed as granting to Congress power to regulate the free flow of commerce that is interstate in nature. Congress has no power to regulate commerce *within* a foreign nation, or a state or territory lands ceded by treaty to an Indian Tribe. Any decisions of the Supreme Court contrary to this amendment are voidable by any Article III court.

Every Bill considered for passage by Congress shall be posted on the Internet on three separate days prior to a final vote.

Every vote shall be recorded electronically. [Comment: The technology is already installed—use it]. It would be simple to record all votes and make the recording available to the public by way of the Internet and/or C-SPAN.

Enforcement: it shall be the duty of the Legislatures of the several States to consider whether any law passed by Congress complies with the requirements of this amendment and the Constitution of The United States generally.

After due consideration, a vote of a majority of the Legislatures of the several States shall nullify any law of Congress *which does not strictly comply* with the requirements of this amendment. PROVIDED HOWEVER, SCOTUS shall have no jurisdiction to review the nullification of an Act of Congress by the several States pursuant to this amendment unless Congress challenges the state legislatures' decision to nullify an act.

The jurisdiction of SCOTUS shall be confined to ruling on the dispute between Congress and the States and shall not include deciding whether the act is constitutional per se.

The United States of America was founded on the desire for individual liberty and for each individual to have the freedom to pursue life, liberty, and happiness without the interference of government. Reverse discrimination has served its purpose, if it ever had one, and is hereby abolished. It is time this nation affirmed Dr. Martin Luther King's dream of a nation which is colorblind.

That right to life, liberty and happiness included the obligation of the government of the United States of America to insure the right to own private property and the right to enter into a contract and to have that contract enforced.

The power of imminent domain shall be used only when the taking is for a government *purpose*. The State, Local, and Federal Governments shall have no power to condemn private property to give to another private entity, no matter what the perceived benefit such a taking would appear to give the government body.

Property seized from any individual or entity using the power of imminent Domain shall be titled in the name of the government entity exercising imminent domain and shall be treated for tax purposes as similarly situated property titled in the name of the government body exercising the power.

Whenever any government entity shall place restrictions on private real property for environmental easements or any other public use, with or without actually seizing title to the land, it shall be considered a taking and just compensation shall be paid pro rata to the landowner for any reduced use or value of the land for personal or commercial purposes.

The prosperity of the United States of America was built on a free market economy. Congress shall forthwith take steps to restore the markets which have been distorted by government intervention. No one is too big to fail. Entrepreneurs risk capital in the expectation of achieving gains. They also must be willing to suffer any losses that risk entails.

4. Balanced Budget

Congress is prohibited from approving more spending that the anticipated revenue in a given year.

Several balanced budget amendments have been proposed—twice the amendment received large majorities in the House and was defeated by a single vote in the senate—and every state except Vermont is on record approving of a balanced budget amendment for the federal government.. The amendment should have an override provision so a supermajority of both houses of Congress could use deficit spending during time of war *declared by Congress* or for other extreme national emergencies or nuclear attack or invasion of American territory, As a point of reference, Hurricane Katrina was not sufficiently severe to trigger deficit spending.

Congress shall have power to impose a Value Added Tax (VAT) for the sole purpose of retiring the national debt. The revenue raised by a VAT shall be used to pay the principle of the debt only and shall not be used for debt service or any other purpose. Interest and costs of serving the debt shall continue to be paid out of the general revenue.

Retirement of the national debt shall be in the shortest time consistent with the Laffer curve.[279]

Upon retirement of the debt, Congress shall have no further authority to impose a Value Added Tax except in time of War, so declared by Congress under its Article I, section 8 powers enumerated in the Constitution.

5. English is the official language of the United States of America.

Article I section 8 of the Constitution contains no authority for the federal government to fund bilingual education in the public schools nor funding to provide translators in transactions between U.S. citizens or residents and the U.S. government. Therefore, Congress is without authority to appropriate funds for this purpose. PROVIDED, HOWEVER, nothing in this amendment shall be construed to restrict the use of translators in dealings between the government of the United States and foreign governments.

I recommend the phase-out of all programs not specifically authorized by Article I, section 8 of the Constitution over fifty years. Congress would have plenary power to set priorities on how to reduce what has come to be called "domestic spending" [for social programs having no relationship to the Article I, section 8 duties of Congress]. A recommended schedule would be to freeze all "domestic spending" at the present level in absolute dollars, with no adjustment for inflation, for the first year after this amendment goes into effect.

At the end of the first year, and each succeeding year, the budget for non-Article I expenditures could be reduced by 2 percent per year. Again, this would be in absolute dollars not adjusted for inflation.

This proposal will doubtless bring down upon the author charges of "racism," "ageism," and "disabled-ism" [is there such a word?], but consider this: When you reduce the federal budget—and bureaucracies—you also cut out that famous "waste, fraud, and abuse" politicians are always talking about.

The states, freed from federal mandates and populated by people with an ever decreasing federal tax yoke, could set up their own programs to take up the slack from the feds, and they could do it more efficiently and far less expensively. Without the federal government sucking all the oxygen [tax money] out of the air, states could actually raise state taxes with a net tax reduction in overall taxes for taxpay-ers—there would be a much smaller federal bureaucracy to support.

James Madison insisted that "[a]s a guide in expounding and applying the pro-visions of the Constitution...the legitimate meanings of the Instrument must be derived from the text itself" (letter to Thomas Ritchie).[280] Chief Justice Marshall confirmed that this was the proper method of interpretation:

> As men whose intentions require no concealment, generally employ the words which most directly and aptly express the ideas they intend to convey, the en-lightened patriots who framed our constitution, and the people who adopted it, must be understood to have employed words in their natural sense, and to have intended what they have said. *Gibbons v. Ogden*, 22 U.S. 1, 188 (1824).The Constitution "is to be interpreted, as all other solemn instruments are, by en-deavoring to ascertain the true sense and meaning of all the terms; and we are neither to narrow them, nor enlarge them, by straining them from their just and natural import, for the purpose of adding to, or diminishing its powers, or bending them to any favorite theory or dogma of party. It is the language of the people, to be judged according to common sense, and not by mere theoretical reasoning."[281]

Justice Oliver Wendell Holmes Jr. said it most succinctly: in legal interpreta-tion, it is impossible to know what the writer or speaker may have had in his mind. Therefore, we only consider what those words "would mean in the mouth of a nor-mal speaker of English, using them in the circumstances in which they were used. (*The Theory Of Legal Interpretation*, 12 Harv L R 417, 417-418 [1899]).

When you read the Constitution, understand that what you read is what the Constitution says. If the Supreme Court says something different, you must exam-ine that difference very carefully in the context of the bias and the agenda of the Supreme Court. The Supreme Court may have got it wrong!

6. Reaffirm Amendments I through X—The Bill of Rights

Another essential step is necessary if we want to take back our country. We need to fully reinstate the first ten amendments, known as the Bill of Rights, and return to the rule of law—which we claim to follow, but in fact do not.

> The truth is, that, even with the most secure tenure of office, during good be-havior, the danger is not, that the judges will be too firm in resisting public opinion, and in defense of private rights or public liberties; but, that they will be ready to yield themselves to the passions, and politics, and prejudices of the day.[282]

The Bill of Rights, then, was intended to restrain the potentially unlimited power of the federal government to interfere with the individual freedom of indi-viduals. It was not meant to restrain the several states. The Supreme Court, again exceeding its constitutional authority, has turned that upside down by using the Fourteenth Amendment as an excuse to say the Bill of Rights *restrains the legitimate power of the states* as SCOTUS shall interpret that power. That is patently false!

During the drafting and ratification of the Constitution, there was much discussion and concern that the document did not guarantee the individual rights and freedom the Revolution was fought to ensure. Many colonies refused to support ratification of the Constitution unless a specific statement of rights was included. Therefore, the agreement to include a Bill of Rights is a condition precedent to ratifying the Constitution.

I contend the Bill of Rights, because it is a condition precedent, enjoys a higher status than ordinary amendments and cannot be repealed by implication. Obviously, any of the amendments in the Bill of rights can be repealed if Congress proposed to repeal a particular amendment and that was ratified by the States. But such an amendment to repeal must be supported by specific language evidencing that intent. I have no legal authority to support my contention; therefore, clarifying language should be added to the Constitution by way of an amendment.

The underlying issue I am addressing is the Supreme Court's interpretation of the Fourteenth Amendment clause that allows Congress to make laws necessary to carry out the intention of that Amendment. However, it was not a broad grant of power to Congress to make laws subjugating the states to the federal government's will. We discussed in Chapter 5 how the Supreme Court used the Fourteenth Amendment to gut the Ninth and Tenth amendments in the Bill of Rights. We also set out how the Court incorporates ex post facto laws into its judge-made laws in clear violation of the Constitution's prohibition of ex post facto laws.

Article I, § 9 of the Constitution, setting forth limits on Congress's powers, specifically identifies ex post facto laws as being forbidden to Congress. Therefore, if Congress is the sole and exclusive legislative power identified in the Constitution, under what authority does the Supreme Court make ex post facto laws? Why does the Court think it has the authority to make laws at all?

The short answer is it has no such power; the Court just made us think it had. We stand by and do nothing so *we* give the Court the *de facto* power to enact law and ex post facto laws.

At common law, Court interpretations were supposed to clarify ambiguous laws—poorly written and ambiguous in meaning. Its role is not to write new laws more to its liking. It is worth saying again: if we are to be a country which believes in the "rule of law," the people need to know what the law is. They should be able to read it, understand it, and therefore be in a position to follow it. They should not have to wait for a Supreme Court "interpretation" to know what the law *really* says. Remember, "the Constitution was written to be understood by the voters; words and phrases were used in their normal and ordinary as distinguished from technical meaning" (United States Supreme Court decision, *U.S. v. Sprague*).

❖   ❖   ❖

In the final analysis, states should not have federal one-size-fits-all mandates on how to care for their citizens; they should be free to design local programs based on local needs.

Chapter 14: "Whether You Think You Can Do a Thing or Not, You're Right."—Henry Ford

Bad politicians are sent to Washington by good people who don't vote.
—William E. Simon, former secretary of the treasury, Nixon and Ford administrations
A citizen of America will cross the ocean to fight for democracy but won't cross the street to vote in a national election.
—William E. "Bill" Vaughn[283]
The American citizen must be made aware that today a relatively small group of people is proclaiming its purposes to be the will of the People. That elitist approach to government must be repudiated.
—William E. Simon.

You, as an individual, personally can do something to change America for the better. This chapter will tell you where and how to start. Please understand, this is an individual effort—if you don't do it, the chances are good that no one else will either.

American patriot Samuel Adams is widely quoted as saying, "It does not require a majority to prevail, but rather an irate, tireless minority keen to set brush fires in people's minds."[284]

To understand what is required will be to understand that the Supreme Court of the United States has turned the Constitution on its head. Couple that with a corrupt Congress, who is singularly unresponsive to the will of the people, and one understands the only way to change the federal government is to amend the Constitution. We must abandon the "Living Constitution," which is the opposite of the rule of law. The "Living Constitution" gives carte blanche to the Supreme Court to amend the original document at will, without honoring the amendment process in Article V. All it takes is five justices' votes.

To amend the written Constitution, to take away the power the Supreme Court usurped from Congress, will be terrifying to the people who trust Congress even less than they do the Court. To restore confidence in Congress will require term limits and an end to gerrymandering, which promotes special interests at the expense of the people as a whole.

What must be done—and how you fit into that process—is simple. A mental health therapist at a Veterans Hospital[285] said, "Keep doin' what you're doin' and you'll keep gettin' what you're gettin'." Let's begin with what may seem like a tangent but is, in fact, essential to get you started.

First, thoughts, behavior, and feelings are like three points on an isosceles triangle. Imagine the triangle as being freely movable in space but the points are fixed in relationship to each other. It is readily apparent if you move one of the points, you necessarily change the position of the other two.

Now, let's apply that to human behavior. Sigmund Freud, the father of psychoanalysis, believed unconscious thoughts gave rise to hysterical symptoms. In other words, thoughts influenced behavior.

Psychologist B. F. Skinner, who is credited with systemizing behavior modification as a psychiatric tool, took the opposite view. He used operant conditioning to change a person's behavior and that was supposed to change how the individual thought about things and how he felt.

I happen to believe they are both right.

It doesn't matter where you start. Just get started with what fits you best. Now, apply that to the task at hand, *i.e.,* to reforming government. Henry Ford's quote, which is the title of this chapter, is dead on. If you believe you can't do anything about it—you're right! You can't do anything about it. Not because you have no *ability* to change how we are governed; it's because *you don't believe* you can bring about change so you don't even try.

If you have a negative thought pattern, it is difficult to change what you think without the intervention of a therapist—or without changing what you do. You *can* change what you think by changing your behavior. If you act *as if* you believe and you see the results of what you do, you will come to see that you really can make the changes you seek and you will come to believe. A good illustration of this is in the lyrics to "Whistle a Happy Tune" from the *The King and I.* If you are not familiar with Oscar Hammerstein's lyrics, go here: www.stlyrics.com/lyrics/thekingandi/iwhistleahappytune.htm.

Successful songs touch us because they reveal some primordial truth we already know intuitively but have not internalized or put into words before.

People need to feel they have some investment in their country and the ability to do something about governing it; if they did, maybe we could get more than half of the eligible voters to the polls to vote. Right now, only about 61 percent of registered voters turn up at the polls.[286] When you consider that many people who are eligible do not bother to register, the figure for *potential* eligible voters who actually vote may be closer to 50 to 55 percent.[287]

Since the electorate is about evenly divided between liberals and conservatives, the president is often elected by not much more than 25 percent *of eligible voters.* To expound further on that subject is beyond the scope of this book, I want to focus here on changing the Constitution to put the federal government into its proper place in a federal republic.

Let's Get Started

The easy part of this is how to start the process. Don't expect to influence the federal government directly. It is far too big, too remote, and if you follow the news on health-care reform and immigration, it is ostentatiously *not* responsive to the voters. We must start at the local level. You need to get in touch with your local delegate to the state legislature or your state senator. This is a political process, and there is no way to avoid politics if you want to do something about the corruption/ special interests' influence with government office holders. The surprise to most newcomers will be how easy it is.

In Jackson County, West Virginia—where I once ran for office—the population was 28,000. Of these, in the 2000 census, 21,237 were listed as eligible to vote. However, in the 2000 primary election, 3,965 people actually voted in the Democratic primary and 3,437 Republicans voted. That works out to 39.9 percent of all eligible voters.

Ordinary citizens do not have much to do with who gets on the ballot. Candidates often are self-selected; even these self-selected candidates seek, and usually get, support from some of the established politicians in the county where they run. Often candidates are approached and offered the backing of the local political parties if they would agree to run.

But who are the local political parties? They are an even smaller group of people who feel passionately about what they do. At the time I ran for office, the sheriff was the "king-maker." Another influential group, however, will have helped the sheriff get elected. It's the county executive committee, themselves elected officials but not a high profile office.

Each county will also have a "Democratic Club" and a "Republican Club," which are open to the public (in some counties there may also be Libertarian, Constitution, Tea Party, or other clubs where like-minded people get together to talk politics and plot strategy) and will most often meet at the same time and place as the executive committee. Everybody gets to know everybody else. It is not necessary to join one of the clubs, but I recommend you do. It is the quickest and easiest way to learn how politics works.

Anyone involved with politics will be eager to recruit new people and you will be welcome. Once you get your feet wet, the next step is to attend as many open functions as you can. Most political organizations on the county or district level will have a "meet the candidate night." Plan to go. Shake hands with each candidate there, chat for a moment if you can. You can expect almost all politicians to be easy to talk to.

Mickey Burriss, a former South Carolina representative, put it this way:

"It should be easy [to talk to your legislators]. It is difficult to get elected if one is hard to talk to. *You* are the boss. not the legislator.

"Q: What is the best way to contact your local state legislator or state senator?

"A: When I was in office the telephone was easiest. I imagine now it is the Internet. Had your question been the most effective way I would have said personal visit to the Reps. office or catch them at the state capitol.

"Q: Did you answer telephone calls from constituents?

"A: I took all calls. I answered at the capitol, I took calls [at home] when transferred to me by the switchboard. Not returning calls is a quick way to lose an election. Why would anyone run for office who does not have a genuine desire to help the constituents? Beats me but some do.

"Q: If you are not available when they call, do you return calls?

"A: Always. If I was accused of not returning a call there was a problem but it was not with me. I usually returned calls immediately to catch them while they were available rather than play phone tag. Some folks will hate you even when you respond so you may as well give them their say and move on. If you do this faithfully the word will get around and when an enemy grouses others will know better. Always return calls. In fact if you can, call to answer letters. Nothing beats personal contact in politics.

"Q: Did you respond to letters?

"A. Don't think of running for office if you will be reluctant to return calls, answer letters or visit constituent's homes. Run *from* public office if you have that attitude or they will chase you out.

"Q: How responsive were you in looking into questions raised by your constituent?

"A: "Do it or don't run. It is called public service. If you think otherwise and run you are a fool.

"Q: Did you pay more attention to people you personally were acquainted with as compared with strangers?

"A: Be interested in all voters.

"Q: How can an ordinary citizen, not yet involved in politics, get to know their representative?

"A: Go shake their hand.

"Q: Do the individual representatives look at donor lists?

"A: They should and thank each donor by phone or letter. I wish everyone had to serve two terms with the threat of losing an election. There would be less verbal abuse of politicians. Just like there is little abuse of military people because so many of us have served and understand. Few people understand the extreme difficulty of being an elected official. Just because someone contributes to a campaign should not mean a politician will throw away their philosophy and honesty. A politician should ask himself with every vote how will I explain this vote back home.

"Q: Do you think there will be a third party movement which catches the public's imagination?

"A. Something needs to happen to awaken the public. The American public can not be relied on to do the best thing for our country. You can count on a bunch to do what's best for them. They want 'something for nothing—for me, damn the country.' "

Who's Paying Attention

The message I took away from that conversation reinforced my belief we have a generation of citizens brainwashed by liberal institutions in this country—and poorly prepared to talk about government and the political process. George Washington said:

> A primary object...should be the education of our youth in the science of government. In a republic, what species of knowledge can be equally important? And what duty more pressing...than...communicating it to those who are to be the future guardians of the liberties of the country.[288]

As pointed out elsewhere in this book, people are busy living their own lives, coping with their own problems, and not paying much attention to what is happening to the country. I have occasion to talk with a lot of young adults. It continues to baffle me why they have so little interest in the country most of them will live in for the rest of their lives. They are ignorant of politics but, more importantly, they are indifferent.

It gets worse.

About five years ago, I began using the opportunity that came along to talk to young people I came to know—cashiers in supermarket lines, workers in fast food restaurants, young adult children of friends, even waitresses at Hooters. I attempted to be low-key and conversational, but I tried steering the conversation to politics and freedom in the United States.

The responses I got were almost universally, "Oh, I don't pay attention to politics," or "I don't care about that stuff," or some similar expression of indifference. This from people I saw regularly, had many pleasant—even animated—conversations with, but who turned off completely when the subject was politics or government.

❖   ❖   ❖

As to your involvement, you need to read different sources of information and understand the problem and the amendment process. There is a wealth of information on the Internet arguing different points of view. Read a sample and understand not only your own pitch but what you might expect in rebuttal. It is very helpful if you talk to other people—family, friends, people in checkout lines at the supermarket—to become comfortable with your message and to see what counterarguments you need to anticipate before you talk to your legislator. You want to sound like you know what you are talking about. To borrow a cliché, "You get only one chance to make a good first impression."

❖   ❖   ❖

While interviewing legislators, I posed a similar set of questions, like ones I asked Mickey Burriss, to Bill Wooten, a member of the West Virginia House of Delegates.

"Q: What is the best way for a citizen to contact a legislator?

Mr. Wooten: "The best way is to call." He added most legislators are always eager to know what citizens have on their minds.

Mr. Wooten is an attorney and has an office where he can be reached; for legislators who may not have an office (one local WV legislator is a school bus driver, another is a school teacher—they may not want to take calls at school), it may be more effective to call them at their office in the capitol. Most capitol switchboards will have the means to transfer the call to whatever number the legislator lists with the switchboard.

On the state level, legislators are still very close to the people they represent. Anyone, I mean *anyone,* can pick up a telephone and talk to their legislator; and if you cannot reach him or her immediately, every one I have ever known, or known about, returned telephone calls to constituents.

Of all the people you ever meet, politicians are the easiest to talk to.

Article V Convention for Offering Amendments

Your initial goal, after you bring your own understanding up to speed, will be to help educate your representative about the Article V process. There is much confusion, and widespread fear, of a convention because some think it may become a "runaway" convention and scrap the Constitution we have. I think that would be impossible. The authority of Article V is to propose amendments to become a "Part of this Constitution." That will prevent scrapping the Constitution we have and starting from scratch.

The Articles of Confederation, which preceded this Constitution, had no such safeguard.

We don't need a new governing document—we just need to compel the Supreme Court and Congress to follow the one we have. We need to clearly state the will of the people from whom the entire federal government gets its authority. Whatever comes out of the convention for offering amendments will still need to be ratified by three-fourths of the states before it becomes a part of the Constitution. That is a high hurdle and will require amendments that a majority in three out of four state legislatures find to be acceptable.

You will also have to overcome the belief that "we can't do anything about it."

There have been at least 750 calls for a convention for offering amendments, according to a Web site, "Friends of the Article V Convention."[289] Some have been a call by a single state asking for a particular amendment; others, like the Balanced Budget Amendment, have garnered support from thirty-nine states (only thirty-four required to meet the two-thirds requirement) over a period of some forty-five years (1955-2000).

The fact that some of these requests for convention were rescinded, then a few of the rescissions were reinstated by some of the states, has led to enough confusion that Congress has been able to ignore the requests.

Some, like the Seventeenth Amendment, drew enough state support that Congress, fearing a convention, passed the direct-election-of-senators bill and sent it out to the states to ratify; it was seen as a way of preempting an Article V convention for offering amendments. It was also a mistake. The Seventeenth is one of the major reasons the federal government has become a cancer, eating up all the individual freedoms that used to be guarded by federalism.

A Model for an Article V Convention

There was a call by Rhode Island for an Article V convention as early as 1790.[290] Obviously, the will of the people is not expressed when an amendment is proposed by one state and may not be supported by other states until more than a century later. All of the people who supported the original call for a convention are dead.

I recommend that a central organization—the National Conference of State Legislators (NCSL) comes to mind, but it could be another organization—take on the project of drafting the call for the convention and submitting it to their member legislatures. The state legislators could use that call as a model for writing their own legislation, or they could pass a bill incorporating the NCSL draft by reference. When thirty-four states call for the convention, the NCSL (or the other organization coordinating the effort) could present that group of documents to the Congress. I believe that would be much more difficult for Congress to ignore.

If Congress continues to ignore the will of the people, as expressed through their state legislators, the states already have the authority to nullify any act which is not specifically delegated in the Constitution. One state, South Carolina, nullified a tariff act as early as 1832,[291] but President Andrew Jackson issued his own nullification proposal that South Carolina's action was unlawful.

South Carolina stood virtually alone, so Jackson's edict ruled the day. I believe if two-thirds of the states nullified an Act of Congress, which act exceeded Congress' delegated authority under the Constitution, the outcome would be different.

It is unclear how the Supreme Court would act if Congress ignored mandatory language in Article V regarding the call by the states for convention.

In common or ordinary parlance, and in its ordinary signification, the term "shall" is a word of command, and one which has always or which must be given a compulsory meaning; as denoting obligation. It has a preemptory meaning and it is generally imperative or mandatory. It has the invariable significance of excluding the idea of discretion, and has the significance of operating to impose a duty which may be enforced, particularly if public interest is involved, or where the public, or have rights which ought to be exercised or enforced.

The Court has sometimes been reluctant to require Congress to do anything, citing the separation of powers doctrine. However, in other cases—*Powell,* [292] for example—the Court has ruled that Congress must seat a member the Congress had just expelled. In the Powell case, Article I, section 5 of the Constitution says, "Each House shall be the Judge of the Elections, Returns and Qualifications of its own Members...."

It seems to me the Supreme Court picked a fight it couldn't win. At any rate, Congress stalled—an election was coming up—and Adam Clayton Powell was re-elected by his constituents to another term and he was seated as a new member so the issue became moot.

Whether Congress would precipitate a constitutional crisis by failing to act on a duty clearly set out in the Constitution is an unsettled point. However, "doin' what you're doin' and gettin' what you're gettin' " is putting this country on the road to socialism, bankruptcy, and anarchy.

ADDENDUM

Since the original printing of this book, there has been a resurgence of interest in repealing the 17th Amendment. That would do away with direct election of U. S. Senators. It would restore the concept and practice of Federalism—the balance of power between the federal government and the states. Without direct election of Senators, the Senate would never have passed Obamacare. Senators would represent their state instead of the K Street lobbyists. For discussion, see: www.flyovercountrypress.com.

Endnotes

Chapter 1: Can We Have a "Living Constitution" *and* the Rule of Law?

1   277 U.S. 438.
2   A line frequently used by comedian Larry the Cable Guy.
3   514 U.S. 779 (1995).
4   Obama's first State of the Union address, January 27, 2010.
5   Attributed to Thomas Jefferson; President Gerald Ford used the phrase in an address to Congress, August 12, 1974.
6   http://www.demossnews.com/manhattandeclaration/press_kit/manhattan_ declaration_signers (drafted on October 20, 2009; accessed November 25, 2009).
7   *Sprague v. United States*, 282 U.S. 716, 731 (1931).
8   Rasmussen Report, http://www.rasmussenreports.com/public_content/poli- tics/issues2/articles/just_17_say_federal_government_represents_will_of_ the_people.
9   *Kelo v. City of New London,* 545 U.S. 469 (2005) *United States*, 282 U.S. 716, 731 (1931).
9   Rasmussen Report, http://www.rasmussenreports.com/public_content/poli- tics/issues2/articles/just_17_say_federal_government_represents_will_of_ the_people.
9   *Kelo v. City.*
10   *Rasul v. Bush,* 542 U.S. 466 (2004).
11   Associated Press wire service story, October 20, 2006. *See, e.g.,* http://www. ftimes.com/main.asp?SectionID=1&SubSectionID=1&ArticleID=37084&T M=45891.52.

Chapter 2: Who Told the Supreme Court It Can Amend the Constitution?

12   530 U.S. 428, 461 (2002); http://www.supremecourtus.gov/opinions/ boundvolumes/530bv.pdf (accessed February 9, 2007).
13   *Ullmann v. U.S.,* 350 U.S. 422, 428 (1956).
14   530 U.S. 538 (2000).
15   U.S. Const. amend. I.
16   *Mine Workers v. Illinois Bar Assn.*, 389 U.S. 217, 222 (1967).

17   *California Motor Transport Co. v. Trucking Unlimited*, 404 U.S. 508, 511 (1972).

18   *Black's Law Dictionary*, 5th ed. West (1979).

19   410 U.S. 413 (1973).

20   See discussion of *Atkins v. Virginia*, Chapter 3, *post*.

21   *University of California Regents v. Bakke*, 438 U.S. 265 (1978).

22   Cummings, Homer S. "Reasons for President's Plan and the Remedy." February 14, 1937. http://newdeall.feri.org/court/cummings.htm (accessed January 23, 2007).

23   *Dickerson*, at 461.

24   http://www.britannica.com/eb/article-2639/George-III (accessed January 23, 2007).

25   *Miranda v. Arizona*, 384 U.S. 436 (1966).

26   *Dickerson* at 444-45.

27   *Id.*, at 442.

28   *Black's Law Dictionary*.

29   *Id.*, at 444.

30   5 U.S.137 (1803).

31   *See, e.g.,* Justice Harlan's dissent in *Sanders v. United States*, 373 U.S. 1, 32 (1963): "I seriously doubt the wisdom of these 'guideline' decisions...However carefully written, they are apt in their application to carry unintended consequences which once accomplished are not always easy to repair."

32   Supreme Court Rule 10. http://www.supremecourtus.gov/ctrules/rulesofthecourt.pdf (accessed January 23, 2007).

33   *Michigan v. Tucker*, 414 U.S. 433, 446-47 (1974) [citing *Elkins v. United States*, 364 U.S. 206, 217 (1960).

34   *Oregon v. Elsted*, 470 U.S. 298, 299 (1985).

35   U.S. Const., Art. 5.

36   See, Miller, Mark C. "Lawyers in Congress: What Difference Does it Make?" *Congress and the Presidency*, 20 no 1 (1993). http://polisci.wisc.edu/~kritzer/teaching/ls415/Miller1993CP.htm (accessed January 26, 2007).

37   Bork, *Coercing Virtue*.

38   Garrow, David J. "Mental Decrepitude on the U.S. Supreme Court: The Historical Case for a 28th Amendment." 67 *University of Chicago Law Review*, 995 (2000).

39   *Id.*

40   Lazarus, Edward. "Supreme Court Roulette." http://writ.news.findlaw.com/scripts/printer_friendly.pl?page=/lazarus/20000802.html.

41   http://www.rasmussenreports.com/public_content/politics/19_say_congress_doing_good_or_excellent_job (accessed June 21, 2007).

Chapter 3: Animus toward Religion

42   http://www.loc.gov/loc/lcib/9806/danpre.html (accessed January 26, 2007).

43   http://pietisten.org/winter02/reliberty.html (accessed c. 2005—unable to access on March 1, 2007).

44   Perry, Wayne, and Gerald Smith. "What part of 'No' don't you understand?" Recorded by Lorrie Morgan. The phrase may have evolved from "won't take no for an answer" in use in American English since the mid-nineteenth century. *See:* http://www.phrases.org.uk/meanings/ what-part-of-no.html (accessed January 26, 2007).

45   Story, Joseph. *Commentaries on the Constitution of the United States,* Book III, §1873; http://www.constitution.org/js/js_344.htm (accessed December 24, 2008).

46   *See,* http://www.history.org/Almanack/life/religion/religionva.cfm (accessed January 27, 2007).

47   http://www.britannica.com/eb/article-79353/Massachusetts (accessed January 27, 2007).

48   *The Works of John Adams*, ed. C.F. Adams, Boston, Little Brown Co.,1851, vol. 4, p. 31.

49   http://www.undergodprocon.org/pop/statereligions.htm.

50   *Wallace v. Jaffree*, 472 U.S.38, 84-85 (1985).

51   The Holy Bible, preface to the new Revised Standard Version. Thomas Nelson & Sons., pub. (1952).

52   *Torcaso v. Watkins*, 367 U.S. 488 (1961).

53   331 U.S. 1 (1947).

54   *Reynolds v. United States*, 98 U.S. 145 (1878).

55   Matthew 22:18 (RSV).

56   *Bradfield v. Roberts*, 175 U.S. 291 (1899).

57   *Quick Bear v. Leupp*, 210 U.S. 50 (1908).

58   *Arver v. United States*, 245 U.S. 366 (1918).

59   *Pierce v. Society of Sisters*, 268 U.S. 510 (1925).

60   *U.S. v. MacIntosh*, 283 U.S. 605 (1931).

61   *Lovell v. City of Griffin*, 304 U.S. 444 (1943).

62   *Jones v. City of Opelika*, 319 U.S. 105 (1943).

63   *West Virginia Board of Education v. Barnette*, 319 U. S. 105 (1943).

64   http://www.loc.gov/loc/lcib/9806/danpre.html (accessed January 27, 2007).

65   Matthew 7: 20 (RSV).

66   *McCollum v. Board of Education*, 333 U. S.203 (1948).

67   *Zorach v. Clauson*, 343 U.S. 306, 312 (1952).

68   *Id.* at 314.

69   *Id.* at 323.

70   370 U.S. 421 (1962).

71   374 U.S. 203 (1963).

72   397 U.S. 664 (1970).

73   403 U.S. 602 (1971).

74   530 U. S. 290 (2000).

75   Goldstein, Laurie. "National Briefing /Midwest: Iowa: Students Win Ban On Lord's Prayer." New York Times.com (May 16, 2002), http://query.nytimes.com/gst/fullpage.html?res=9A06E0DA1139F935A25756 C0A9649C8B63 (accessed June 21, 2007). NOTE: During a final cite check, the author had difficulty accessing the site. If the URL doesn't work, try a Google search for "Students Win Ban on Lord's Prayer."

76   http://www.ed.gov/policy/gen/guid/religionandschools/prayer_ guidance. html?exp=0 (accessed January 27, 2007.

77   *ACLU v. Black Horse Pike Reg'l Bd. Of Educ.*, 84 F.3d 1471 (1995).

78   *Cole v. Oroville Union High Sch. Dist.*, 228 F.3d 1092 (9th Cir. 2000).

79   *Adler v. Duval County Sch. Bd.*, 250 F.3d 1330 (11th. Cir. 2001), cert. denied, 122 S. Ct. 664 (2001)

80   530 U.S. 290 (2000).

81   *The Heritage Guide to the Constitution,* 285 (5,000 amendments); http://www. centeroncongress.org/learn_about/feature/qa_role.html and http://usgovinfo. about.com/library/blconstamend.htm (10,000 amendments).

Chapter 4: What Does "Five-to-Four" Mean?
(It Depends on Whose Gore is Being "Oxed")

82   *Atkins v. Virginia,* 536 U.S. 304, 313 (2002).

83   *Id.* at 338 Justice Scalia, dissent .

84   *Thompson v. Oklahoma,* 487 U.S. 815, 873 (1988).

85   *Id.*

86   Lazarus, Edward, "The Real Story Behind the Release of Justice Blackmun's Papers and Tapes," http://writ.news.findlaw.com/lazarus/20040318.html (accessed June 22, 2007).

87   *Harvard Law Review,* Vol. 117, No. 1, p. 501, November 2003.

88   O'Connor, Sandra Day. Speech delivered to the Southern Center for International Studies, Atlanta, Georgia, October 28, 2003. http://www.bgct.org/TexasBaptists/Document.Doc?&id=1500 p. 2 (accessed February 9, 2007).

89   543 U.S. 551 (2005).

90   O'Connor, Sandra Day. Keynote address at the proceedings of the Ninety-Sixth Annual Meeting of the American Society of International Law, March 16, 2002, http://www.humanrightsfirst.org/us_law/inthecourts/ASIL_Keynote_Add_2002_Just_O'Connor.pdf.

NOTE: International Law is the body of law which "regulates the intercourse of nations." *Black's Law Dictionary*, 5th ed. International law is not the same thing as "foreign law," although by her own admission Justice O'Connor uses both and bases her decisions, in part, on the internal domestic laws of France, Germany, and other European nations.

91 O'Connor's October speech in Atlanta (*ante*, at Note 63).

92 *Chisolm v. State of Georgia*, 2 U.S. 419, 450 (1793).

93 *Atkins* at 304.

94 *Black's Law Dictionary*, 5th ed., s.v. "Amicus curiae."

95 *Atkins* at 322.

96 *Id.* at 347-48.

97 *Id.* at 348.

98 Woodward, Bob, and Scott Armstrong. *The Brethren*. Simon & Schuster Paperbacks, New York (1979) 69.

99 *Atkins* at 304.

100 Jefferson or Hamilton, Federalist Papers No. 51, http://thomas.loc.gov/home/histdox/fed_51.html (accessed January 27, 2007).

101 *Id.*

102 Sirovich, Lawrence. "A Pattern Analysis of the Second Rehnquist U. S. Supreme Court." *Proceedings of the National Academy of Science*. 100, No 3 (2003): 7432

103 *Id.*

104 http://goldberg.law.northwestern.edu (accessed March 3, 2007).

105 Bork, Robert H. *Coercing Virtue: The Worldwide Rule of Judges*, 9. AEI Press, Washington, DC 2003.

106 *University of California Regents v. Bakke*, 438 U.S. 265 (1978).

107 Goodman, Ellen. *Boston Globe*. "The Supremes: Just nine politicians in black robes." December 14, 2000. http://www.mindfully.org/Reform/Supremes-Nine-Politicians.htm.

108 347 U.S. 3 (1954).

109 *Bush v. Gore*, 531 U.S. 98 (2000).

110 *Planned Parenthood of Southeastern PA v. Casey*, 505 U.S.833 (1992).

111 http://goldberg.law.northwestern.edu/mainpages/bio.htm.

Chapter 5: Judges Decide, Criminals Slide

112 *Board of Comm'rs Waubaunsee County, Kansas v. Umbehr*, 518 U.S. 668, 689 1996), http://www.supremecourtus.gov/opinions/boundvolumes/518bv.pdf (accessed February 10, 2006).

113 *Miranda v. Arizona*, 384 U.S. 436 (1966).

114   In *Wong Sun v. United* States 371 U.S. 471 (1963), the Supreme Court ruled that any physical evidence that is recovered as the result of an unlawful confession must be suppressed along with the confession.

115   *Nix v. Williams*, 467 U.S. 471 (1963).

116   *New York v. Quarles*, 467 U.S. 469 (1964) (1984).

117   166 F.3d 667 (1999).

118   530 U.S. 428, 445.

119   The decision in *United States v. Dickerson* acknowledged the conflicting evidence about exactly when the *Miranda* warnings were given. The trial court found that the confession was voluntary and as a result refused "Dickerson's motion to suppress the evidence found as a result thereof, e.g. the statement made by Rochester identifying Dickerson as the getaway driver." 166 F.3d at 676. However, because of the dispute over when the *Miranda* warnings were given, the confession itself was suppressed by the court.

120   Lockhart, B., Kamisar, Y., Choper, J., Shriffin, S. *Constitutional Law*, 6th ed. West Pub. (1986).

121   Strazella, James A, Reporter. "The Federalization of Criminal Law." 9. Washington, DC. American Bar Association, Criminal Law Section. 1998.

122   286 U.S. 652 (1925).

123   *Gitlow v. New York*, 286 U.S. 652 (1925), [Freedom of speech and freedom of the press]; *Cantwell v. Connecticut*, 310 U.S. 396 (1940), [free exercise of religion]; *Everson v. Board of Education*, 330 U.S. 1, (1947), [establishment of religion].

124   287 U.S. 45 (1932).

125   211 U.S. 78 (1908).

126   *Black's Law Dictionary*, 5th ed., s.vv. "stare decisis."

127   Woodward, Bob, and Scott Armstrong. *The Brethren*. P. 69. Simon & Schuster Paperbacks, New York (1979).

128   302 U.S. 319 (1937).

129   332 U.S. 46 (1947).

130   401 U.S. 222 (1971).

131   467 U.S. 649 (1984).

132   378 U.S. 478 (1964).

133   319 U.S. 105 (1943).

134   166 F.3d 667 (4th Cir. 1999).

135   Lincoln, Abraham. Gettysburg Address.

Chapter 6: Taxation *and* Legislation Without Representation

136   http://www.yale.edu/lawweb/avalon/presiden/inaug/lincoln1.htm.

137   "Boston Tea Party" Microsoft® Encarta® Online Encyclopedia,2006. © 1997-2006 Microsoft Corporation. All Rights Reserved. http://encarta.msn.

com/encyclopedia_761565150/Boston_Tea_Party.html (accessed February 11, 2007).

138   Lossing, Benson, John, Craig Hugh. *Our Country. A History of the United States for All Readers from the Discovery of America to the Present Time.* Vol. 2, New York: Johnson & Bailey, [c1834].

139   http://www.britannica.com/eb/article-9057651/James-Otis.

140   "Intolerable Acts," Microsoft® Encarta® Online Encyclopedia 2006 http:// encarta.msn.com © 1997-2006 Microsoft Corporation. All Rights Reserved. http://encarta.msn.com/encyclopedia_761579222/Intolerable_Acts.html (accessed February 11, 2007).

141   Lossing.

142   http://64.226.34.179/Editorial%2010%2030.htm.

143   Bier, Thomas, Ph.D. Appearing before the Committee on the Judiciary, Subcommittee on the Constitution, September 18, 1996. http://judiciary.house. gov/judiciary/255.htm (accessed February 11, 2007).

144   Brandeis, Louis, Dissent in *Olmstead v. U.S.*, 277 U.S. 479 (1928) [*see:* Preface, *ante*].

145   Jeremiah, 25:8-11.

146   *Black's Law Dictionary*, 5th ed.

147   Jefferson, Thomas. Declaration of Independence. http://www.archives.gov/ national-archives-experience/charters/declaration_transcript.html (accessed February 11, 2007).

148   347 U.S. 483 (1954).

149   *See:* documents and proclamations at http://www.eisenhower.archives.gov/dl/ LittleRock/littlerockdocuments.html (accessed February 11, 2007).

150   *See:* FN 105 *ante*.

151   Miller, Mark, J.D., Ph. D "Lawyers in Congress: What Difference Does it Make?" *Congress and the Presidency*, 20:1-24 (1993). http://polisci.wisc.edu/-kritzer/ teaching/ls415/Miller1993CP.htm [Note: Originally accessed c. 2005. Unable to access February 11, 2007.Try a Google search for "Lawyers in Congress: What Difference Does it Make?"]

152   Some state and local jurisdictions allow nonlawyers to preside over traffic courts or small claims courts, but all federal judges were lawyers first in order to became judges.

153   Fox News/Opinion Dynamics Poll conducted September 25-26, 2007.

154   243 F. Supp. 527, 536 (2002).

155   *Hamdi v. Rumsfeld*, 542 U.S. 507 (2004).

156   542 U.S. 466 (2004).

157   Miller, *ante* at FN 118.

158   Bork, Robert H., *Coercing Virtue: The Worldwide Rule of Judges.* The AEI Press, Washington (2003).

159   The author finds it of more than passing interest that even as the law ab-
       jures religion and morality, it cannot even *define* every day issues of concern to
       American citizens such as pornography. See, e.g., Justice Potter Stewart's re-
       marks in *Jacobellis v. Ohio*, 378 U.S. 184, 197 (1964), wherein he says: "I shall not
       today attempt further to define [pornography].... But I know it when I see it."
       The Court would doubtless be just as confused today when it tries to explain
       why it projects the same due process values onto foreign terrorists, at war with
       the United States, that it affords America's domestic criminal defendants.

Chapter 7: The End of Representative Government

160   Thomas Jefferson Papers Series 1, General Correspondence, 1651-1827.
161   5 U.S. 137, 179 (1803).
162   Jefferson, Thomas. Letter to Charles Hammond, August 18, 1821. *The Writings
       of Thomas Jefferson*, ed. Andrew A. Lipscomb, Vol 15, pp. 331-32 (1903) .
163   *See*: speech delivered to Congress on March 19, 1867 in support of H.R. 20.
164   http://en.wikipedia.org/wiki/Thaddeus_Stevens .
165   *See*, generally: http://www.phmc.state.pa.us/ppet/stevens/page1.asp?secid=31;
       see, also: *The Writings of Thomas Jefferson*, ed. Andrew A. Lipscomb, Vol 15, pp.
       331-32 (1903).
165   *See*: speech delivered to Congress on March 19, 1867 in support of H.R. 20.
165   http://en.wikipedia.org/wiki/Thaddeus_Stevens.
165   *See*,generally:http://www.phmc.state.pa.us/ppet/stevens/page1.
       asp?secid=31http://en.wikipedia.org/wiki/Thaddeus_Stevens (accessed August
       8, 2007).
166   . http://www.supremecourthistory.org/02_history/subs_history/ 02_c04.html
       (accessed June 27, 2997).
167   http://www.liv-ol.ac.uk/pa09/europetrip/brussels/neimoller.htm.
168   *Mattox v. United* States, 156 U.S. 237 (1895).
169   Cited in http://www.heritage.org/Research/LegalIssues/HL553.cfm.
170   330 U.S. 1 (1947).
171   Bork, Robert H. *Coercing Virtue: The Worldwide Rule of Judge*. 8. AEI Press,
       Washington, DC 2003.
172   *Everson* at 18.
173   Jefferson, Thomas. Letter to the Baptist Association in Danbury, Connecti-
       cut. *Writings of Thomas Jefferson*, Vol XVI, pp281-82 (1904) http://www.loc.gov/
       loc/lcib/9806/danpre.html (accessed June 25, 2007).
174   *Reynolds v. United States*, 98 U.S. 145, 164 (1878).
175   *Everson* at 16.
176   *Id.* at 18.
177   472 U.S. 38, 98 (1985).

178   *Id.* Note 4 at 104.

179   *Id.* at 99.

180   *Id.* at 92.

181   http://religiousfreedom.lib.virginia.edu/sacred/vaact.html (accessed February 12, 2007).

182   *Id.*

183   Berger, Peter L. ed. "General Observations on Normative Conflicts and Mediation." Bolder, CO (1998) [quoted in Bork, Robert H., *Coercing Virtue*" p. 5].

184   *Id.*

185   Prager, Dennis. "The Culture War is About the Authority of a Book." Jewish World Review, December 27, 2006/6 Teves 5767. http://www.jewishworldreview.com/1206/prager122706.php3.

186   O.K. For the military purists, I know it is now the 101st *Airmobile* but I choose to maintain the symbolic continuity with President Eisenhower's actions in integrating the Little Rock schools.

187   http://www.time.com/time/magazine/article/0,9171,900914,00.html (accessed January 22, 2007).

188   *Cooper v. Aaron* 358 U.S. 1, 18 (1958).

189   *Dred Scott v. Sandford*, 60 U.S. 393 (1856).

190   530 U.S. 428, 432 (2000).

191   http://www.yale.edu/lawweb/avalon/presiden/inaug/lincoln1.htm.

192   Garrow, David J. "The Brains Behind Blackmun," *Legal Affairs,*" May/June 2005   http://www.legalaffairs.org/issues/May-June-2005/feature_garrow_mayjun05.msp].

193   *Employment Div.,Ore Dept. of Human Res. V. Smith*,494 U.S. 872, 893 (1990).

194   42 U.S.C. § 2000bb (complete text at: http://religiousfreedom.lib.virginia.edu/sacred/RFRA1993.html (accessed June 25, 2007).

195   *City of Boerne v. Flores*, 521 U.S. 507 (1997).

196   277 U. S. 438, 479 (1928).

197   Webster, Noah. http://www.duke.edu/~gnsmith/quotes/quotes03.htm.

Chapter 8: *Marbury v. Madison*: How the Imperious Court Got That Way

198   5 U.S. 137 (1803).

199   *Hylton v. United States* 3 U.S. 171 (1796).

200   *Marbury v. Madison*, 5 U.S. 137, 154 (1803).

201   Ward, Paul W. "Washington Weekly," *The Nation*, Vol. 144, No. 3, pp, 63-64, January 16 1937; http://newdeal.feri.org/nation/na37144p063.htm at ¶ 7 (accessed June 28, 2007).

202   Bork, Robert H. *Coercing Virtue: The Worldwide Rule of Judges.* p. 8.

203   *Griffin V. School Board,* 377 U.S. 218, 233 (1964).

204   347 U.S. 483 (1954).

205   *Missouri v. Jenkins,* 515 U. S. 70 (1995); *Missouri v. Jenkins,* 495 U. S. 33 (1990); and *Missouri v. Jenkins,* 491 U.S. 274 (1989).

206   White, Tanika, and Kate Beem. *Kansas City* (MO) *Star,* National/World sec., Metro ed., p. A1, August 22, 1999.

207   219 U.S. 346 (1911).

208   Ciotti, Paul. "Money and School Performance: Lessons form the Kansas City Desegregation Experiment." Cato Institute Policy Analysis No. 298, March 16, 1998. http://www.cato.org/pubs/pas/pa-298.html.

209   *Missouri v. Jenkins,* 495 U.S. at 34-35 (1990).

210   *Id.* at 35-36.

211   *Id.* at 57.

212   *Id.,* at 58-59.

213   Ciotti .

214   *Id.*

215   "After the Bell: Education Solutions outside the School" June 4-5, 2001 The NYU Center for Advanced Social Science Research & The Jerome Levy Economics Institute of Bard College. http://www.nyu.edu/fas/cassr/conf01.htm.

216   http://www.mackinac.org/print.aspx?ID=3263#_edn1 [citing *The Case for Choice in Schooling*].

Chapter 9: The Court Empowers Terrorists—Then PC Takes Over

217   *Terminiello v. City Of Chicago,* 337 U.S. 1 (1949).

218   *Rumsfeld v. Padilla,* 542 U.S. 426 (2004),

219   Sullivan, Laura. "U.S. Fears al-Qaida Drafting American Prisoners." Baltimore Sun, November 30, 2002.

220   Id.

221   Padilla v. Rumsfeld, 03-2235 (L); 03-2438 (Con.) (2003).

222   www.mental-health-matters.com/articles/ article.php?artID=469-97k.

223   http://www.geocities.com/kidhistory/index.htm.

224   http://www.princeton.edu/pr/pwb/01/1022/.

225   "One Missed Call" *The Wall Street Journal* March 28, 2008, p. A8. http://online.wsj.com/article/SB120674959280273345.html?mod=djemEditorialPage (accessed March 30, 2008).

Chapter 10: The "Living Constitution"

226   The Federalist, 29 September 2004, Federalist Patriot No. 04-39 Wednesday Chronicle.

227   Graglia, Lino A., "Rigged Justice" American Enterprise Institute, (July-August 2002).

228   http://www.house.gov/judiciary/2127.htm.

229   Hatch, Orin. "The Balance of Power," *The Washington Times*, Editorials/Op-Ed September 17, 2004.

230   http://www.house.gov/judiciary/gaziano101002.htm.

231   http://www.usdoj.gov/olp/judicialnominations108.htm#courtofappeals.

232   http://www.nationalreview.com/york/york200505130859.asp.

233   "En banc:"the hearing of a legal case where all judges of a court will hear the case (an entire "bench"), rather than a panel of them....

234   http://www,cfif/htdocs/legislative_issues/federal_issues/hot_issues_in_congress/confirmation_watch/olati_johnson_complaint.pdf.

235   Id.

236   Id., Page 2 of 11.

237   Id., Page 3 of 11.

238   Lincoln, Abraham. First Inaugural Adddress.

239   http://www.liv-col.ac.uk/pa09/europetrip/brussels/neimoller.htm.

240   *Wickard v. Filburn*, 317 U.S. 111 (1942).

241   545 U.S. 469 (2005).

242   *Richmond Newspapers, Inc. v. Virginia*, 448 U.S. 555, 596 (1980).

243   *O'Hare Truck Service, Inc., Et Al. V. City Of Northlake et al.*, 518 U.S. 712 (1996).

244   67 U. Chi. L. Rev. 995 [2000]).

245   http://www.oyez.org/justices/anthony_kennedy/ The Web site for Oyez reveals "The Oyez Project is a multimedia archive devoted to the Supreme Court of the United States and its work." All of the audio recordings made in the Court since 1955 are available for public access through Oyez.

Chapter 11: Who Do You Trust?

246   Hughes, Charles Evans. Speech before the Chamber of Commerce, Elmira, New York, May 3, 1907. *Addresses and Papers of Charles Evans Hughes, Governor of New York, 1906–1908*, p. 139 (1908).

247   Wood, Gordon S. Comment on *A matter of Interpretation*.

248   Federalist # 51.

249   *Black's Law Dictionary*, 5th ed. West Publishing, St Paul (1979).

250   495 U.S. at 58-59.

251   The author's calculations are based on an average of twelve national polls conducted by various media organizations and the Gallup polling organization. http://www.pollingreport.com/CongJob.htm (accessed February 17, 2007).

252   Rasmussen Report, "19% Say Congress is Doing a Good or Excellent Job." June 13, 2007. http://www.rasmussenreports.com/public_content/ politics/19_say_congress_doing_good_or_excellent_job.

253   http://www.rasmussenreports.com/public_content/politics/ congressional_performance (accessed July 27, 2007).

254   http://online.wsj.com/article/SB117752895118782401.html? mod=politics_primary_hs (accessed July 7, 2007).

255   http://www.congress.org/congressorg/bio/userletter/?id=497& letter_id=1281425861 (accessed July 13, 2007).

256   *United States v. Sprague*, 282 U.S. 716, 731 (1931).

257   Lincoln, Abraham. The Gettysburg Address.

258   Lincoln, Abraham. First Inaugural Address.

Chapter 12: Restoring the Balance

259   Hand, Learned, Speech at "I Am An American Day," Central Park, New York (May 20, 1945) [reprinted in Spirit of Liberty; papers and addresses, collected and with an introd. and notes, by Irvin Dilard].

260   Matthews, Jay, "A Battle on the WWII Knowledge Front," *Washington Post*, May 28, 2004. http://www.washingtonpost.com/wp-dyn/articles/A61803-2004May27.html (accessed 6/24/2006).

261   Title 5 of the U.S. Code.

262   Payne, Thomas. Rights of Man, (1791). Reprinted: Penguin Books, New York (1985).

263   *United States v. Sprague,* 282 U.S. 716, 731 (1931).

264   http://www.capitolhillblue.com/Aug1999/081999/criminalclass4-081999.htm.

265   http://www.yale.edu/lawweb/avalon/washing.htm (accessed July 15, 2007).

266   Woodward at 69 [quoting Chief Justice Warren Burger].

267   http://www.rasmussenreports.com/premium_content/historical_ data/supreme_court_congress_history (accessed July 15, 2007).

268   *In re Opinion of the Justices,* 172 S.E. 2d 474, 204 N.C. 806.

269   *Hollingsworth v. State of Virginia,* 3 U.S. 378 (1798).

270   282 U.S. 716 (1931).

Chapter 13: The Rule of Law

271   http://usinfo.state.gov/dhr/democracy/rule_of_law.html.

272   29 U.S. Code 652(5).

273   "To retain respect for sausages and laws, one must not watch them in the making." Attributed to Otto von Bismarck, quoted by the Florida Supreme Court in *In re Petition of Edward T. Graham,* 104 So.2d 16 (1958).

274 Scalia, Antonin. *A Matter of Interpretation*, p. 34. Princeton University Press, Princeton, NJ (1997) [citing: 128 Cong. Rec. 16918-19, 97th Cong., 2d Sess. (July 19, 1982), quoted in *Hirshey v. F.E.R.C.*,777 F.2d.1, 7 n.1 (D.C. Cir. 1985) (Scalia, J. concurring)].

275 *Id.*

276 *The Hill,* April 29, 2008.

277 http://www.foa5c.org/file.php/1/Amendments.

278 282 U.S. 716, 731 (1931)

279 The Laffer curve represents the theory that at low tax rtes an increase in taxes increases revenue. However, there is an optimum point after which further raising taxes actually *decreases* revenues.

280 September 15, 1821, 3 *Letters and Other Writings of James Madison* 228 (Philip R. Fendall, ed., 1865).

281 Story, Joseph. *A Familiar Exposition of the Constitution* (1840).

282 Story, Joseph. *A Familiar Exposition of the Constitution* (1840).

Chapter 14: "Whether You Think You Can Do a Thing or Not, You're Right."

283 Author, syndicated columnist for the *Kansas City Star* until his death in 1877.

284 A Google search reveals 84,000 references to this quote; none cite an original source.

285 In the interest of full disclosure, she is also my wife.

286 http://elections.gmu.edu/turnout_rates_graph.htm.

287 http://www.fairvote.org/?page=262.

288 *The Writings of George Washington.* John C. Fitzpartick, ed. Vol. 35:316. GPO, (1931-44).

289 http://www.foa5c.org/file.php/1/Amendments.

290 *Id.*

291 http://www.ushistory.org/us/24c.asp.

www.ingramcontent.com/pod-product-compliance
Lightning Source LLC
Chambersburg PA
CBHW081415270326
41931CB00015B/3281